Nuclear War: Philosophical Perspectives

NUCLEAR WAR
Philosophical Perspectives

An Anthology Edited by

MICHAEL ALLEN FOX
and
LEO GROARKE

(Second Edition)

PETER LANG
New York · Berne · Frankfurt am Main · Paris

Library of Congress Cataloging in Publication Data
Main entry under title:

Nuclear War.
  Bibliography: p.
  1. Nuclear warfare – Moral and ethical aspects –
Adresses, essays, lectures.   I. Fox, Michael Allen.
II. Groarke, Leo,
U263.N779 1985   172'.42   85-4274
ISBN 0-8204-0209-5

CIP-Kurztitelaufnahme der Deutschen Bibliothek

Nuclear war: philos. perspectives; an anthology /
ed. by Michael Allen Fox and Leo Groarke.– 2. ed.–
New York; Berne; Frankfurt am Main; Paris: Lang, 1987.
  ISBN 0-8204-0209-5

NE: Fox, Michael Allen [Hrsg.].

Cover design: Robin Fox
Illustration: from Honoré Daumier

Printed by Weihert-Druck GmbH, Darmstadt (West Germany)

Contents

Acknowledgments

The editors would like to thank the Research Office at Wilfrid Laurier University for an Initiatory Research Grant and a Book Preparation Grant, and also the Advisory Research Committee, Queen's University at Kingston, for a Research Award.

The following publishers and authors have kindly granted permission to reprint material:

From *The Observing Self*; copyright © 1982 by Arthur Deikman; reprinted by permission of Beacon Press. From *Hiroshima*, by John Hersey; copyright 1946 and renewed 1974 by John Hersey; originally appeared in *The New Yorker*; reprinted by permission of Alfred A. Knopf, Inc. and Penguin Books Ltd. (UK). From Brooke Medicine Eagle in Joan Halifax, ed., *Shamanic Voices*; reprinted by permission of E.P. Dutton, Inc. From *The Nuclear Delusion: Soviet-American Relations in the Atomic Age*; copyright © 1983 George F. Kennan; reprinted by permission of Pantheon Books, A Division of Random House, Inc. From *The Prevention of Nuclear War*; ed. T.L. Perry; reprinted by permission of Physicians for Social Responsibility, British Columbia Chapter. From "What Would Happen to Canada in a Nuclear War?", by Don Bates et al.; in Regehr and Rosenblum, eds., *Canada and the Nuclear Arms Race*; reprinted by permission of James Lorimer & Company. From *Social Psychology: An Applied Approach*, by Ronald Fisher. Copyright © 1982 by St. Martin's Press, Inc., and reprinted by permission of the publisher. From *Fathering the Unthinkable*, by Brian Easlea; reprinted by permission of Pluto Press. From "Three Main Fallacies in Discussions of Nuclear Weapons," by W.B. Gallie; in Blake and Pole, eds., *Dangers of Deterrence: Philosophers on Nuclear Strategy*; reprinted by permission of Routledge & Kegan Paul. From *The Risks of Unintentional Nuclear War*, by Daniel Frei; reprinted by permission of United Nations External Publications. From *In a Different Voice*, by Carol Gilligan; reprinted by permission of Harvard University Press. From Ralph K. White, "Images in the Context of International Conflict: Soviet Perceptions of the US and the USSR," in Herbert C. Kelman, ed., *International Behavior: A Social Psychological Analysis*; reprinted by permission of Holt, Rinehart and Winston. From *The Fate of the Earth*; copyright © 1982 by Jonathan Schell; reprinted by permission of Alfred A. Knopf, Inc. From *Poetry, Language, Thought*, by Martin Heidegger. Translation copyright © 1971 by Harper & Row, Publishers, Inc., and reprinted by permission of the publishers. From *The End of Philosophy*, by Martin Heidegger. Translation copyright © 1973 by Harper & Row, Publishers, Inc., and reprinted by permission of Harper & Row and The Souvenir Press Ltd., London. From "Alienation and Economics," copyright © 1971 by Walter Weisskopf. Reprinted by permission of the publisher, E.P. Dutton, Inc. From *Indefensible Weapons: The Political and Psychological Case Against Nuclearism*, by Robert Jay Lifton and Richard Falk. Copyright © 1982 by Basic Books, Inc., Publishers. Published in Canada by CBC Enterprises/Les Entreprises Radio-Canada. Reprinted by permission of the publishers. From H.J.N. Horsburgh, "The Claims of Religious Experience," *Philosophy East and West*, 19/2 (April 1969); reprinted by permission of the University of Hawaii Press. From *Limited Nuclear War*; copyright © 1982 by Ian Clark; reprinted by permission of Princeton University Press. From *Nuclear Illusion and Reality*; copyright © 1982 by Solly Zuckerman; reprinted by permission of Viking Penguin, Inc. and Penguin Books Ltd. (UK). From Herbert Scoville, Jr., "A Clear and Present Danger – West." Reprinted by permission of *Bulletin of the Atomic Scientists*, a magazine of science and world affairs. Copyright © 1981 by Educational Foundation for Nuclear Science, Chicago, IL 60637.

The editors also express appreciation to Paul Valerry for giving permission to use two of his illustrations in Michael Allen Fox's article "The Nuclear Mindset: Motivational Obstacles to Peace."

Preface

It is difficult to comprehend the horrors of nuclear war. One way to gain a perspective is to note the existing megatonnage, the numbers of weapons on both sides and other similar statistics. Statistics, however, cannot capture the pain and agony of nuclear war. If we wish to appreciate its nature, we will do better to remind ourselves of what did happen when nuclear weapons were used against Japan. The following excerpt from John Hersey's *Hiroshima* captures one man's encounter with the bomb. More than any statistic, it conveys the real horror of a nuclear confrontation.

Mr. Tanimoto, fearful for his family and church, at first ran toward them by the shortest route, along Koi Highway. He was the only person making his way into the city; he met hundreds and hundreds who were fleeing, and every one of them seemed to be hurt in some way. The eyebrows of some were burned off and skin hung from their faces and hands. Others, because of pain, held their arms up as if carrying something in both hands. Some were vomiting as they walked. Many were naked or in shreds of clothing. On some undressed bodies, the burns had made patterns – of undershirt straps and suspenders and, on the skin of some women (since white repelled the heat from the bomb and dark clothes absorbed it and conducted it to the skin), the shapes of flowers they had had on their kimonos. Many, although injured themselves, supported relatives who were worse off. Almost all had their heads bowed, looked straight ahead, were silent, and showed no expression whatever.

After crossing Koi Bridge and Kannon Bridge, having run the whole way, Mr. Tanimoto saw, as he approached the center, that all the houses had been crushed and many were afire. Here the trees were bare and their trunks were charred. He tried at several points to penetrate the ruins, but the flames always stopped him. Under many houses, people screamed for help, but no one helped; in general, survivors that day assisted only their relatives or immediate neighbors, for they could not comprehend or tolerate a wider circle of misery. The wounded limped past the screams, and Mr. Tanimoto ran past them. As a Christian he was filled with compassion for those who were trapped, and as a Japanese he was overwhelmed by the shame of being unhurt, and he prayed as he ran, "God help them and take them out of the fire."

He thought he would skirt the fire, to the left. He ran back to Kannon Bridge and followed for a distance one of the rivers. He tried several cross streets, but all were blocked, so he turned far left and ran out to Yokogawa, a station on a railroad line that detoured the city in a wide semicircle, and he followed the rails until he came to a burning train. So impressed was he by this time by the extent of the damage that he ran two miles to Gion, a suburb in the foothills. All the way, he overtook dreadfully burned and lacerated people, and in his guilt he turned to right and left as he hurried and said to some of them, "Excuse me for having no burden like yours." Near Gion, he began to meet country people going toward the city to help, and when they saw him, several exclaimed, "Look! There is one who is not wounded." At Gion, he bore toward the right bank of the main river, the Ota, and ran down it until he reached fire again. There was no fire on the other side of the river, so he threw off his shirt and shoes and plunged into it. In midstream, where the current was fairly strong, exhaustion and fear finally caught up with him – he had run nearly seven miles – and he became limp and drifted in the water. He prayed, "Please, God, help me to cross. It would be nonsense for me to be drowned when I am the only uninjured one." He managed a few more strokes and fetched up on a spit downstream. ...

Mr. Tanimoto found about twenty men and women on the sandspit. He drove the boat onto the bank and urged them to get aboard. They did not move and he realized that they were too weak to lift themselves. He reached down and took a woman by the hands, but her skin slipped off in huge, glove-like pieces. He was so sickened by this that he had to sit down for a moment. Then he got out into the water and, though a small man, lifted several of the men and women, who were naked, into his boat. Their backs and breasts were clammy, and he remembered uneasily what the great burns he had seen during the day had been like: yellow at first, then red and swollen, with the skin sloughed off, and finally, in the evening suppurated and smelly. With the tide risen, his bamboo pole was now too short and he had to paddle most of the way across with it. On the other side, at a higher spit, he lifted the slimy living bodies out and carried them up the slope away from the tide. He had to keep consciously repeating to himself "These are human beings." It took him three trips to get them all across the river. When he had finished, he decided he had to have a rest and he went back to the park.

As Mr. Tanimoto stepped up the dark bank, he tripped over someone, and someone else said angrily, "Look out! That's my hand." Mr. Tanimoto, ashamed of hurting wounded people, embarrassed at being able to walk upright, suddenly thought of the naval hospital ship, which had not come (it never did), and he had for a moment a feeling of blind, murderous rage at the crew of the ship, and then at all doctors. Why didn't they come to help these people?

The Hiroshima bomb was small by today's standards. Any full-scale war would now involve thousands of Hiroshimas, disastrous ecological consequences, and an outside world without the means to help or communicate. The need for a solution to the nuclear problem cannot be overestimated. It is this need which motivates the present volume.

Our work on the collection began with the conviction that the possibility of nuclear war presents a problem which it is important, indeed morally obligatory, for philosophers to address. Philosophical commentary seems particularly appropriate given that philosophers possess a unique set of skills which may shed light on a very complex issue. In light of this conviction, our aim was to solicit articles from some of today's most able philosophers on different aspects of the arms race. No consideration was given to their political stance or final conclusions, and anyone familiar with contemporary moral and political philosophy will see that the articles reflect very different political perspectives (both "right-wing" and "left-wing" views, to use a somewhat crude distinction). That intelligent individuals writing from such diverse perspectives all conclude that present nuclear war and weapons policies are mistaken reflects the weakness of those policies rather than the editors' personal outlooks. The reader is in any case encouraged to undertake his or her own critical assessment of the arguments presented in each article. As aids to this endeavor, and to generate discussion in classroom and other settings, we have included commentaries on each selection, as well as issues to think about and discuss, and an extensive bibliography. Our hope is that a better-informed public will increasingly demand of our political leaders serious, meaningful efforts to negotiate disarmament and the destruction of nuclear weapons. If the present volume can make some small contribution to the realization of this goal, our labors as editors will be amply rewarded.

With only four exceptions, as indicated in the text, all contributions to this volume appear in print here for the first time.

In conclusion, it should perhaps be said that the issues involved in the arms race are intricate and puzzling, and that while one does not need to be an expert to possess a well-founded opinion, certain factual information is essential for those who wish to understand and discuss it intelligently. We believe that much of this information is contained in the articles making up this collection. However, we also recommend that one or more of the following publications be consulted or read along with *Nuclear War.* (Publishing information for all works cited in this book may be found in the bibliography.)

Common Cause. *Up in Arms: A Common Cause Guide to Understanding Nuclear Arms.*
Freeman, Harold. *This is the way the world will end, this is the way the world will end, unless ...*
Ground Zero. *Nuclear War: What's in it for You?*
Harvard Nuclear Study Group. *Living With Nuclear Weapons.*
Nield, R. *How to Make up Your Mind About the Bomb.*
Sivard, Ruth Leger. *World Military and Social Expenditures 1983.* (Published annually.)
Stockholm International Peace Research Institute. *The Arms Race and Arms Control.*

Suddaby, Adam. *The Nuclear War Game: Facts and Information Everyone Should Know.*

Tobias, Sheila et al. *The People's Guide to National Defense (What Kind of Guns Are They Buying for Your Butter? A Beginner's Guide to Defense, Weaponry, and Military Spending).*

Tsipis, Kosa. *Arsenal: Understanding Weapons in the Nuclear Age.*

Turner, John. *The Arms Race.*

M.A.F. & L.G.
December 1984

Part I Nuclear Delusions

Nuclear "War" Is Omnicide

JOHN SOMERVILLE

Let us begin with a touch of linguistic analysis. The first thing that must be understood about nuclear war is that it is not war. Once this fact is understood, the rest is, in terms of theory, relatively simple and easy, though the application to social practice remains difficult. What we are dealing with is, first of all, a massive case of linguistic self-deception which arises out of the fact that we have gone on using an old and familiar word – war – to denote a new thing that has a superficial resemblance to the old thing called war, but which in reality has been transformed into something qualitatively different. The adjective "nuclear" is by no means sufficient to express the new quality; a new noun is needed. To see why, let us turn to empirical description.

The social phenomenon we have always called war, a phenomenon as old as human history, is understood by everyone as a form of physical conflict between large groups of people, after which it was usually possible to identify a winning and a losing side. Most important of all, it was always possible to count on the fact that there would be human beings and a habitable Earth left when the war was over. Retrospectively, we can see that it was precisely this contextual fact which was the absolute precondition of considering any problems at all about war, whether the problems were ethical, legal, political, social, religious, psychological, artistic, dramatic, patriotic, economic, or any other kind. That is, whenever we spoke of war prior to World War II we were referring to an activity that presupposed the possibility of a human future. Therefore, there is no theoretical or logical difficulty in seeing that when we begin to deal with an activity which, like nuclear combat, could eliminate the very possibility of any kind of future for anyone at all, we should not call such an activity

Reprinted, with slight changes, by permission of the author and the editor, from *Peace Research: A Canadian Journal of Peace Studies,* 14 (1), April 1982 (original title: "Human Rights, Ethics and Nuclear 'War'").

a "war." To continue to use the word "war" misleads people into thinking that the same ethical, legal, political, economic, or other judgments and attitudes they may have arrived at concerning war must essentially apply to the new activity, only perhaps in some quantitatively bigger way.

There was a failure, quite understandable in the beginning, to realize that in the closing stages of World War II, when nuclear weapons were first used, they brought into being a phenomenon as qualitatively different from war as death is from disease. Even though death can occur in the closing stages of disease, death is not a severe form of disease, any more than strangling a student in the closing stages of a course would be a severe form of education. Different nouns were needed in both cases. For reasons of this kind I propose a new word to replace the misleading term "nuclear war." Since we already have a series of nouns which denote successively wider ranges of killing – suicide for killing oneself, infanticide for killing infants, genocide for killing national or ethnic groups – and since nuclear weapons can now kill all human beings and obliterate all human creations in one relatively brief conflict, it seems appropriate to call such a conflict *omnicide*.

It is said of Confucius that when he was asked the secret of good government he answered, to call things by their right names. It is clear that the need to call things by their right names in matters concerning government was never greater than it is today because it is precisely governments that possess the nuclear weapons. For example, would it not help all of us, morally and logically, instead of saying, "our government is preparing for nuclear war," to say, "our government is preparing for nuclear omnicide"? Would the government be inclined to argue that it could win omnicide, or that the people could survive omnicide, or that the best way to avoid omnicide is to prepare for omnicide? In the United Nations the US government has on occasion refused to vote for, and has in fact blocked, a resolution that would outlaw nuclear weapons and nuclear war, although, for example, poison gas is outlawed. Would it not be more difficult for any UN member to oppose a resolution that would outlaw omnicidal weapons and omnicide? Would anyone be inclined to argue that omnicide is in the national interest, is patriotic or is economically profitable? Surely, these questions answer themselves. When nuclear war is called by its right name – omnicide – it must be acknowledged to be the greatest, most inclusive and least forgivable violation of human rights that could possibly be conceived. In terms of ethics, whether naturalistically or supernaturalistically conceived, nothing could fulfill the requirements of absolute evil so perfectly as omnicide, which can exterminate all human values without exception. In a supernaturalistic perspective, could there be a greater sin than to dare to end the whole human world that God created, and to end it in the hitherto undreamed of sufferings and agonies foreshadowed by Hiroshima and Nagasaki, now multiplied billions of times?

Yet the supremely ironic fact is that today we live in fear and in possible sight of the human committing of this crime so unspeakable that it does not even have a name, this crime so enormous it can be committed only once. The historical truth is that in the 1940s the splitting of the atom and the production of the atomic bomb took everyone by surprise, and very few were prepared to think through its consequences. But we philosophers have always had a special obligation to think in terms of the totality: what is common to all its parts, its possible purpose, its possible beginning and its possible end. To do this in the modern scientific period we must above all put the results of the special sciences together, and show their consequences for the totality. When we do this today we see that the whole human world is facing a crisis of truly unique depth and urgency – a crisis that suggests nothing less than the problem of eschatology, arising out of the scientific-technological progress that created omnicidal weaponry as a political by-product. Put in scientific-philosophical terms, what we now so desperately need, on pain of universal extinction, is a preventive eschatology, an eschatology that is preventive in the same sense that criminology is preventive, wherein the goal of the study is to prevent the occurrence of the object of study.

What can be said more concretely about this contemporary version of the old philosophical-religious discipline of eschatology? The first thing we can say is that religion should play as important a role in it as it did in the older discipline. Religious emotion, feeling, dedication, and faith must be united with scientific methodology, efficacy and practicality in order to prevent the ending of the human world. All of the social sciences and disciplines should be drawn upon – sociology, political science, law, education, psychology, what we call the humanities, and the immensely influential fine arts and popular arts, all forms of literature, drama, theater, film, television, the electronic media, and the printed press. As omnicide threatens everything, everything capable of resisting must resist. Omnicide is not a class problem nor a regional problem nor a sectarian problem. It is an *all-human problem,* one which demands that all competitiors join forces in order to preserve the very possibility of competition.

Because of the urgency of the case, I think the short-term aspect of the problem should concern us first. Defined in its most concrete sense, the short-term problem is to convince the governments which possess omnicidal weapons (*a*) that these weapons must not be used in any circumstances; (*b*) that they must, by treaty agreement, be abolished and outlawed. How can this be done? Probably the quickest way would be by a combination of education and political pressure. That is, what is needed first of all is to convince more and more people – students and the general public as well as people in the government – that they must really believe the central facts which, in one degree or another, they already know, but do not allow themselves fully to believe: that these weapons can and will end the human world by killing every single individual on Earth in the cruelest and most painful manner imaginable. St. Anselm of Canterbury long ago acutely pointed out the almost paradoxical relation between understanding and believing. "I do not understand in order to believe; I believe in order to understand." A contemporary way of applying his point is to recognize that belief is a matter of degree, so that the more deeply a person actually believes the omnicidal facts already known, the more quickly he will take the action they call for. This means that the known facts must be repeatedly communicated by all the existing means and techniques of reason and art, affectively and cognitively, always truthfully, but always remembering that truth needs art as faith needs work in order that they may flower and bear fruit in human life. The truth can indeed make you free, but only on condition that you believe and act upon it.

The truth about today's omnicidal, eschatological crisis has been documented beyond any possible doubt, but it is still extremely difficult for most people to believe it, as I can testify from my own experience. In 1975 I published a book called *The Peace Revolution: Ethos and Social Process* in which I tried to set forth the relevant facts and the precise documentation. One of the central facts – in some ways the most important and incredible fact – is that the executive leaders of the Kennedy administration in 1962, during what was called the Cuban Missile Crisis, deliberately made a decision which they admittedly expected to result in the annihilation of the human race – the decision to bomb the Soviet missiles if they were not removed from Cuba. We know all the details of that decision because President Kennedy's brother Robert, who was then Attorney General of the United States and a leading figure in the executive group that handled the crisis, wrote a small book about it called *Thirteen Days: The Story About How the World Almost Ended.* In it he tells the whole incredible truth; and the government has never denied his account. In fact, all succeeding us administrations have adopted the same policy which, if we call things by their right names, is a policy of *omnicidal blackmail.*

Robert Kennedy's account was also printed in a popular family magazine where it was read by millions of people. But the strange thing was that neither the book nor the magazine publications caused any outcry of indignation, though the text demonstrated, in the most explicit detail, that the president and the other leaders "expected"[1] the ultimatum they sent the Soviets would not be obeyed, and that the resulting world conflict would be "the end of mankind."[2] It further demonstrated that the only reason the result did not come about was that the Soviets unexpectedly complied with the ultimatum. I concluded that the reason there was no outcry of public indignation at the us government's decision was not only the success of the blackmail, but the fact that the readers could not really believe it happened that way.

In order to make this situation more real in the affective sense I decided to write a play about it, a play that would include all the relevant documentation given by Kennedy, but would put it in the mouths of the actual leaders he had written about, in just the way he had reported that the decision was made. I called the play *The Crisis,* but found that no publisher would print it in my own country. Perhaps the drama made the truth too believable. However, the play was published in Japan where people are more ready to believe the omnicidal truth, and sold 50,000 copies in three months. It was staged in Tokyo, and also in a state theater in Sweden. In the United States I published it myself, circulating an edition which is now being used as study material in an increasing number of universities. I recite these facts not because my work has attained any observable success in changing the policy of the us government, which is actually growing worse, but because my experience may throw light on problems that confront us in the psychology of belief. I should add that when I dealt with the problem of the Cuban Missile Crisis in a symposium at the xvth World Congress of Philosophy the Soviet speakers emphasized that their government would never again yield to nuclear blackmail.[3]

A similar instance relevant to the problem of omnicide is what happened to a proposal made on four separate occasions by the ussr as leader of the Warsaw Pact states to the us as leader of the nato states for a mutual treaty that neither side would be the first to use nuclear weapons. The first of these offers was made in 1976 from Warsaw, the second in 1979 from Budapest, the third in 1980 from Moscow, the fourth in 1982 from the United Nations. The fact is that the first three were all rejected by the us government behind closed doors, without any discussion in Congress or any explanation to the public, the vast majority of whom are entirely unaware that the proposals were ever made, since they were so little reported by any of the media. The fourth, as is well-known, was publicly rejected amid worldwide criticism of the us. At the same time, the us government has been on record since 1975 with public declarations of its willingness to be the first to use nuclear weapons.[4] Here the problem is sheer ignorance of the facts rather than disbelief of known facts. Elementary education is lacking.

A classic formulation of human rights in the American Declaration of Independence states:

We hold these truths to be self-evident, that all men are created equal, that they are endowed by their Creator with certain unalienable rights, that among these are life, liberty and the pursuit of happiness. That to secure these rights governments are instituted among men, deriving their just powers from the consent of the governed, that whenever any form of government becomes destructive to these ends, it is the right of the people to alter or to abolish it, and to institute new government.

In other words, human rights include the right of revolution. In fact, this very right of revolution is the only one that is also referred to as a *duty,* for the Declaration adds that when any government persistently violates the human rights of the people, "it is their right, it is their duty, to throw off such government." The actual violation of human rights which occasioned this Declaration and the Revolution which implemented it in socio-political practice in 1776 had to do mainly with the right to liberty. However, it is not accidental but entirely logical that the Declaration puts the right to life first of all, since all else, including liberty, depends on life. The conclusion is inescapable that people threatened by omnicide have more justification for revolution than people threatened by any other form of despotism. The solution of the problem of omnicide, therefore, is crucial to the protection of all human rights.

This most urgent planetary need has two aspects: (*a*) the need to prevent a first use of nuclear weapons; and (*b*) what may be equally important, the need to prevent a second use in retaliation against the first. The human world could not be ended by one nuclear strike; it could be ended only by a series of nuclear exchanges. This means that two infinitely fateful moral facts have now emerged on the stage of human history: (*1*) The government that now makes first use of nuclear weapons will be guilty of the most enormous and unspeakable crime that could be committed against humanity. (*2*) The government of the nuclear power against which the nuclear attack was made will then be forced to decide whether the human world shall be ended or shall continue. No government has ever faced a moral dilemma of such agonizing depth and scale, of such totality.

If the victim of a nuclear attack decides to fight back with conventional weapons, with strategies and tactics that do not end the human world, it will have to suffer initial defeat, and risk foreign domination and occupation for an unpredictable period. But its national life will continue, and it will have the chance to regain its sovereignty. History shows many examples of temporarily conquered, occupied or dispersed nations which win back their freedom and independence, however hard or long the struggle. On the other hand, if the victim of a nuclear attack retaliates with nuclear weapons and all-out nuclear combat, it must expect the result to be omnicide – the annihilation not only of the belligerents and their allies, but of all humankind. The inevitable question poses itself: In both logical and ethical terms, can self-defense include the use of weapons that utterly destroy the defenders themselves and the entire human family? Obviously not, and it is equally self-evident that no wrong done to any part of humankind could justify a retaliation which annihilates everything human. I believe that Marx, Engels, and Lenin, as well as Jefferson, Franklin, and Washington were they alive today, would agree with this answer, not because they were revolutionaries, but because they were sane.

City University of New York (Professor Emeritus)

NOTES

1 See Kennedy, p. 109. After detailing how he delivered the American ultimatum to the Soviet Ambassador, Kennedy says, "I returned to the White House. The President was not optimistic, nor was I. He ordered 24 troop-carrier squadrons of the Air Force Reserve to active duty. They would be necessary for an invasion. He had not abandoned hope, but what hope there was now rested with Khrushchev's revising his course within the next few hours. It was a hope, not an expectation. The expectation was a military confrontation by Tuesday and possibly tomorrow." See also p. 106. Reporting the President's view, Kennedy says, "The thought that disturbed him the most, and that made the prospect of war much more fearful than it would otherwise have been, was the specter of the death of the children of this country and all the world – the young people who had no role, who had no say, who knew nothing even of the confrontation, but whose lives would be snuffed out like everyone else's."

2 *Ibid.,* p. 23. Robert Kennedy characterizes the crisis as " a confrontation between the two giant atomic nations, the US and the USSR, which brought the world to the abyss of nuclear destruction and the end of mankind."

3 See Somerville, ed., esp. Chaps. 1 and 2.

4 See the *New York Times* July 2, 1975 (press conference of Secretary of Defense James Schlesinger). See also the *New York Times,* October 5, 1977 (text of President Carter's address to the United Nations).

Nuclear War: Public and Governmental Misconceptions

WILLIAM C. GAY

From a philosophical perspective, the nuclear debate seldom reaches the level of genuine argument. As a first step toward more rational debate, both public and governmental misconceptions about nuclear war need to be exposed. In this essay I try to clarify and criticize some of the misconceptions that are common in the American debate. Specifically, I consider the public view that nuclear war is improbable, unsurvivable, and unrecoverable, and the governmental view that total destruction is avoidable, control feasible, and victory attainable. My analysis focuses on the ways in which both the public and the government accept exaggerated claims. Public views tend to be overly pessimistic and alarmist and cite worst-case estimates as evidence, while governmental views tend to be overly optimistic and reassuring and cite best-case estimates as evidence.

Despite their exaggerations, public and governmental misconceptions about nuclear war often stand as unquestioned assumptions and decisive premises in many arguments in the nuclear debate. Because each of these perspectives is frequently taken for granted by a particular group, I term these misconceptions "myths." When that which a community takes for granted is termed a "myth," however, distinctions concerning the origin and function of the myth are crucial. Myths may arise from prophetic visions and convey illuminating symbols or from scientific theories that generate testable predictions, but many myths have less noble origins and functions. Hence vested-interest groups may seek to manipulate the political process and develop myths which serve as effective propaganda tools. Regardless of the origin and function of specific myths, myths guide the thinking of their "converts." Conclusions, policies, and actions fall neatly, albeit rashly, into place.

Reprinted, in revised form, by permission of the author and the editor, from *Philosophy and Social Criticism,* 9, Summer 1982 (original title: "Myths About Nuclear War: Misconceptions in Public Beliefs and Governmental Plans").

Ideally, philosophers avoid "living by myths" or, at the least, subject them to critical examination. Given their concern for truth and cogent argument, philosophers have a special responsibility to expose and criticize that which is taken for granted in their community. Since much of the nuclear debate involves appeals to myths which are incompatible, a "battle of myths" is one mode of resolution. In an effort to avoid such a resolution, philosophers can endeavor to "demythologize" the viewpoints, thereby facilitating more logical discussion. To demythologize public and governmental myths, I will reformulate them as each characterizes the other. The government perceives public views to be full of emotional fervor, and the public perceives governmental views to be cold and calculating. These interpretations convey common perceptions which I will take for granted. Because of the contrasts that these interpretations convey, however, my demythologizing will distinguish myths which are false from those which are "half-truths."

Insofar as the emotional vs. calculative contrast holds, the public has tended to make universal claims, e.g., "no one will survive (any) nuclear war," while the government has tended to make particular claims, e.g., "(some) nuclear wars will not result in total destruction." Logically, the government has the easier type of assertion to support and typically argues for the contradiction, not the contrary, of the public's categorical assertions. Since it is sufficient to point out that some survivors are likely, for example, the government need not argue for such a prepostrous contrary as "everyone will survive a nuclear war." If the counter-examples which are used to contradict the public's categorical claims are reasonable, the public myths are dismissed as false and governmental myths are posed as true. If governmental claims are true, however, they are true under very limited conditions, and, because they omit much of the truth about nuclear war, are properly termed half-truths. A half-truth, though true so far as it goes, may be more pernicious than a falsehood because of its effects on people.

Public Myths

Many people believe that nuclear war is (*1*) improbable, (*2*) unsurvivable, or (*3*) unrecoverable. On the one hand, these beliefs function as public myths which short-circuit critical reflection on the arms race. On the other, they function as emotional, yet factually questionable fulcrums for criticizing the nuclear establishment.

Before proceeding to my own analysis, it is necessary to provide the definition of nuclear war against which I will assess public views. To be comprehensive, I define "nuclear war" as "any conflict, international or subnational, in which one or more of the parties employs weapons which rely on fission and/or fusion."[1] If one reflects on the fact that by this definition World War II was a nuclear war (albeit a one-party nuclear war in which the use of nuclear weapons was very limited and late), one immediately sees two important, yet often neglected aspects of nuclear war: (*1*) only one party need have and employ nuclear weapons and (*2*) only a few nuclear weapons (perhaps of low yield) need be used.

Many people imagine nuclear war to be nothing less than a massive exchange of high-yield nuclear warheads by two nations, viz., an all-out exchange between the US and the USSR. Since this could become reality, concern about such a grim prospect is appropriate. Nevertheless, six or more nations already have nuclear weapons, while nuclear reactors in other countries produce radioactive waste that can be converted into material for nuclear weapons. I will not detail the numerous scenarios of how nuclear war could begin, what combinations of parties could be involved, or what levels of destruction might occur.[2] Rather, I will, in light of these possibilities, analyze several misconceptions about nuclear war. While I will, for the most part, assess data on a major exchange, i.e., one involving about 10,000 megatons (MT), I hasten to add that the probable falsity of these public myths increases as the tonnage in a nuclear exchange decreases. A minor power nuclear war could, for example, involve considerably less than a 100 kiloton (KT) exchange – 100,000 times less explosive force and correlative heat and radiation than that which would result from all-out nuclear war.

1 The Myth of the Improbability of Nuclear War. For many people after World War II, "nuclear" was linked to "peace," not "war."[3] Public fears and myths followed the initiation of post-war, above-ground testing and the development of fusion weapons. The public myths emerged as US and Soviet nuclear arsenals rapidly increased and Cold War ideology intensified. Many resorted to "psychic numbing," refusing to pay attention to the arms race and relegating nuclear war to the "unthinkable" among US strategic options.

So far as initiation of an all-out nuclear war is concerned, nuclear war may well be improbable. Since the Soviets developed a modest nuclear arsenal, initiation of all-out war has never been considered a viable strategic option. Yet surrender has also been dismissed. Since both have been rejected,[4] limited nuclear war has been proposed as the only viable alternative when conventional forces are inadequate. Given the degree to which the full range of US ground, sea and air forces have been nuclearized, it should be obvious that nuclear war is not improbable.

Even if policy statements and weapons developments were insufficient to demonstrate the falsity of this myth, the historical record settles the matter. Nuclear weapons were originally built to be used, and they have been used. Since the bombing of Hiroshima and Nagasaki, the US has continued to produce more weapons and has threatened or contemplated their use on several occasions. The US has, for example, seriously contemplated the use of nuclear weapons during the Korean and Vietnam Wars, was prepared to use them during the Cuban Missile Crisis, and sanctions NATO first use of nuclear weapons against large-scale (yet conventional) Warsaw Pact advances. Outside government several studies detail the increasing probability of nuclear war and within government one faction explicitly pursues calculations about the conduct and consequences of nuclear war.[5] The informed citizen must therefore drop the myth that nuclear war is improbable and concede that nuclear war is regarded as a viable strategic option. One may hope that the further use of nuclear weapons will be avoided, but it is a mistake to assume that the option to use nuclear weapons is not taken seriously by governmental planners.

2   *The Myth of the Unsurvivability of Nuclear War.* The assertion that nuclear war is unsurvivable is not true by definition. Logically, one can just as easily assert that nuclear war will have survivors. The conflict between these assertions is settled by evidence, not by definition. Before considering the evidence, however, one must reflect on the sensibility of the following hypotheses: (*1*) If any nuclear war will kill all human beings, then civil defense and post-attack planning are a waste of money and energy that could be applied instead to prevention. (*2*) If all or only some nuclear wars can have survivors, then civil defense and post-attack planning are appropriate at some level, at least from a humanitarian viewpoint. Since the affirmation or denial of survival has such contrasting policy implications, the myth of unsurvivability receives considerable defense and criticism in debate.

Nevil Shute's novel *On the Beach* is a classic articulation of the myth of the unsurvivability of nuclear war. Regardless of its literary merit and political impact, Shute misunderstood the mechanics of fallout and miscalculated the levels of fission. Bernard Feld, a major critic of nuclear weapons who has done extensive research on both fission and fallout, terms Shute's image of total destruction "1 beach" and calculates that such destruction would require one million megatons of fission.[6] Though not altogether reassuring, current global stockpiles are closer to 50,000 MT, and even a major exchange would probably involve only part of this total.[7] At any rate, most scientific calculations show that current blast and radiation potential is insufficient to guarantee human annihilation in any war.

Of course many other significant, yet less researched factors complicate the potential for survival.[8] These factors include: fire storms, ozone depletion, spread of communicable diseases, inadequate life supports, and the carcinogenic/mutagenic effects of radiation. Electromagnetic pulse can also damage communication, and adversaries could attack nuclear reactors. Such unknowns and their interaction do significantly lessen one's confidence in predicting consequences, yet their significance decreases as the level of exchange decreases.

Two of the most prominent of the pessimistic assessments of nuclear war are those of Jonathan Schell and H. Jack Geiger.[9] Despite their graphic and highly gloomy portrayals, neither categorically claims that no one can survive an all-out exchange (though both reject social survival as feasible even if moderate biological survival is likely). Moreover, they omit or dismiss several factors which militate against the possibility of biocide. Given the presence of some national blast protection programs, the precautions of the survivalist movement, the lesser effect of a nuclear war in the non-involved hemisphere of the globe, and the presumed existence of some governmental and non-governmental underground shelters capable of sustaining inhabitants for years, many analysts contend that human annihilation is not highly probable even after a major nuclear war, let alone a minor power, low-yield confrontation.[10]

Most recently, Carl Sagan has presented an even more pessimistic view. He warns of a "nuclear winter" following a nuclear war involving 500 to 2000 strategic nuclear weapons.[11] Especially as a result of the soot from fires, average hemispheric temperature could quickly drop to around -20°C and remain below freezing throughout several months of constantly night-like skies, possibly resulting in the extinction of numerous species – among them *Homo sapiens*.

Sagan calculates that if nuclear winter occurs, as many as 500 trillion people might "not live," i.e., never be born. Assuming biocide to occur, he calculates how many people would have lived if our population rate remained constant, our lifespan averaged 100 years and our species were to have lasted the 10 million years typical of successful species. Of course to deny life to 500 trillion people is wrong. But must it be possible for nuclear war to deny life to billions or trillions before it is clearly wrong? This question is crucial since Sagan proceeds to sketch, though he does not endorse, a scheme in which the use of nuclear weapons would not, on environmental grounds, threaten the survival of the human species. In citing the technical feasibility and environmental tolerability of "sub-threshold" nuclear arsenals (i.e. new systems with several thousand very low-yield, high accuracy, earth-burrowing warheads), even Sagan gives scientific support to the view that nuclear war is, on several levels, strategically viable, survivable, and recoverable.

So long as the myth of unsurvivability is false under many, if not all, scenarios, humane persons should not dismiss too flippantly the propriety of planning for even marginal human survival, though the general propriety of such planning is distinct from a justification of current civil defense planning.

3   The Myth of Unrecoverability from Nuclear War. Assuming nuclear war will have survivors, it makes sense to project into the future the question, "Did any communities recover?" In the social sense, if human life goes on, societal recovery can be pursued.

Pessimism about recovery is epitomized in Khrushchev's remark that after nuclear war, "The survivors will envy the dead." Even more than the myth of unsurvivability, the myth of unrecoverability presents great potential for verbal disagreement, i.e., with different definitions of "recovery," the same evidence can support opposite conclusions. Put simply, to the degree that the myth of unsurvivability is false, the prospect for long-term species survival increases. Given species survival, higher levels of eventual societal recovery are likely as well. In fact, the recoverability debate often ends with disagreement over "how much and how soon."

One of the most pessimistic fictional estimates can be found in Russell Hoban's recent novel, *Riddley Walker.* More than two thousand years after what is termed the "1 Big 1" the inhabitants of England are living not merely under pre-industrial conditions but even largely in a hunting-gathering culture. The novel ends with the rediscovery of gunpowder and the foreboding that civilization is embarking again along the path toward the 1 Big 1. In comparison, the pessimistic academic treatments of J. Carson Mark and John Kenneth Galbraith are much less severe since they paint a picture of a predominantly medieval-style economy. [12] At the opposite extreme stand governmental studies, one of which pictures a recovery of ⅔ of the pre-attack GNP in 9 years, followed by a 4 percent yearly growth rate. [13] Such rapid recovery plans raise serious ethical questions when they involve not only martial law but also reurbanization and remilitarization. [14] The human and economic costs of such endeavors do not so much undercut the possibility of recovery as they undercut the concept of political obligation.

4   The Use of Public Myths by the Anti-Nuclear Movement and by Governments. My treatment of the public myths runs counter to the arguments of some very reputable and respectable anti-nuclear scholars. Generally, their arguments for one or more of the public myths come later than the governmental rejection of these myths and have a different function than the myths in their original, naive forms. My aim is not to undercut their attempt to motivate the peoples of the world to protest the nuclear arms race and the threat of nuclear war. I fully concur that if their interpretations are correct, there are more than sufficient grounds for protest. Such near or actual worst-case interpretations are not, however, necessary for an adequately grounded protest. Two alternate strategies are worth noting. On the one hand, rational and moral objections can be raised cogently even against nuclear wars in which less than everyone is killed or after which marginal recovery is possible. The logical advantage of successful argument on this level is obvious: whereas the unjustifiability of a worst-case nuclear war is not sufficient to imply the unjustifiability of nuclear wars at low levels is sufficient to imply unjustifiability at all higher levels. Of course, some anti-nuclear writers do address limited nuclear war, but they find it difficult to avoid grounding their criticism of limited nuclear war on the prospect of its escalation to all-out war. In that case, the critique of the lower-level conflict does not stand on its own. For me, the articulation of sufficient grounds against less-than-worst-case nuclear wars seems an especially appropriate enterprise for ethicists and moralists worth their salt. Failure to articulate sufficient grounds on this level would bespeak a real theoretical crisis in the adequacy of contemporary moral and ethical philosophy. At the same time, a critical analysis of the politico-military approach can demonstrate contradictions within its framework. Such internal criticism begins with the assumptions of the nuclear establishment and demonstrates its inadequacy and impropriety even on its own terms.

Governmental Myths

Regardless of the extent to which the growth of nuclear stockpiles decreases the probability that the public myths are false, the theory of deterrence and capabilities for waging war with nuclear weapons were forged before the anti-nuclear movement's affirmation of the public myths. Within military and governmental circles there is a widespread belief that the public myths are false. In their place many hold (*1*) that MAD (mutually assured destruction) can be rejected; (*2*) that controlled nuclear war can be waged; or (*3*) that victory can be achieved. When these beliefs fail to include an appreciation of their very limited truth, they function as governmental myths which threaten vast numbers of people. Although I concede that these myths contain some truth, I contend that from the falsity of the public myths, governmental sources make invalid inferences, confusing necessary for sufficient conditions in their pursuit of successful nuclear policies.

1   The Myth of Rejecting MAD. For two decades and largely unknown to the public, systems analysts have been refuting (at least on paper) the doctrine of mutually assured destruction (MAD). As their studies have become more widely disseminated, some military and political figures have become more bellicose, claiming that nuclear war can be limited or that an all-out nuclear war can be sustained.[15]

Many people are shocked by such claims because they believe that "MAD" refers to a US-Soviet strategic stalemate which is facilitated by each side's possession of such vast numbers of incredibly lethal weapons that dumbfounding overkill capacities exist. Most of us have heard someone say, "We have enough nuclear weapons to kill everyone in the world seven times over."[16] This view of MAD and the present stalemate cannot be correct if the myth of unsurvivability is false.

In fact, the public has generally misunderstood – whether through invalid inference on their part or by self-serving design on the government's part – the technical meaning of "MAD" and "overkill."

"MAD" is not equivalent to "biocide." The notion of "assured destruction" was developed in the 1960s by the American Secretary of Defense, Robert S. McNamara.[17] He argued that the potential of the US to destroy 20-25 percent of the Soviet population and over 50 percent of Soviet industry would be sufficient to deter Soviet attack. Such destruction only required delivering one or two nuclear warheads to each of the 200 largest Soviet cities. In terms of policy statements by governments, MAD became a key doctrine once the Soviets had a similar capacity for attack or retaliation. The assumption was that the damage of nuclear war would be too high a price for either side to pay. Of course, mutual nuclear destruction was possible much earlier. Shortly after the Soviet Union entered the nuclear club in 1949, it developed the ability to destroy the major urban and industrial targets in the US in an all-out first strike. The Soviet Union took two decades to stockpile enough weapons to achieve such destruction if it were struck first, though the US has maintained a second-strike capacity since 1949.

The meaning of "overkill," then, is not senseless stockpiling of nuclear weapons beyond a level sufficient to achieve biocide. Rather, "overkill" refers to nuclear capacity beyond the requirements for "assured destruction"; specifically, it is linked to potential delivery failures. US strategy illustrates the "logic" of overkill. By dispersing over 9000 strategic nuclear weapons across the Triad (i.e., ICBMs, SLBMs and bombers), the US assumes that even a surprise attack would be unlikely to knock out enough missiles to reduce retaliatory capacity between 2000 warheads. Assuming a 25 percent failure rate, an overkill of nearly four times would still be available.[18] Such levels of overkill supposedly make even a surprise attack unacceptable. Such a second-strike retaliatory nuclear capacity constituted what was once the US's strategy of "minimum deterrence."

Even under MAD, governments assumed that after nuclear war both sides would have some survivors and could pursue some recovery. With MAD the US monopoly on nuclear weapons ended, however, and the credibility of a nuclear threat was jeopardized, especially in the European theater. The US therefore moved from its policy of "massive retaliation" to a policy of "flexible response."[19] As weapons and scenarios for limited nuclear conflict proliferated, analysts inferred that, in addition to developing an anti-ballistic missile system (ABM), a nation contemplating the use of or fearing subjection to nuclear attack might first try to disperse its population and harden its industry in such a manner that a nuclear attack would have less effect. At the extreme, some argued that such precautions could eliminate the possibility of assured destruction even in a major nuclear exchange. Civil defense became an essential part of strategic planning.[20] "Deterrence" was still desirable, but for the new breed of planners use was also feasible. In rejecting MAD, however, planners give the *impression* that damage will be well below "assured destruction" levels, whereas their own studies place fatality estimates in the millions for even limited exchanges.[21] For this reason alone, the myth of rejecting MAD involves a half-truth and it is not surprising that the reasoning behind "anti-MAD mythology" is sometimes called NUTS – an acronym for "nuclear utilization targeting strategies" or "nuclear use theorists."[22]

2 The Myth of Control in Nuclear War. In the US, public awareness of the governmental view that limited and controlled nuclear war can be waged largely followed the Carter administration's official sanctioning of those views in July 1980. The Reagan administration's plans for "protracted" nuclear war are a further example of post-MAD or NUTS logic.[23] Regardless of which administration is pursuing it, control is credible only if one accepts that several distinctions used by strategy planners involve real contrasts in approach and outcome. Central among these supposedly non-vacuous contrasts are:

(*a*) *Countervalue strategy.* A nuclear strike aimed primarily against populations and industry (MAD, especially in relation to minimum deterrence, relied on this strategy).

(*b*) *Counterforce strategy.* A nuclear strike aimed primarily against military targets, especially those with nuclear strike capacity. (This strategy, when used as a form of "surprise attack," is presented as a "debilitating first strike" that lessens the potential of the victim to achieve a successful second strike.)

(*c*) *Countervailing strategy.* A military strike selected from enhanced conventional options or nuclear options which include strategic countervalue and/or counterforce capacities as well as non-strategic or theater nuclear capacities (such as KT-level howitzer-launched tactical weapons and neutron bombs). (Such a strategy conveys the view that conflict may be controlled and that successful nuclear use may be facilitated.)

Countervailing strategy is current US nuclear policy.[24]

Before the Carter and Reagan official policy shifts, some analysts claimed the Soviets were making advances in counterforce and civil defense which might by the mid-80s give them capacities the US would not share.[25] In addition to a supposedly effective ABM system, the Soviets were developing strategic weapons of such numbers, yield and accuracy that they could be interpreted as designed for or capable of a counterforce attack. (This supposed counterforce potential would be against US ICBM forces and not against US SLBM forces. Bear in mind as well that whereas only 23 percent of US nuclear forces are land-based, 71 percent of Soviet forces are land-based. These facts bring out a very different asymmetry from the one usually publicized in the US and put in a different light the relative threat of counterforce strikes against the ICBM forces of the US and the USSR.[26] On the other hand, the Soviets, who for years had been spending twenty times more on civil defense than the US, were developing a population protection program which, when coupled with a first strike counterforce attack, might offer a buffer against a US second strike.[27] Supposedly in response, the US is now refining its counterforce potential with the Pershing II, MX and cruise missiles and altering its approach to population protection with the Crisis Relocation Program. It has also begun exploring various space-based ballistic missile defense systems and anti-satellite systems.

These factors, along with others in the US's countervailing strategy, make evident the government plan to be ready for many levels and types of nuclear conflict. In conjunction with such plans, it is suggested that these conflicts can be controlled.[28] Of course the *possibility* that nuclear conflict *can be* controlled *does not* imply the *probability* that nuclear conflict *will be* controlled. Critics typically focus on problems in C-3 systems (communications, command, control). Recent attention has stressed (perhaps too restrictively) the possible negative implications of EMP (electromagnetic pulse) in maintenance of C-3.[29] Many in the anti-nuclear movement scoff at talk of control and insist any nuclear conflict will inevitably or most probably escalate to an all-out nuclear war. In response, those who affirm the myth of control stress that there is no physical, political or strategic necessity that once nuclear weapons are (again) used the conflict will escalate to an all-out nuclear exchange. While such statements are true, the myth of control involves a half-truth, because undesired escalation may occur and because contrasts between counterforce/countervalue strikes and strategic/tactical weapons may turn out to be more imaginary than real. (For example, almost any counterforce strike will have countervalue implications, and many so-called tactical weapons are as destructive as the Hiroshima bomb.[30]) Because there are some conditions under which MAD can be rejected and controlled nuclear war can be waged, however, there may be some cases in which victory is possible. Such is the wager of NUTS thinking and countervailing strategy.

3   The Myth of Victory in Nuclear War. The view that nuclear conflicts can be won received its classic public expression in the essay, "Victory Is Possible," by Colin S. Gray and Keith Payne.[31] Unless evaluation of this claim is restricted to semantic considerations or to question-begging premises (as some in the anti-nuclear movement would desire), then it makes sense to explore the conditions under which and the degree to which it can be true.

For victory in nuclear war to be possible, it is necessary, but not sufficient, that the public myths be false. Victory requires more than some survivors and recovery potential. Among other things, a victorious nation must preserve key national institutions and retain political obedience, i.e. it must not end in anarchy.[32] Even if the public myths are false under all scenarios, nuclear war will not necessarily have a winner.

While I concede that there are restricted cases in which one side could emerge as a victor, I deny Gray and Payne's assumption that "the distinction between winning and losing would not be trivial."[33] Some distinctions *are* trivial, and to deny that winning versus losing a major nuclear war would be trivial is to transform such terms into potentially empty categories of ideological rhetoric.

That the myth of victory also involves a half-truth should be obvious. Realistically, almost all nuclear war scenarios involve massive destruction. Moreover, nuclear war is grossly inefficient with respect to the prospect of sparing noncombatants and, in countervalue strategies, specifically aims at noncombatants. Plans for waging nuclear war increasingly appear as the pursuit of Pyrrhic victory. When "acceptable" death tolls for the "victor" can run from 20 million to 100 million and even more,[34] semantic considerations become relevant. If one makes "victory" narrowly quantitative, then one side may well "win" even a major nuclear war. One would therefore expect that post-attack military and political figures of the "victorious" nation will stress such quantitative distinctions as lesser death toll and lower industrial destruction. When "victory" is confronted in its broad qualitative dimensions, however, the sentiment of citizens in the surviving national remnants may well be that the distinction between "winning" and "losing" is trivial and that few will find significant evidence of victory.

4   The Use of Governmental Myths by Pro- and Anti-Nuclear Forces. The calculating arguments of the NUTS faction are not generally cited in government statements. Instead, claims about "everyone losing" in nuclear war or the possibility of "prevailing" (rather than winning) abound. Not surprisingly, many citizens do not realize that current strategic doctrine is based on the rejection of MAD. Insofar as citizens are unaware that the public myths have been rejected by many in politico-military circles, governments need not defend anew the foundations on which current planning rests. Nevertheless, much of the information on such planning is unclassified, and through the efforts of various antinuclear organizations, rapidly growing numbers of citizens are aware of these changes.

For many the question is not whether, but how to alter nuclear policies. Even on the assumptions of the politico-military establishment, representatives of the anti-nuclear movement can attack the cogency of the governmental myths about nuclear war. One can concede some elements of truth or, at least, possibility in the government's assumptions. By indicating how much significant information is omitted, one can expose the governmental myths for the half-truths they are. The task at this point passes beyond logical clarification, however, and involves ideological considerations. In politics the elevation of persuasion above truth is propaganda, and nuclear propaganda and the half-truths which fuel it have become increasingly sophisticated over the past decade. Increased public education could facilitate a dramatic turn from propaganda to rational argument.

Conclusion

My analysis of public and governmental myths about nuclear war suggests, at the very least, that none of these myths ought to be taken for granted. They are not self-evident or self-supporting, yet they often function as pivotal premises in arguments over public policy. My analysis goes beyond saying that these myths cannot be taken at face value, however. Hence I have also argued that they misrepresent the facts. For this reason, I cannot support the use of any of the myths, except in very restricted and properly qualified contexts.

In stronger terms and going beyond what I could adequately argue for in this brief essay, I contend that false consciousness results from public myths, that political propaganda results from governmental myths, and that neither is wise: the public myths foster helplessness among citizens and the governmental myths countenance foolhardiness among our leaders. Regardless of the charges of false consciousness and propaganda, the debate needs to move beyond falsity and half-truth and beyond the prospect that such misconceptions result in helplessness and foolhardiness.

The nuclear debate, if it is to be rational, must occur between the extremes of public and governmental myths. If my critique discredits specific postures on both sides, several other important points follow. The government's critique of public myths as false does not imply that current nuclear policies are reasonable, and the public's critique of governmental myths does not imply that current anti-nuclear proposals are reasonable. It is irresponsible to argue *against* current nuclear policy on the basis of myths that are false or to argue *for* current nuclear policy on the basis of myths that are half-truths. Even if the debate avoided such fallacious and irresponsible arguments, however, the factual evidence will not itself demonstrate which policy options, if any, are rationally justifiable.

Many of the relevant factual issues are either unknown or undeterminable. Despite the use of the language of probability, numerous other crucial factual issues cannot be treated by either classical or relative frequency theories and must be relegated to the dubious realm of subjective probability. Where empirical data are incomplete and probability calculus is imprecise other relevant considerations, like prudence, may properly play the decisive role. What is responsible in the nuclear debate is to recognize that *facts alone cannot settle the policy issues*. Facts are relevant; they can show some views to be false and others to be half-truths, but the accumulation of facts is insufficient in the nuclear debate.

Within the parameters I propose, citizens and leaders who seek rational resolution of the nuclear debate still face a formidable challenge. The challenge is not merely how the public and government can, without exaggeration, argue about the facts. The challenge also includes the problem of how to recognize and resolve value issues in the debate. These considerations include general and external issues such as the morality of war, and particular and internal issues such as prudence in the face of inconclusive factual data. Indirectly, my argument supports the relevance of the diverse work by philosophers who seek to apply logical, political, and ethical theories to the nuclear debate. While *Realpolitik* has tried to dismiss moral arguments or to relegate them to secondary importance, my argument shows that the separation of fact and value and the restriction of focus to matters of fact leaves logically insoluble the problem of justifying nuclear policy. Of course it is also fallacious to presume that the addition of any specific set of value premises is either adequate or appropriate. It is for this reason that philosophers are the professionals who are most qualified to address such questions.

It is possible that the nuclear debate can have a rational resolution, and at this point in the public debate, genuine possibilities for rational resolution deserve serious consideration. Since increased philosophical sensitivity in the treatment of the factual and value issues could make the difference in the nuclear debate (and our future), let us hope that it becomes more philosophical.

University of North Carolina at Charlotte

NOTES

1 Definitions of nuclear war are scarce. Among US government sources, neither *The Effects of Nuclear Weapons* nor *The Effects of Nuclear War* defines nuclear war. My definition is consistent with what these classic (and value neutral) texts say about the nature of nuclear weapons and the scenarios for nuclear war.

2 For information on global arsenals, nuclear technology and routes to and effects of nuclear war, see especially the UN's *Nuclear Weapons* and Beres, *Apocalypse*. Also helpful, but presenting its nuclear establishmentarian analysis as the first "realistic, non-emotional and non-partisan" investigation, is the volume by the Harvard Nuclear Study Group.

3 For a satirical view of this period, see the movie "The Atomic Cafe," produced and directed by Kevin Rafferty, Jayne Loader, and Pierce Rafferty. The movie is composed of clips from films, radio and TV broadcasts, and speeches of the 40s and 50s. For a serious treatment, see Wasserman and Solomon.

4 Cf. Gray and Payne on the strategic rejection of "surrender or all-out nuclear war."

5 For outside government, see sources in note 2. For within government, see the US government, *Nuclear War Strategy, Planning US Strategic Nuclear Forces,* and *Countervailing Strategy,* as well as more publicized comments by key military and political figures.

6 Feld, "The Consequences of Nuclear War," p. 13. See also his essay "The Mechanics of Fallout."

7 UN, *Nuclear Weapons.*

8 See Adams and Cullen, eds., and the US Government, DCPA *Attack Environment Manual.* Especially detailed on these issues is the study by the Committee for the Compilation of Materials on Damage Caused by the Atomic Bombs. Concerning electromagnetic pulse (EMP), see the articles by Broad and by Holden. Concerning attacks on nuclear reactors, see Ramberg.

9 See Schell, *The Fate of the Earth;* Jack Geiger, *"Illusion and Survival,"* in Adams and Cullen, eds.; and the pieces by Somerville and Santoni in this collection.

10 Among US Government sources, see *Civil Defense* and "Questions and Answers on Crisis Relocation Planning." For survivalist planning, see especially Clayton.

11 See Sagan, as well as two selections by Turco et. al. and one by Ehrlich et. al. For a scientific critique, see Singer.

12 See J. Carson Mark, "The Consequences of Nuclear War," in Griffiths and Polanyi, eds.; J.K. Galbraith, "Economics of the Arms Race–and After," in Adams and Cullen, eds.

13 Cf. DCPA *Attack Environment Manual,* Chap. 8.

14 These points are implicit or explicit in the hypothetical case and analysis done for DCPA by Brown. They are also made in many other sources.

15 For an early study and critique of such "systems analysis," see H. Green. For recent strategy sources in government, see note 4. For a critique of these government sources, see Buchan, and Beres, *Mimicking Sisyphus.* See also Shrader-Frechette's article, this volume.

16 Even Caldicott makes this claim (Nuclear Madness, p. 67).

17 Cf. UN, *Nuclear Weapons* and the US Government, *The Economic and Social Consequences of Nuclear Attacks.*

18 Cf. Lewis.

19 To see how far from these strategies their architects have moved, i.e., to support for "no first use," see Bundy et. al.

20 Cf. US Government, *Civil Defense.*

21 See *ibid.,* Bellenson, and Beres, *Mimicking Sisyphus.*

22 Recent issues of the *Bulletin of the Atomic Scientists* have addressed this focus. Cf. also Joseph.

23 Cf. *Countervailing Strategy,* pp. 1, 10-12, and Halloran.

24 For a "pro" and "con" discussion, see the US Government, *Nuclear War Strategy,* and Beres, "Presidential Directive 59."

25 Cf. Huntington's testimony in US Government, *Civil Defense.*

26 Cf. UN, *Nuclear Weapons.*

27 Cf. Huntington's testimony in US Government, *Civil Defense.*

28 For sources in government, see note 4.

29 See Miller, "Existing Systems of Command and Control," in Griffiths and Polanyi, eds.; and the articles cited in note 8.

30 Cf. UN, *Nuclear Weapons.*

31 Even more "NUTS" than Gray and Payne's article is that by Bellenson and Cohen. For another leading NUTS analysis, see Luttwak.

32 Cf. US Government, *The Economic and Social Consequences of Nuclear Attacks,* and Brown.

33 Gray and Payne, p. 14.

34 Ibid., pp. 25-26.

Commentary: Somerville, Gay and Limited Nuclear War

LEO GROARKE

John Somerville equates nuclear war with the total destruction he calls "omnicide." In contrast, William Gay argues that it is a mistake to think that nuclear war is unsurvivable or impossible to recover from. It is, I think, possible to find a middle ground between these views. On the one hand, Gay is surely right in suggesting that a nuclear war might not encompass all-out combat, and that this is not necessary to make it morally unacceptable. On the other, Somerville is right to suggest that the possible consequences of a nuclear war are on a plane far beyond anything previously imagined. Even if the worst case scenario did not entail omnicide (which it might if ecological damages were severe enough) it would entail billions of casualties and pain and suffering on a scale hitherto inconceivable. Logically speaking, it is possible that nuclear war could be limited, though this does not (as Gay points out[1]) make it a viable military strategy. I shall argue that the possibility of escalation into the scenario Somerville describes makes ethically unacceptable any talk of limited war between the superpowers. It is important not to forget that nuclear proliferation means that nuclear war might be waged by minor powers (or even terrorist groups), though I leave a discussion of such a possibility for elsewhere.

The view of limited war espoused by the superpowers is in some ways unclear, though it is American policy which has most straightforwardly endorsed the notion. The American administration has made conflicting statements, but a commitment to limited nuclear war is evident in prevailing military strategy.[2] Such a commitment is, for example, illustrated by the American refusal to follow the Soviets in a pledge of no first use; the NATO endorsement of the use of tactical weapons in Europe (a policy based largely on an exaggeration of Soviet conventional strength[3]); the continuing buildup of the American stockpile of more than 20,000 tactical weapons (some 5000 to 8000 more than the Soviets have deployed); and the development and deployment of intermediate range weapons (e.g. the Pershing II) which make sense only in the context of first strike and limited nuclear war. It is in view of such trends that the possibility of limited nuclear war is at the heart of American military planning.

It is best to begin an examination of limited nuclear war by noting that debate on the issue has proceeded in a somewhat peculiar way. Those who have proposed the notion have suggested it as an obvious alternative which needs no special scrutiny or examination. In answer to their claims others have argued that limited war is an untenable military option. These two trends have created the impression that the onus is on those who reject the notion to prove it inconsistent, though nothing could be further from the truth. Thus the consequences of a failure to keep a limited war limited are so severe that the moral onus is squarely on the shoulders of those who propose the notion to prove (not assume) it is a viable alternative. If there is one chance in ten that a limited nuclear war would not escalate, for example, then any particular confrontation might not escalate though it would be reckless to put much faith in such a possibility. Given that a failure to keep a war limited could entail omnicide or something very similar, it cannot be justified on the off chance it may succeed.

The kind of responsibility which must be borne by leaders who endorse the idea of limited nuclear war can be illustrated with examples which might seem initially unrelated. A variety of examples come to mind, but one which is particularly perspicuous is the use of the drug thalidomide by pregnant women during the late 1950s. Sold as a cure for morning sickness, it produced babies without arms and legs, and with a variety of horrific birth defects. The important point for us to note is that the producers of thalidomide were morally obligated to insure that it did not have negative side effects *before* it was put on sale and their failure to do so was the ultimate cause of birth defects. By failing to submit the drug to sufficient tests, they gambled with the lives of pregnant women and their offspring, and this is morally unacceptable.

To move from thalidomide to limited nuclear war, we might note that the responsibility for insuring that something has acceptable consequences increases as its potential harm increases. Safety checks on airplanes, not taxi cabs, take place before every trip because the results of mechanical failure are much more serious. Thalidomide was a tragedy because the birth defects it produced caused so much mental and physical hardship. They are, however, nothing when compared to the billions of casualties; the pain and agony; the destruction of homes, cities, and industries; and the ecological damage which would occur if a nuclear confrontation were to escalate. It immediately follows that those military and political leaders who suggest limited nuclear war as a military strategy have an even greater responsibility to prove that such a strategy will not fail. Given that the failure of limited nuclear war would, as Somerville suggests, entail more dire consequences than anything else imaginable, no other gamble is more reprehensible and no other activity requires more certainty about its outcome.

Despite the enormous onus on those who propose the viability of limited nuclear war, they have provided little evidence for their claims. On the contrary, all the evidence suggests that a limited engagement would lead to all-out war. To see why, we may note that there are serious problems with the limitation of any war, though the real point is that they become virtually insurmountable in the nuclear context. An example may illustrate this point.

One way in which conventional war has been limited is by so-called "combat by champions." Practiced in one form or another for some four thousand years, it replaces conventional war with personal combat between champions from opposing sides. In this way it avoids the casualties and injuries which would result from all-out war. A variant of champion combat which illustrates its weaknesses is the battle between Argos and Sparta over the territory of Thyreae during the sixth century BC. To avoid all-out combat, both sides agreed that six hundred hand picked men would do battle and that the winners would take Thyreae. Leaving the chosen to do battle, the two armies returned to their encampments to insure that they did not interfere with the fighting. Despite their careful precautions, their attempt to wage a limited war was not successful. Hence the battle was so fierce that two Argives and one Spartan were all that survived the fighting. The two Argives immediately returned to their army to announce their victory, but the Spartan Othryadas remained to strip the bodies of the Argive dead, carrying their equipment to his own camp. When the armies met to officially declare a winner, both claimed victory – the Argives in virtue of their two survivors and the Spartans in virtue of the fact that their survivor had stripped the bodies of the dead. The argument eventually turned to blows and a new battle ensued.

The lesson to be learned from the Argos-Sparta conflict is that the most carefully planned limited war can go askew. This raises the possibility that the attempt to wage limited nuclear war might not succeed, though the ramifications are much worse than this. Hence the Spartan-Argive attempt to limit war is – despite its failure – an admirable attempt to specify clear and precise limits to the conduct of a battle. These limits were not precise enough, though they constitute a more serious attempt to limit battle than anything that has been proposed by the proponents of limited nuclear war. The stakes in a nuclear confrontation would be infinitely greater, yet the United States and the Soviet Union have *no* agreement whatsoever on how to conduct a limited nuclear war. Instead of clear and precise limits establishing what tactics are and are not permissible, those who support limited nuclear war rely on the vague and indeterminate suggestion that an all-out attack should be avoided – though even this suggestion is not the basis of international agreements. The standard view seems to be that the use of nuclear weapons should be limited to the extent necessary for victory, but this does not set a definite limit and asks for escalation. It is only naiveté which could allow one to believe that the Soviets would not respond with a similar strategy, and this entails a gradual escalation as each superpower ups the ante to avert defeat. Given no established limit beyond which neither party may progress, it is hard to see how such a situation can avert disaster. One might try to establish such a ceiling – by limiting the number or the size of nuclear warheads – but it is hard to see how violations can be monitored. The only clearly viable limit is *no* nuclear weapons, and any deviation from it is dangerous and indeterminate. Even if other limits were inherently plausible, the inability of the superpowers to reach arms control agreements makes it difficult to expect any more success on ground rules for limited nuclear war. The suggestion that limits can be established during an actual confrontation is founded on the notion that compliance becomes more likely in circumstances where experience shows just the opposite is the case.

The very notion of strict rules for limited nuclear war is inherently implausible. The usual scenario suggests the careful monitoring of an enemy attack and retaliation with an appropriate response. Such a scenario has little basis in reality, however, and is more in keeping with a game of chess than a war. In an actual confrontation, the use of nuclear weapons would take place in the confusion of battle, where there is no time for careful assessment and calculated response, and where it is difficult – if not impossible – to control thousands of nuclear warheads operated by a variety of military commanders. The fact that centers of communication and command would be among the primary targets would contribute to the confusion. Indeed, some commentators have suggested that such attacks would be so destabilizing that both sides will specifically refrain from them, though there are no explicit policies in this regard and conventional military wisdom sees such actions as most likely to secure the enemy's defeat. If military and political leaders are reckless enough to attempt to fight a limited nuclear war, one cannot place too much confidence in their ability to feel the force of such considerations.

One problem with limited nuclear war which warrants special mention is the electromagnetic pulse – the so called EMP effect – which accompanies nuclear explosions. It causes such severe side effects that it is likely a single Soviet warhead detonated over Nebraska would knock out unprotected communications equipment throughout the United States. Such equipment can to some extent be hardened to protect against the EMP effect but is at present vulnerable. As Dr. Steinbruner, a senior researcher at the Brookings Institute remarks, this vulnerability and the "precariousness of command channels" it implies "probably means that nuclear war would be uncontrollable, as a practical matter, shortly after the first tens of weapons are launched."[4] Those who argue for limited war maintain that EMP problems can be overcome, though similar reassurances were made in the early 1960s, and have never been fulfilled. In 1980 the Federation of American Scientists devoted a special edition of its newsletter to the problem, remarking that "We ought not to kid ourselves that we are prepared to fight a protracted nuclear war when no plausible improvement in command, control and communications is likely to permit it; countervailing strategies with numerous complicated options that cannot, in fact, be carried out could become an expensive kind of self-delusion."[5] In addition to the problems EMP creates for the control of nuclear warfare, it encourages the adoption of a "use them or lose them" policy which would see the early use of the American – or Soviet – nuclear arsenal in order to insure that problems with communications do not render it unusable.

A second problem with the mechanics of limited nuclear war is the likelihood that long-term consequences will be forgotten in the heat of battle. As Basil Lidell Hart puts it, military commanders "will always tend to use every weapon available if it looks likely that their troops will be overrun. In that immediate concern they tend to lose sight of wider issues. By taking the narrow view they have often in the past marred the aims of higher policy. Now, they could wreck the world."[6] Solly Zuckerman, the chief scientific advisor to the British Ministry of Defence from 1960 to 1966 and the chief scientific advisor to the British Government from 1966 to 1971, agrees. His recent book *Nuclear Illusion and Reality* describes a series of NATO war games he organized to test the use of tactical nuclear weapons in Europe. It is worth our while to quote his conclusions at length. He writes:

There are no rules in nuclear or any form of warfare like those which apply in the boxing-ring.

... Both the logic of the situation and the results of war games show that escalation to all-out nuclear war is all but implicit in the concept of fighting a field war with "tactical" and "theatre" nuclear weapons.

... A field commander would tend to use more and more weapons if it became apparent that a previous weight of attack was not having the desired effect of halting the enemy. Once the weapons he used included nuclear warheads, the likelihood is that more would be used.

... the only conceivable reason why a nuclear battlefield would not escalate to an all-out nuclear exchange would be because both sides simultaneously stopped to consider what the further consequences might be.

... But for this to happen command and control, as well as the scope of intelligence and reconnaissance, would for both sides have to be considerably better technically than they are now, at the same time as the psychological reactions of the contestants would have to be the reverse of what has been the pattern in previous wars.[7]

Zuckerman goes on to list a number of military specialists who have reached similar conclusions, among them Lord Mountbatten, who in 1979 remarked that the belief that nuclear weapons could be used in field warfare without triggering an all-out exchange is "more and more incredible. ... In all sincerity, as a military man I can see no use for any nuclear weapons which would not end in escalation, with consequences that no one can conceive." Admiral of the Fleet Lord Hill-Norton, Field Marshal Lord Carver and Marshal of the RAF Sir Neil Cameron – all former Chiefs of the British Defence Staff – agree. On the American side, Herbert Scoville, a former Technical Director of the American Armed Forces, writes the following of his "experience" with limited nuclear war:

When I was in the government, back in the 1960s, I used to participate from time to time in so-called "war games" that the Joint Chiefs of Staff held. On two occasions we dealt with the European situation. These war games started with the Red Team carrying out some kind of aggressive act in Germany. Then the Blue Team wasn't doing very well, and so it said, "We've just got to show the Reds we are serious." So it dropped one nuclear weapon on a Red Team tank battalion and wiped it out. The Blues thought that was going to convince the Reds to back off and that there would be no further aggression. Unfortunately, the Red Team said "We're not going to be bluffed by this sort of thing; we're going to show them that we really mean business." And they dropped five atomic bombs on five of the Blues airfields, knocking out the planes. The action then zigzagged back and forth, escalating at each step. The net result of the war game was not only that there was no Europe left; there was also no Soviet Union, no United States, at least as modern societies.

There is just no way one can count on keeping a limited nuclear war limited. ... We don't want any kind of war, but one of the things that is absolutely certain is that we cannot rely on nuclear weapons to win a conflict.[8]

Such comments do not allow much room for confidence in our ability to keep a limited war contained.

The most likely cause of a limited nuclear war would be the use of tactical or "battlefield" weapons in a conventional war in Europe. It is this which is discussed by Zuckerman and Scoville. An alternative scenario would see the use of strategic weapons in an attempt to destroy an enemy's warheads before they can be used. It is the American military which is closest to achieving the capability for a so called "disarming first strike," though there is no reason to put much faith in such a possibility. Hence its success would require a Soviet failure to detect incoming missiles and a completely unrealistic success rate in finding and destroying Soviet submarines, bombers and land based ICBMs. If only 99 percent of all Soviet missiles were prevented from reaching their targets (a phenomenal rate of success) the West would still experience millions of casualties and a medical disaster. However successful, such an attack would leave the Soviets to dispose of their tactical weapons as they saw fit while recent research suggests that it would produce a nuclear winter which would wreak havoc on the North American environment. Military strategy founded on the limited use of strategic arsenals is no more plausible than that founded on the use of tactical nuclear warheads.

We might finish our discussion of limited nuclear war by noting the problems with the common claim that humanitarian considerations would not allow a limited war to escalate. Any such suggestion exaggerates the role that humanitarian considerations play in times of war. If one needs any indication of the lack of concern for pain and suffering which is its natural consequence, it is provided by the principle of noncombatant immunity and its fate during World War II. Arguably a part of the international laws of war, much has been made of the fact that it was respected at the beginning of the war, but as Ian Clark writes:

The capacity of stylized conventions to limit war could not be thought encouraging in light of earlier precedents in the course of the Second World War. As is well known, the precision bombing with which Britain prepared to conduct the war rapidly took the form of indiscriminate area bombardment as Bomber Command groped for an operational policy which was consistent with its role as an independent force and with the technical limitations of its bomber fleet. It is difficult to conceive that the very Bomber Command which was to devise the saturation bombings of Berlin, Hamburg and of Dresden had but a few short years before prevented its aircraft from bombing German navel vessels at Wilhelmshaven, as they were considered too close to the shore to be attacked without collateral civilian damage. The conventions of aerial bombardment were, therefore, to be the most spectacular casualties of the war. Likewise, although the United States Air Force had a slightly cleaner record in its offensive against Germany, by early 1945 it was heavily engaged in the fire-bombing of Japan with massive civilian loss of life.[9]

The failure of the Allied forces to respect civilian immunity during World War II cannot inspire much confidence in the ability of humanitarian considerations to prevent the escalation of a limited nuclear war.

The best analogy for limited nuclear war is the game "chicken" – a life-and-death game where two drivers, typically adolescents, drive at one another at breakneck speed. The winner is the driver who does not alter his course, while the loser is the driver who "chickens out" and drives off course. In any particular game, the two drivers must weigh their desire to prove themselves against the chances that they will kill themselves in the impending collision. No driver will intend to kill himself, but he may be willing to take a chance in order to win the game – particularly if the stakes are high (pride itself has sufficed). To compare this to limited nuclear war, note that it too amounts to a decision to proceed down a path of mutual destruction (possibly omnicide) in the hope that the other superpower will turn off course and admit defeat. What is more likely to happen is that the other side will up the ante in an attempt to intimidate its opponent. Given the resoluteness of both sides and all that is at stake, it is hard to see how this can lead to anything but disaster. We would quite rightly reprove teenagers who participate in chicken; how much more should we reprove military and political leaders who are playing not only with their lives, but all of ours as well.   *Wilfrid Laurier University*

NOTES

1 There is some tension in Gay's paper in this regard. Hence he criticizes other commentators for rejecting limited nuclear war on the grounds that it might escalate, though he himself advocates prudence and attacks governmental views because they accept the "myth" that nuclear war can be controlled. It should in this regard be noted that an appeal to the likelihood of escalation does provide the strongest moral basis for a rejection of limited nuclear war. To take an analogous case, one could argue that it would be wrong to shoot a terrorist if one or two bystanders might be shot in the crossfire, though the case against shooting is much stronger if hundreds or thousands of hostages are likely to die as well.

2 For a discussion of Soviet views, see Kaplan, *The Dubious Specter.* Re: the inconsistency of American views, note President Reagan's October 1, 1981 statement that "It's difficult for me to believe there's a winnable nuclear war." (Cockburn, p. 99), a statement which contradicts his earlier claim that the notion of limited nuclear war made such winning possible.

3 See Cockburn.

4 See Broad, "Nuclear Pulse (III)," 1248.

5 *Ibid.,* 1249.

6 Solly Zuckerman, p. 62.

7 *Ibid.,* pp. 65-69.

8 Herbert Scoville, Jr., "West – A Clear and Present Danger," in Adams and Cullen, eds., pp. 67-68.

9 Clark, pp. 233-34.

Part I   Issues to Think About and Discuss

1   Somerville asserts that nuclear war is "as qualitatively different from war as death is from disease." Evaluate this claim.

2   Do you think that the American Declaration of Independence, as cited by Somerville, obliges us citizens to resist their government's preparations for nuclear conflict? If so, to what extent? If not, why not?

3   State, in your own terms, one governmental myth and one public myth about nuclear war. Find an example of each in the media or in something else you have read, a political speech, etc. What effects have these myths had? (Refer to Gay's article.)

4   Is it morally irresponsible to advocate limited nuclear war? Defend your answer. (Refer to Groarke's commentary.)

Part II The Individual and the State

Noncombatants, Indiscriminate Killing, and the Immorality of Nuclear War

RICHARD WASSERSTROM

The idea that even in time of war there are certain things it is wrong to do is neither an unintelligible nor an unfamiliar one. Even in the more total, quite unrestrained armed conflicts of this century, certain limits on the conduct of the wars, on the ways they were fought, were both acknowledged and adhered to. Members of armed forces who surrendered were taken prisoner rather than killed, the neutrality of certain countries was recognized and respected, and weapons, such as poison gas, were not employed (at least in World War II). In addition, of course, after the end of World War II, the victorious Allied powers conducted trials based in part upon the idea that some individuals had in the course of the conduct of the war violated important norms and principles prohibiting certain kinds of wartime conduct – violations of the laws of war. And members of the armed forces of the United States, as well as many other countries, are taught that there are certain specifiable things they may not do in war; some, though not very many, have been disciplined and punished for having done them.

Those who have sought to make moral as well as intellectual sense out of the idea that even in time of war there are some ways of fighting it which are impermissible and wrong have proceeded along several distinct lines of analysis and argument. One approach takes the existing conventions, treaties and practice which establish prohibitions upon the forms and kinds of warfare and weapons as providing the exhaustive content of what it is impermissible to do in the conduct of war. A second, potentially more fruitful approach is the view that such prohibitions' having been accepted and agreed to is evidence that they reflect or embody those moral considerations and values that continue to have place and application in time of war. I have on other occasions endeavored to indicate and explain what I take to be the problems with both approaches, and I will not pursue such questions here. Rather, I will assume, what I take to be

in fact the case, that the existing laws of war do not clearly prohibit nuclear weapons from being used in war. At the very least, if it would always be wrong to use them it is not because the Hague or Geneva Conventions or the principles accepted and applied after World War II expressly govern and prohibit their use. Hence, my aim is to try to develop a plausible theory about what considerations matter most in time of war, about what it is wrong to do in time of war and why, and about why nuclear weapons are impermissible to use.
ble to use.

The distinction that is a central part of the tradition of moral thought about the laws of war and that is, I think, still the central distinction that properly holds in time of war is the one expressed in and through the ideas that even in time of war there are differences between combatants and noncombatants, that these differences give rise to, explain, or justify the different moral status of each, and make it wrong to do to noncombatants what it may not, in wartime, be wrong to do to combatants. Sometimes this gets expressed in terms of the innocence of noncombatants and in terms of principles or considerations having to do with the claims they have and with things that it is wrong to do to or with them. But, without explication, the sense of "innocence" which is relevant here is neither clear nor obvious, and without further thought and argument the relevant principles or considerations concerning the innocent are neither apparent nor manifestly correct. So, there are at least two questions that must be investigated: (*1*) Are there differences, even in wars that are total, that in fact make it possible to identify and distinguish the combatants from the noncombatants?; and (*2*) If there are, do these give rise to a defensible moral position concerning things that it is wrong to do to noncombatants, even in time of war?

If the combatants in question were only those individuals who were members of the armed forces and if all members of the armed forces were to wear distinctive uniforms, then we could identify them accordingly and distinguish them from the noncombatants who were not so garbed and not so specially engaged in conducting (i.e. fighting) the war. And we could then also develop an account of their differences in moral standing or status and of the reasons why things it would be permissible to do to combatants would be wrong to do to noncombatants. For in war the armed forces of each side are at least prepared, under a claim of right, to subdue the opposing armed forces. Under such circumstances it seems surely appropriate that members of the armed forces of each side view and regard members of the armed forces of the other side as their prospective killers. They are *armed* with weapons of deadly force and the arms are the means by which armed forces fight, and battles and wars are won and lost. So it seems quite reasonable to think and to argue that once it is a war that is going on, it is not wrong, for reasons that borrow upon familiar ideas of self-defense, that

members of the armed forces of either side should either intentionally or knowingly seek to kill those similarly situated on the other side – at least, surely, unless
and until they have surrendered and laid down their arms, so that they no longer
possess the ability, as well as the intention (which they still may, of course,
possess), to kill or otherwise subdue them. As long as they have that ability and
that intention constitutive of membership in the armed forces the use and
employment of weapons of deadly force against them seems a part of the internal logic and morality of war.

Noncombatants are different. Because they are not armed they cannot kill
and are not committed to killing in the same way. They do not constitute the
same kind of danger, and therefore the case, if there is one, for justifiably, intentionally, or knowingly killing them in time of war must be different and not
founded in the same relatively secure fashion upon relatively familiar ideas concerning the permissible use of deadly force in self-defense.[1]

It can, though, be argued that the distinction between noncombatants and
combatants is not so easily made out nor the difference in moral status so easily established. One might hold that wars, especially total wars, require the
organized support, energies, and activities of large numbers of persons not
themselves members of the armed forces. Weapons and armaments need to be
designed, manufactured, and supplied to the armed forces. The members of the
armed forces need to be clothed, fed, and housed. And even their morale is an
important component of how effectively and well they will fight. It is the so-
called "noncombatants" of the country who can be and are engaged in doing
all of these kinds of things. If they were not supporting the armed forces in all
sorts of ways, both material and ideological, by and through their own intentional and knowing actions, the war would be a short and unsuccessful one
because of the failure of the effort required to sustain it. The point is that the
causal chains which lead to the wielding and employment of the weapons of
war by the members of the armed forces are longer, more complex, and less clear
than appeared at first, and it is no longer either obvious or right that the targets
of these weapons be only those who are most immediately or distinctively in
the position to employ them, and hence to constitute a deadly danger.

What is more, just as it does not and cannot matter, once a war is underway,
whether the members of the armed forces volunteered or were conscripted under
circumstances that left them no real choice, so too it does not and cannot matter much whether the noncombatants working in the factories or the fields are
enthusiastic supporters of the war or are there because they have no real choice.
If they are there, they are doing things, acting in ways that aid, help, contribute
to, and are parts of the causal chains that go to make up the fighting and the
waging of war. And if they are not there, but in their beds asleep, they will be

there the next day. They are still tightly connected to the war and the war effort, just as are members of the armed forces when they are asleep at night. In war, especially in total war, the distinction between combatants and noncombatants, so this line of argument concludes, is not a clear-cut or coherent one; nor is it one that can or should have moral weight; nor is it one that could possibly be maintained in practice, even if there were theoretical distinctions that could, in the abstract, be identified and defended. That is why, for example, there was nothing wrong *per se* with the saturation bombing of cities in World War II. The war effort was at work in Dresden as well as in the battlefield, and there was no way to identify and destroy the factories and the factory workers effectively, except in this way.

Nor is this the only argument that could be advanced. Even if there are noncombatants in the sense so far considered, there are other things to take into account. Any number of noncombatants may have opted for the war in the first place and it will of course be impossible to tell which ones. They may have supported it and helped to bring it about. They may support it still. If so, then there are different causal chains within which they are enmeshed and a different moral dimension since it was or is their actions that played a role in bringing about the situation in which the weapons of war are what they now confront. And if the war that they favored and helped to bring into being is a wrongful or unjust one, then they are, still more clearly, morally culpable for their places in these causal chains and what they produced. If they are culpable in this way, their special moral status as noncombatants is undermined further. Bearing some responsibility for the war and its unusual dangers, it is permissible that the dangers and risks so created be borne by them rather than by those on the opposing side. In the imperfect moral world of war, killing them, even if they are noncombatants, is permissible as the only kind of punishment they are likely to receive and do deserve. In all these ways persons can be and are noncombatants without being morally innocent, and for that reason distinct from the rest who may not permissibly be killed in time of war.[2]

And finally, there is just the matter of practicality. Even if there were theoretical distinctions that in the abstract could be made, they could not possibly be maintained in practice. Innocent noncombatants, if there are any, do not wear special uniforms or keep to special places. If a war is to be waged at all effectively, perhaps it is wrong to try deliberately to kill them if we do know who and where they are, but that is all that morality in war can or should require.

I do not think these lines of argument are right, despite their apparent plausibility and despite the difficulties and complexities which provide that plausibility. One of the guiding ideas is that of self-defense *in* war, extended, as we have seen, to the peculiar and special circumstances of what is and must be true of war. But the extension goes too far and in ways that morality does not licence. No matter how extensively and complexly the causal chains are extended back from the actual possessors and employers of the weapons of war, they do not and cannot reasonably be thought to include all persons living within a country at war, or even all activities in which persons within a country may be engaged. There are differences of degree as well as kind, and both matter when the case for intentional and knowing killing rests upon the permissible use of deadly force as a matter of self-defense *in* war. If persons are not causing, producing, or constituting in any way a threat to life it is hard to see how killing them on grounds of self-defense, no matter how that notion be relaxed or loosened, can itself be maintained or defended.

If the things that link noncombatants to the war and to armed combatants are matters that have to do with their causal relationship to the war, with ideas having to do with assumption of risk, perhaps, or just with a fair and reasonable redistribution of risk in the light of the dangers they helped to create or favored, then these are ties and connections which must in fact exist and must not merely be asserted. I do not know how loose the ties and connections can be in reasoning about these matters when the relationships are between individual action, acquiescence, or enthusiasm, on the one hand, and the behavior of groups and collective action and conduct, on the other. Nor do I know how and to what extent that relationship, if and when it holds, properly shifts or imposes liability to being deliberately killed on the individuals tied and connected in these more tenuous, but still real and intelligible ways. But it cannot be correct that just because they are *there,* in a country at war, they are sufficiently tied and hence permissibly killed. There must be some basis in fact for the assertion of a further connection before this way of reasoning becomes plausible.

To regard the intentional or knowing killing of noncombatants as justifiable as a kind of summary capital punishment requires, surely, a stronger, tighter connection. It is one that has to do, at the very least, with the moral culpability of the individuals executed in this way for their wrongdoing. Perhaps in war and in the absence of enforceable municipal laws and courts, our ideas about the conditions for permissible punishment can be appreciably loosened and relaxed here too. But there must be here, as well, some basis in fact for the assertion of an actual culpability before this way of reasoning can assert a legitimate claim to be considered.

If these very general and only partially explicated considerations and conclusions are correct, then there are, I believe, real and deep problems with all of the lines of argument offered in support of the permissibility of the deliberate killing of noncombatants, especially in indiscriminate fashion. For among the classes of noncombatants that we might identify as those possessing none of the characteristics that might affect or alter their moral status, children, of whom there are many in all countries, are fully noncombatants in all of the senses challenged, and clearly so. They are innocent in each and every one of the senses in which a lack of innocence might be relevant to the permissibility of acting to kill those who are not. They exist in large numbers, they are alive and most if not all of them are, just as fully as adults, persons whose lives are as valuable as those of any other persons. It is as wrong to kill them, intentionally or knowingly, as it is to kill other persons. More so, I am inclined to think, in part because they have most of their lives still before them, and in part because they are defenseless and even more unable to protect themselves from dangers, especially from the dangers of war when it occurs.

If they are reasonably young children, they literally cannot fight and in that way be a danger to others, nor do they engage in any of the other activities that might be thought to have the requisite causal connection with the more direct activities of making war. Their lives, their continued existences, even given the duration of wars such as World War II, are not (in any reasonably extended sense of "now") *now* a threat to the lives of any of those on the other side. To kill them intentionally or knowingly is not to kill them within the context of justifiable self-defense no matter how relaxed the standards may be thought to become, given the inner dictates and morality of war and the justifiability of such killing in war. Typically, too, they had no hand or choice whatsoever in being wherever they happened to be once war begins, or as it continues. And given the way social, institutional, and political life is organized in all countries, they played no role at all in bringing about the occurrence of war. A large and indeterminate number of them are fully noncombatants and wholly innocent in each and every one of the relevant senses. Children are the clearest kind of case, I think, but there are surely many other individuals in all countries to whom these descriptions and accounts apply. Perhaps, though, the problem is with the indeterminacy of the numbers and the identification of the individuals.

To be sure, given the features of urban life, or even those of contemporary societies more generally, those who possess the characteristics I have just described and which seem to me to have the moral significance I have indicated, are not individually identifiable or distinguishable so that one can tell at a distance exactly who or where they are. But when it can most surely be known that they are at a place, and there in numbers, as children are in the cities and towns of every country, then to kill them deliberately along with others who may more rightly be killed is to do something wrong, and seriously so. To intend to destroy a populated city, particularly if there is no warning and no shelter, is to intend to kill its inhabitants. If the answer is that that is what bombs do and what is involved, in, say, the adoption and pursuit of the tactic of the saturation bombing of cities, then this seems to me not to settle things at all but rather to call quite directly into question whether that is not the wrong, rather than the permissible way to fight a war.[3] And if such a tactic is not impermissible under the existing laws and conventions of war, that may be one reason to think there is something morally unsatisfactory and wrong about such standards.

A nuclear "war" is the limiting case of all this, if it is a war at all in any proper or meaningful sense.[4] It would, I believe, be clearly wrong to act so as to cause such an event in virtue of the absolutely indiscriminate, massive killing that everyone must know would occur. Were the nuclear missiles and bombs of the USSR and those of the US to be launched and detonated there would not be, nor could there be, a differentiation either intended or expected among the individuals who would be killed by the explosions, the fires, and the radiation. Nuclear "weapons" are surely among the very small number of weapons least capable of being used, no matter where aimed and how targeted, in a way by which any person or group might claim to distinguish between combatants, in any of the meaningful though extended senses, and noncombatants. As they are deployed and aimed at present, they embody neither the intention, desire, nor capability in any way to do so. I do not therefore see how their use in such circumstances could be anything but the deliberate wrongful killing, the murder, of vast numbers of wholly innocent persons on a scale and in a fashion that is barely comprehensible. I do not see how it could possibly be thought other than absolutely wrong to use them, and the choice to engage in nuclear "war" of the sort I have described seems to me to be the morally worst and most despicable act conceivable.

If what I have said so far is plausible or right, I do not think that the cause for which a war is fought, the justness of going to war, matters as much as is often supposed in the contexts that are now relevant. Let us grant that the clearest, most justifiable case in which it is right to go to war is that of national self-defense. Let us grant, too, that it is self-defense in the sense that if the country against which war is being made does not go to war in order to keep the aggressor from being successful, its citizens will be killed wrongly by the aggressor country, acting through its armed forces using weapons of mass destruction, or acting with and through some other means and other individuals in order to accomplish its murderous aims. Let us suppose further, although I think it somewhat more problematic, that wars of national self-defense are sometimes justifiably pursued for reasons other than to prevent the wrongful killing of the individuals in the country being aggressed against.[5] And let us suppose, finally, that when it is self-defense (individual or national) which is at stake, deadly force may be used to prevent death (or permanent or very serious injury, or enslavement) from occurring without requiring that the aggressor be morally culpable in any of the usual senses.

There is still, I believe, the problem of what may justifiably be done under the legitimate claim of self-defense, either in the individual or the national case. In the individual case the circumstances and conditions under which lethal force may permissibly be used in self-defense (or in defense of others under attack) are, surely, appropriately more restrictive than those which apply in the case of national self-defense – and for the kinds of reasons suggested earlier: there is no background of international criminal law, of international police and of international courts (of the right analogous sort). And because countries act, aggressively or otherwise, through the complex, coordinated actions of many individuals, both the causal networks and the networks of culpability relating individual actions to the collective actions of countries are different, and looser, than those which must reasonably be thought to hold in the individual case before the use of lethal force in self-defense legitimately comes into play. Yet even in the case of national self-defense there must be *some causal or analogous connections* that are reasonably thought to hold, and some defensible theory about why these are the sufficient connections that do in fact hold, between the individuals against whom deadly force is used in self-defense and the danger which that use of deadly force seeks to prevent. If our ideas about national self-defense and the permissible use of deadly force on its behalf are to have any connection with our ideas about individual self-defense, the individuals against whom such force is used in the case of a war of self-defense must have some causal or closely analogous connection with the danger at hand before they are intentionally or knowingly killed by the weapons used in a war of self-defense. And if, as I think is surely the case for the reasons I gave before, there are many such individuals in any country, no matter what its character as an aggressor, who have no such connections, then the deliberate use of weapons of indiscriminate mass destruction against them is not and cannot be a part of an intelligible or defensible recourse to ideas of legitimate national self-defense.

Perhaps there is an account of permissible national self-defense which can be constructed, developed, and defended and which can make a place for the actual use of weapons of indiscriminate mass destruction in wars of self-defense; and if there is such an account, then it is of course possible that it would also be able to explain how it is permissible, rather than wrong, actually to *use* nuclear "weapons" indiscriminately to kill the inhabitants of an aggressor country as a matter of national self-defense. I, however, am unable to construct such an account, or even to anticipate at all clearly what the plausible lines of argument might be. I certainly do not understand in what sense it could be right – that it would be better and not wrong – for us all literally "to be dead, not red," or even better, that tens or hundreds or millions of the inhabitants of the USSR, the children as well as the adults, the farmers as well as the Comissars, should be killed so that those of us in the US and in other countries should not be "red" if that is in fact the only choice at hand.

The only other possible lines of argument I can think of are the three which follow, and while (c) might possess certain merits, neither of the other two seems to me to be at all plausible or ultimately defensible and creditable.

(a) In war, as well perhaps as in other contexts, the nation-state is essentially a unitary entity composed of, in part, but neither morally nor in other ways reducible to, the individuals who are its members or who reside within its borders. In war it is this entity which makes war and fights it, and it is this entity against which another nation-state, at war with it, uses deadly force in order to defend itself. As long as such force is used against the aggressor country (and, perhaps, as long as only reasonable deadly force is used), there is no further issue. Countries, so conceived, are the only relevant entities which act, and no reductions to the more micro-level of individual actions, interests, claims, or places in the causal and analogous chains have central meaning or moral significance.

(b) Because children are tied and connected to their parents in various and obvious ways, they are necessarily tied and connected, regrettably perhaps, in other ways as well. If the parents chose to go to war, or if they are involved in waging it, then it is their fault and their problem if their children get killed in war. The parents are more the cause of their children's deaths than are their opponents, especially if the war is not a war of self-defense. Moreover, putting issues of causality and assumptions of risk to one side, the connections between parents and children are simply such that children's good and bad prospects and chances cannot be separated from those of their parents. Simply because the children are *theirs,* the children are linked to the parents in ways that make it closer to and more like injuring or killing the parents to kill their children than to kill others who are not so connected. Somehow this matters morally because in killing the children the injury is being inflicted upon a part, an extension or a possession of the adult parents whom, in self-defense, it would be right or permissible to kill.

(c) In cases of very great, extraordinary emergency or peril, on either the individual or the international level, it is sometimes permissible to do wrong or to treat persons unjustly in order to prevent a still greater wrong or injustice. If the differential magnitudes of loss of life, say, are great enough, that may itself make the moral difference, while still giving sense to the idea that something seriously wrong and regrettable was done. It is hard, and morally not very plausible, whatever one's worries about utilitarianism, not to allow consequences at least to matter mightily in this way in circumstances such as these – especially when the calculations are concerned with magnitudes all having to do with innocent lives and their preservation. And all of this is to say nothing about how, even if such is not justifiable, it may come very close to being so because it is so easily and so understandably excusable. If the stakes are really high enough and the options really bleak enough, we can understand why otherwise innocent persons do act so as to save themselves rather than suffer death, even if other innocent persons must be killed to do so.

I think that there is something plausible here, and that the plausibility increases as the differential magnitudes become greater, the danger more imminent and the choice genuinely this bleak and limited. I do not see, however, how the unleashing of massive nuclear devastation of the sort described could possibly satisfy these conditions.

Kresge College, University of California, Santa Cruz

NOTES

1 I think that this general line of argument which I try to elaborate in greater detail in the remainder of this essay is similar to that advanced by Nagel and by Walzer. It is, in my view, a more plausible and satisfactory approach than that taken by Paskins and Dockrill who take as central the idea that combatants are different from noncombatants in that the former, in virtue of the activities they are engaged in, can regard the prospect of their own deaths as a consequence of their own actions, while the latter cannot. They link this idea to that of a meaningful death to develop a theory of the moral difference between killing combatants and killing noncombatants. I think the idea of a meaningful death is a hard one to explicate, and a dubious one, for this as well as other reasons, upon which to rest matters of this kind of moral significance.

2 A position such as this is taken by Mavrodes. He argues that the laws of war are best understood as analogous to conventions or rules of the road, and that the distinction between combatants and noncombatants is anything but a deep one. The restrictions of the laws of war, and especially the restrictions connected to the immunity of noncombatants, are not, according to Mavrodes, justifiable for their own sake in the way in which the prohibition upon murder is. Instead, like conventions of the road, they are justifiable because and to the degree to which they minimize social costs, such as death and injury, over what they otherwise would have been. For the reasons I give in the remainder of this discussion I think this position is a mistaken one.

3 A powerful criticism of saturation bombing during the Second World War is to be found in Ford. My concern with the Catholic tradition of thought about war and the killing of the innocent is that the doctrine of double-effect always seems liable to the tendency to place too much emphasis upon an unduly narrow intention, describable in terms of what is directly sought, or aimed for, by the actor rather than upon the kind of broader intention in action which is morally more central, and which has to do with the known and clearly foreseeable consequences of the action. Of course, as Ford makes plain, it need not. Nonetheless, as I try to illustrate by the entire argument of this section, I doubt there is any one moral principle or distinction that can

bear the full weight required in thinking correctly about the range of cases having to do with deadly force and killing, either in war or in civil society.

4 See the essay by Somerville that opens this collection.

5 I discuss this matter, although not very adequately, in "On the Morality of War: A Preliminary Inquiry." I have set out my disagreements with Walzer's arguments and conclusions on these sorts of issues in my review of his *Just and Unjust Wars*.

Commentary: Noncombatants and Hostages

MICHAEL MC DONALD

In his examination of the morality of waging nuclear war, Richard Wasserstrom focuses on the normative distinction between combatants and noncombatants. He is particularly concerned with those who claim that this distinction is of no real importance and to that extent diminish a significant moral inhibition against waging a nuclear war – a war which would involve the indiscriminate obliteration of combatants and noncombatants alike.[1] In this connection, Wasserstrom looks at arguments that purport to show that there are no noncombatants in modern wars.

Here Wasserstrom centers on the conceptual and normative relationship between the state, a juridical collectivity, and its people, the state's constituent "parts." This relationship is central if we make two highly reasonable assumptions: (*1*) that states, not individual persons as such, make war; and (*2*) that a collectivity like a state only acts through its members. Making a third, normative assumption (*3*) that self-defense in war is *prima facie* permissible, Wasserstrom wants to discern who may be a legitimate target of such self-defensive actions. Clearly, on assumption (*1*), the enemy state is the ostensible target. But on assumption (*2*), this means striking at the state's people. The question then is whether all or only some of these people are legitimate targets, and if only some, which ones?

Wasserstrom's response is based on a spelling out of the concept of self-defense (*3*) and establishing its limits. He begins with the notion that self-defense allows us to harm those who are trying to harm us. In war this would limit the targets of lethal self-defensive actions to those trying to kill the combatants in question. This raises the question whether there is anyone left over, i.e., whether anyone in the enemy state is a genuine noncombatant, which involves Wasserstrom in a consideration of (*2*), essentially factoring out as noncombatants those who are not engaged in or assisting the lethal, hostile efforts of

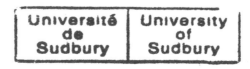

the enemy. Even though the criteria used in such factoring are somewhat loose, especially given the inadequacies of the international legal system that he describes, Wasserstrom finds a clear and important class of genuine noncombatants – namely, children.

Wasserstrom is quite correct in his reasoning here: on the argument presented children are indeed noncombatants. I shall use this basic argument to identify other significant groups of noncombatants. In carrying out this exercise, I will also be identifying those who can plausibly be regarded as enemy combatants, namely, those who are trying to kill us. A noncombatant would perforce be someone who (*a*) is not in a position to kill (or injure) us, or (*b*) is not trying to do so. I will propose three groups as noncombatants to add to Wasserstrom's case of children.

Case #1: Designated Noncombatants. We could look at the laws of war to find classes of individuals designated as noncombatants: group (*a*), those not in a position to harm us, would include prisoners of war, the seriously injured and the shipwrecked; while group (*b*), those not trying to harm us, includes chaplains and medical personnel.[2] Now someone might want to object that in some respects both groups present some sort of threat to us. For example, POWs might escape and medical personnel can be seen as part of a "total" war effort. I will take up the total war question later, but for the former group (*a*) suffice it to say that POWs are no *immediate* threat to us. If the argument from self-defense is going to work, it will have to be against immediate threats. It is an "our-lives-or-theirs" argument and not one justifying preemptive strikes.

Case #2: Neutral Nations. When we reflect on the nature of modern, especially nuclear warfare, we realize that there is another, much larger group of noncombatants than in Case #1, viz., the neutral citizens of neutral states and the neutral states themselves.[3] For simplicity's sake I will speak about the ensemble of a state and its people as "a nation." My concern, then, is with neutral nations. These necessarily fall into category (*b*), those not trying to kill us. For by definition "neutral nations" are noncombatants; hence, combatants may not use the self-defense argument to legitimate attacks on neutral nations in order to strike at their enemies. Because neutral nations are not trying to harm us, we may not harm them on grounds of self-defense against a third party, e.g., as Germany did by invading Belgium in 1914 to strike at France.

You may at this point object that we must carefully distinguish the genuinely neutral from those who only seem to be so. It is, after all, possible that a state and some of its citizens may "lean" toward one of the combatants to such a degree that the noncombatant status of the whole nation is called into question.

I would respond that while this distinction may be crucial in the context of conventional warfare, it is a matter of considerably less, and perhaps even

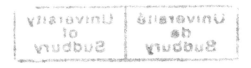

negligible importance in the case of nuclear warfare. Imagine that the Soviets concede that Finland is a neutral nation but call into question Swedish neutrality. The facts of nuclear warfare are such that a nuclear attack on the one will have devastating effects on the other. Indeed, assuming that scientists are correct in their predictions of a "nuclear winter" following a major nuclear exchange between the superpowers, even the most remote neutral nations would be the victims of "self-defensive" nuclear attacks.

Case #3: "Us." This puts me in a position to determine who would be a combatant in a nuclear war between the US and the USSR. I now want to show that on Wasserstrom's argument most of us would not be combatants in such a war and hence would not be legitimate targets for a "self-defensive" nuclear strike by either side. Under the term "us," I am including citizens of the superpowers and their allies. I am not differentiating here among allies that have their own nuclear weapons (e.g. Britain and France), those that have nuclear bases on their soil (e.g. Italy and Poland), and those that have neither (e.g. Canada and Japan). To make this case, I need to consider the general position that Wasserstrom is at such pains to refute.

This is the *total war* argument, i.e., the argument that every individual in a warring country contributes to the war effort and is, as a consequence, not entitled to noncombatant status. Here, it is necessary to distinguish two ways in which a war can be said to be "total." First, a war can be total in its *effects* by being pervasively devastating. One might think of General Sherman's "march to the sea" in the American Civil War or the Soviet's "scorched earth" retreat from Western Russia and the Ukraine in World War II. Second, a war can be total in respect to *means*. That is, all the warring parties' energies are devoted to the war effort. Talk about a nation as a "fighting machine" reflects this sort of totality. Recent examples can be found in both World Wars and in some smaller, recent wars like the current Iran-Iraq conflict or, from the point of view of the Vietnamese but not the Americans, the Vietnam War.

Using "total war" in the first sense, I have just considered the noncombatant status of neutral nations. It is fair to say that in this sense, nuclear war has the highest total of all total wars. However, this is not the way in which Wasserstrom's antagonist would appeal to the concept of total war. Rather, he would be concerned with the means by which a war is waged. For the objection gets whatever plausibility it has from the truth of the claim that the entire enemy nation, the state and its people, are directly or indirectly combatants. That is, civilian activities have ceased in that society and the only noncombatants are designated noncombatants and neutral nations.

Now it might be thought that since nuclear war is a total war in one sense (its effects), it is necessarily a total war in the other sense (its means). But this, I think, misses the real differences between events like the Second World War and a major nuclear war. The former were protracted events, involving large numbers of combatants, and a large-scale (nearly "total") mobilization of national resources for the war effort both before and during combat. But a nuclear conflict is likely to be over *quickly* (in minutes for Europe and not much longer elsewhere), highly *centralized* (directed from a few American and Soviet command centers), and involving a *minuscule* and highly *specialized* portion of either side's population. Where once, e.g., with the Manhattan Project, it might have been plausible to think of vast resources and energies being devoted to developing and using a nuclear war-fighting capability, it is now implausible to think of either superpower's nuclear war-fighting capacity as dependent on anything like the degree of effort involved in fighting the Second World War. This is not to say that the amounts of money or number of personnel involved are insignificant. It is rather to point out that nuclear weapons' explosive power beggars description.

Once we see this, we realize that the total war objection cannot plausibly be advanced for nuclear war. Even taking the widest group possible for the actual number of people involved in either preparation for or the waging of nuclear war on either side, we find that the proportion of the total population is quite small–some scientists and engineers, supply personnel, those manning the weapons, as well as military and civilian command personnel.

I would claim that everyone who is not an integral part of these *strategic* nuclear forces is in the relevant sense a noncombatant. For it is only the strategic nuclear forces that pose the threat against which the so-called "self-defensive" nuclear response is urged.[4] Only strategic nuclear weapons pose the sort of threat that could conceivably justify a self-defensive nuclear response. But the only legitimate targets of such a response are the few people on the other side who are engaged in conducting a nuclear attack. One may not engage in an indiscriminate nuclear attack against the whole enemy people on the grounds that a few of them pose a lethal threat to us.

Now someone might object to this conclusion by arguing that it is simply an unfortunate "side effect" of a nuclear response that noncombatants perish along with combatants. On these grounds, the objector would in effect deny any privileged status to children, designated noncombatants, neutral nations, as well as those in the enemy nation who are not a part of the strategic nuclear forces. Here, like Wasserstrom, I want to claim that there are moral limits to the steps one may take to defend oneself. You may not, for example, lob a hand grenade into a crowd of innocent bystanders to kill a gunman who is trying to shoot you. There is an utter disproportion here–and in the nuclear war case–between the end envisaged (viz. your self-defense) and the means adopted (viz. the annihilation of many bystanders).

This leads me to a final observation. I have already pointed out that in the case of nuclear war the total war argument fails because very few people on either side would be combatants. This I think not only extends the range of Wasserstrom's argument, but also reveals a major source of the widespread sense of despair about nuclear war. We realize that we would inevitably be victims of such a war, though not its agents. To that extent we would be denied the significant moral choices available to agents. If we are to have any role in determining our fate in this regard, it must be in some quite different respect than that of an agent who is faced with a choice of self-defensive actions. We would do well to reflect on what effect ordinary citizens can have on the real agents of nuclear war.   *University of Waterloo*

1 I am assuming that the tactical use of nuclear weapons will involve some spill-over unto noncombatants, especially in highly populated areas, and would probably escalate into an all-out nuclear war. I am also assuming that "star wars" type battles outside the Earth's atmosphere would simply be preparatory to nuclear war on Earth.
2 See, for example, the Stockholm International Peace Research Institute and Best.
3 I owe this point to Seager.
4 Presumably conventional attacks can be responded to in a conventional (non-nuclear) way. As I said in note 1 the problem with a nuclear response to a conventional attack is that it is likely to escalate into an all-out nuclear conflict and spill over to noncombatants. If I am wrong about both claims, then there would be a legitimate self-defensive role for tactical nuclear weapons as a response to conventional attack.

Commentary: Doing the Morally Unthinkable

KAI NIELSEN

Richard Wasserstrom and Michael McDonald do a convincing job of distinguishing combatants and noncombatants.[1] Given this distinction, they argue to the claim that innocent noncombatants could not rightly be killed even in the most justifiable of wars (assuming there are such). Children constitute the paradigm case of such noncombatants, but, carrying out the logic of the argument and appealing to a few uncontroversial facts, McDonald interestingly argues that everyone who is "not an integral part of these strategic nuclear forces is in the relevant sense a noncombatant." Even *if* there were circumstances in which a strictly strategic and very limited nuclear defensive response could be justified, it would only be justified if it were directed exclusively against those on the other side engaged in a nuclear attack. All the rest in a nuclear war are noncombatants.

One can be impressed by the moral force of this – it is plausibly argued and squares with deeply embedded considered moral judgments – and still feel it doesn't get to the heart of the matter. To capture the rationale for the claim I have just made is to explain a dissatisfaction I feel with both articles.

It is, I think, tolerably evident that there is just no way of carrying out a strategic nuclear attack and only hitting the few people on the other side who are themselves engaged in conducting a nuclear attack. There is, as McDonald puts it, going to be the "unfortunate 'side effect' of a nuclear response that non-combatants perish along with combatants." The dead would very likely include children, who, as noted earlier, are the most paradigmatic of innocent noncombatants. Yet this plainly morally relevant fact would not, under certain circumstances, deter even a morally sensitive and determined defender of a limited nuclear strategy who had a certain picture of what his enemy was like. Consider a "better-dead-than-red" American. He will see "the evil communist empire" as an inexorable and implacable expansionism that would, if it is not forcefully checked, turn the whole capitalist world into a Gulag. Under Soviet world hegemony the good of self-respect and human autonomy would be utterly undermined. Concentration camps would be extensive and people would be regimented into a kind of slavery under something like an oriental despotism. The whole world, given his view of things, would be rather like the picture that most of us have of the Third Reich or Orwell's 1984.

Suppose this was a true picture of the world or at least a picture that might probably be true, and suppose the Soviets made a strategic but limited nuclear strike with tactical nuclear weapons or that they made a conventional (non-nuclear) attack; suppose further that either attack, if not responded to by an American strategic nuclear strike, would lead to the Soviets gaining control of the capitalist world and subjecting it to just the kind of tyranny sketched above.

What, in such a circumstance, would be the best thing to do? It would be perfectly possible for someone to favor a strategic nuclear response on the part of the Americans and still agree with Wasserstrom and McDonald about the distinction between combatants and noncombatants and that vast numbers of utterly innocent people would be killed in such a war. They could, that is to say, agree with Wasserstrom and McDonald about those things and still intelligibly argue that here we are in one of those tragic, almost unthinkable situations in which we have to choose the lesser evil, though here we have to choose between evils of unprecedented magnitude. Children and the noncombatants of neutral nations would be massively struck down. They would be killed though they were in no way responsible for what happened. Still, that is, a "better-dead-than-red" advocate would contend, the price we must pay to avoid enslavement. The survivors, though they may be few and genetically threatened, would at least be free. [2] Better, some would say, the death of a not inconsiderable number of innocents than that the whole world should be enslaved. [3]

McDonald remarks – trying to get a model case – that you may not "lob a hand grenade into a crowd of innocent bystanders to kill a gunman who is trying to shoot you." That is fair enough, but what if innocent children were surrounding Hitler and this was very likely your only chance to lob a hand grenade at him or the only chance that anyone who might do so would be likely to have? Is it so terribly obvious that you must, categorically, not throw it? Here Herbert Marcuse, Jean-Paul Sartre, and Maurice Merleau-Ponty were far more perceptive than conventional moralists. There are human situations – terrible human situations – where sensitive, committed moral agents may very well have to do horrendous things to keep even more horrendous things from happening. To insist on "clean hands" at all costs here is not moral purity but moral evasion. And while this does indeed involve rough calculations, the making of such calculations does not commit one to any form of utilitarianism. A Rossian deontologist could in perfect consistency reason in that way. To show that the "better-dead-than-red" attitude is beyond the moral pale we need a stronger argument than that under certain circumstances it licences the killing of the innocent.

Wasserstrom addresses himself to this question in the last two paragraphs of his essay. In the penultimate paragraph, he comes very close to conceding the point I have been concerned to make, although in the form of an abstract moral point. Thus Wasserstrom says, in considering what I suggest (given a certain reading of the facts) is morally justifiable, that even if such a thing is "not justifiable, it may come very close to being so because it is so easily and so understandably excusable." I think that here Wasserstrom is just less resolute in "telling it like it is."

In his final paragraph, Wasserstrom makes a forceful and, I believe, correct point, but one that nonetheless shifts significantly the grounds of his argument. To the argument that there can be circumstances where moral agents could justifiably kill innocent persons, Wasserstrom remarks: "I think that there is something plausible here, and that the plausibility increases as the differential magnitudes become greater, the danger more imminent and the choice genuinely this bleak and limited. I do not see, however, how the unleashing of massive nuclear devastation of the sort described could possibly satisfy these conditions." Wasserstrom's last sentence is the sentence which carries the day. It makes a *factual* claim but a factual claim of immense moral relevance. Given the moral truism that human suffering is something to be avoided, and an understanding of what nuclear war would very likely come to (including the dangers of strategic nuclear war), the crude calculations of the consequences that we can make count heavily against the "better-dead-than-red" claim. The human devastation to "victor" and "vanquished" alike is just too great to make it a morally tolerable option. On moral grounds it is intolerable and on prudential grounds it is insane. But the moral case here does not rest on accepting some morally questionable absolute prohibitions. Even if the most gulagish conception of Soviet world domination were accepted as plausible, that domination, that enslavement, could not last forever and would plainly be the lesser evil to the human destruction that would be unleashed by nuclear war.

It is, I think, unrealistic to suppose that claims made by the "better-dead-than-red" person about the Soviet Union are correct, but the crucial point here is that even *if* they were, it would not justify or in any way excuse nuclear war. It would not even justify the very risky business of tactical nuclear war. The devastation to life involved in nuclear war is just too extensive for anything like that. What it would very likely come to makes it too dangerous to play a kind of brinksmanship by engaging in a strategic nuclear war.

These are old points. Indeed they hark back to debates between Sidney Hook and Bertrand Russell decades ago. But in the kind of debates about nuclear war unleashed by Wasserstrom and McDonald it is arguments of this sort, rather than arguments about killing the innocent, that are morally fundamental.

The argument to which Wasserstrom and McDonald have addressed themselves is a fundamental one. I think, however, that there is a different cluster of considerations that, at least from a practical point of view, are still *more* fundamental. Many people, taken by the kind of strategic reasoning that goes with taking seriously the application of the prisoner's dilemma to nuclear strategy, would agree with Russell that a nuclear war under any circumstances is utterly unthinkable, while still consistently contending, in terms of iterated prisoner's dilemmas, that our best defense against the likelihood of nuclear war is to continue the arms race. Others, following a tit-for-tat strategy, argue, still following the logic of prisoner's dilemma situations, that the safest alternative is phased, slow, mutual reduction of nuclear weapons. I am perhaps something of a Luddite, deeply suspicious of such moves. They seem to me too much like the ancient slogan, "The best way to achieve peace is to prepare for war." Freeze positions or unilateral positions seem to me the better options. In choosing between the alternatives, however, we do not have a deep difference in moral vision, moral sensitivity, moral philosophy, and the like. Our disagreements may be technical ones about prisoner's dilemmas.[4] More likely they are differences about how societies operate, how wars are likely to occur, differences about politics, human nature and perhaps about what human rationality is like and what it is to rely, in such concrete political contexts, on human reason. The answers here are not easy to come by and posturing about who is or is not being tough-minded with a good sense of *Realpolitik* is little more than *hubris*. Yet it is the various practical alternatives, with all the messy problems that they bring in tow, that very much need to be thought through, and it is just such issues that philosophy, particularly moral philosophy, so ill prepares us to face. Our beliefs about the direction that our political struggles should take concerning what to do to avoid nuclear devastation turn in part on what we think here. Yet what to think is not so evident that all people of good will will clearly know what is to be done. I do not say that the issue is intractable if we get clear about the facts, but short of a better understanding of the situation than most of us at present have, moral insight will not carry the day.

I want to finish by commenting very briefly on a crucial observation in McDonald's last paragraph. He adverts there to the widespread sense of despair about nuclear war. So few of us would be combatants, so few of us would have any control over what was done or not done, yet if combatants start a war we will all be devastated.[5] We have – or so it seems – no control here. We are victims but not agents. The moral of this is that the nuclear issue is overwhelmingly a political issue. Begging, for the nonce, some issues brought up in the previous paragraph, I would maintain that our safest bet to avoid nuclear destruction is to mobilize politically so that we-that is, citizens of the various countries-have control over what can be done. We need this, along with a clear sense, hardly afforded under our present political climate, of what the real situation is and what the options are. Given the present political situation, there is room for despair here too, though again the old story about the pessimism of the intellect and the optimism of the will should not be forgotten. What I also think evident, and in reality not a partisan judgment on my part, is that there is little chance of movement in a way that would defuse the nuclear peril within the political frameworks that many people have come to regard, for the forseeable future, as inevitable. Fortunately, the track record for such judgments of inevitability is not very good.   *University of Calgary*

NOTES

1 See the articles by Wasserstrom and McDonald in this volume.
2 It seems to me that such a position only has to be clearly stated to show its absurdity.
3 Elizabeth Anscombe and Lesek Kolakowski think that to reason in such a way shows a corrupt mind. That, I think, is little more than moral evasiveness on their part.
4 See the essay by Groarke in Part v of this collection.
5 The hyperbole here is excusable.

Thoughts from Under the Nuclear Umbrella

TRUDY GOVIER

Every month I read about something new and interesting about the universe that some scientist has discovered, such as what it was that caused the extinction of the dinosaurs sixty-four million years ago. It is really wonderful, the world, and one wonderful part about it is that there are sentient beings here who are able to appreciate the wonders of the world, to understand them! So I feel we have a duty to try and prevent the nuclear war, to reverse this situation. I believe that it can be done. (Linus Pauling, in a speech given at the Hotel Vancouver, October 1982; quoted in Perry.)

Philosophers examining issues of nuclear weapons and nuclear war have been fascinated by the problem of nuclear deterrence. Whether it can ever be morally right to threaten to do something which it would not be morally right to do is a vexing question which underlies the ethical appraisal of nuclear deterrence. But while this issue is profound and important, it has been explored by many other philosophers. I propose, therefore, to take a different direction in this paper. I shall discuss an argument which has been popular in the political debate about cruise missile testing in Canada and use that argument to raise some issues about the risks of nuclear deterrence and the role that allies have in seeking change in the pace and direction of the arms race.

The argument I have in mind may sound small and insignificant, but I believe it carries considerable weight with many Canadian citizens. I suspect that appropriately adapted versions of it are found compelling in Britain and Europe as well. For American readers, I hope that the discussion will be useful in showing how nuclear issues appear to those outside superpower countries. The argument I refer to maintains that those who shelter under a "nuclear umbrella" should not criticize the manufacturer. Rather, they should help him with his business, when requested, and refrain from skeptical comments. To criticize is presumptuous, ungrateful, and exploitative; if we get protection from the American nuclear umbrella, that benefit gives us an obligation to assist

American defense programs when we are asked to do so. As minor players and beneficiaries, we cannot do otherwise.

Prime Minister Trudeau gave a brief statement of this argument in his open letter to Canadians on the cruise testing issue, published on May 9, 1983: "It is hardly fair to rely on the Americans to protect the West, but to refuse to lend them a hand when the going gets rough. In that sense, the anti-Americanism of some Canadians verges on hypocrisy. They're eager to take refuge under the US umbrella, but don't want to help hold it."[1] This response was, in particular, aimed at cruise missile protesters who had urged that the cruise was a destabilizing war-fighting weapon which would not contribute to nuclear deterrence. In essence, Trudeau maintained that as beneficiaries of American nuclear policies, Canadians must toe the line and do what Americans ask us to do or be hypocritical freeriders, failing to hold up our end of the sheltering umbrella provided by our beneficent allies. He assumed, in effect, that criticism of nuclear policy was inappropriate for Canadian citizens. As minor players in the nuclear arms race, our proper role is to be loyal allies and do as we are told, hoping against hope that things will turn out in the final analysis.

One aspect of such reasoning is effectively satirized by W.B. Gallie in a recent essay entitled "Three Main Fallacies in Discussions of Nuclear Weapons."[2] Gallie questions the common belief that only the superpowers who control the present nuclear arms race can have a constructive role in ending that race and resolving its problems. The view, apparently realistic and commonsensical, rests, he says, on assumptions whose enormity is difficult to appreciate. It is necessary to expose "the innocent hugeness and naivety of the habit of thought which they disclose." To expose the assumptions, Gallie offers a fable about giants and cave-dwellers. A derelict remnant of the human race, surviving in caves after a nuclear holocaust, is divided between two rival giants who each have a cache of highly explosive devices which are most effective when released in a cave. The cave-dwellers are constantly at risk of being devastated by these super-rivals.

What, then, should the cave-dwellers do? Wait in hope for the rival giants to see the light, forego their rivalry, and bury their grenades in a "place of safety"? Or should they humbly petition the giants to do so? Or, judging the giants to be irreconcilable, should they take their pick between them, and put their relatively slight strength behind the one whom they think more likely to win out and more likely to befriend them if he proves victorious? Or should they look around for more – even if probably dud – grenades to increase their usefulness as allies of the giant of their choice? What these suggestions have in common is this: they all present the problem of the cave-dwellers' survival as primarily dependent upon what the giants will do. And, on the face of it, the giants, who rely upon their grenades, have already decided to settle the issue between them by means which threaten the very existence of the group, the giants themselves included.[3]

Gallie argues that we need not assume that superpowers must find the way out and that minor powers, such as Britain and Canada, must act as the cave-dwellers in the fable. Minor players can seek to influence the superpowers. If they fail, they can withdraw their cooperation from a system which will involve their own ultimate destruction. "In fine, because one party has the power to destroy the other, it by no means follows that the former is wholly immune to effective pressure from the latter."

We have no evidence that Trudeau read Gallie's essay, but his overall position on the role of allied powers in determining nuclear policy underwent change. In the fall of 1983, only a few months after the publication of his open letter, he had undertaken a "peace initiative" and had made public criticisms of NATO's first use policy and of the American invasion of Grenada. Nevertheless, his original argument is a popular one, used by many people, and merits exploration. Gallie did not extend his fable to cover the circumstance that exists when a cave-dweller has willingly accepted the protection of one giant for a period of time and is hesitating about the details of further alliance. The essence of the pro-cruise argument used by Trudeau and other defense establishment people is that the recipients of a benefit have obligations to their benefactor; that Canadians benefit from the American nuclear umbrella; and that Canadians have, accordingly, obligations to participate in, and assist, American defense activities. I propose to use this common argument as a take-off point for examining various dimensions of the nuclear debate as it occurs in the political realm. There are moral aspects to this debate, certainly, but they do not primarily concern the morality of nuclear deterrence.

The point of the argument Trudeau used is not that there is a legal obligation, in the NATO treaty, or in a specific treaty between the United States and Canada, to do some specific thing such as testing cruise missiles or manufacturing parts for the MX missile. Nor is it that Canada has no choice but to accommodate American requests, due to her economic and political powerlessness in comparison to the United States. Those are different arguments, and they are not moral arguments. It is possible that in some contexts, the moral argument is a cloak for the coercion argument, which people are embarrassed to express.[4]

If Canada has no choice but to accede to American requests, because the United States would bankrupt the country, or invade, or take over the Arctic, there would indeed be no decision for Canadians to make. There are significant strands of this thinking in Canada–and no doubt in other allied countries as well. In "Canada and the US Nuclear Arsenal," Ernie Regehr quotes a 1945 Canadian policy document which allowed that "The pressure which would be brought to bear on Canada by the United States in the event of Canada seeming reluctant or refusing to cooperate with [the United States] in continental defence would be very substantial and might be difficult to resist."[5] These considerations, taken very seriously, might make any moral argument otiose. But whatever the impact of the strictly moral argument on real political decision-making in the highest circles, it is significant in public debate. It does influence many people and affects policy decisions.

Some nevertheless question the meaningfulness of moral analysis and reflection in the domain of international politics. For a variety of reasons, people have seen such analysis as misplaced, naive, and inappropriate. A prominent line of thought is that international relations occur in a Hobbesian world – a set of states in a state of nature, so to speak – where there is no operative moral order. Because this is the case, there is no morality in international relations, and any moral analysis of foreign policy is misplaced. This account ignores the extensive cooperation, trust, and orderliness that do exist in international affairs: in trade, communications, shipping, weather prediction, development activities through the United Nations, and many other areas. It also ignores the practical use of moral argument to defend national actions. There are constant appeals, in the rhetoric of international affairs, to abuses of human rights, the failure of systems to attain economic equality, unwarranted invasions, illegitimate regimes, and so forth. Moral discourse on international affairs is appropriate to expose and assess such comments, if for no other reason.

Another line of reasoning tells us that actions such as those of political leaders are necessary – inevitable – and beyond meaningful moral analysis. It is in this vein that we may be told that there was no real alternative to using the first atomic weapon at Hiroshima, given the investment in the Manhattan Project, the enormous bureaucratic momentum built up during the Project, and the previous conventional bombings of Dresden and Tokyo.[6] In *Just and Unjust Wars,* Michael Walzer effectively criticizes this necessitarian line of thought. He points out that even when it has retrospective plausibility, it ignores the fact that decisions were made by moral agents. Even in crises, there were alternatives, though they may not have seemed feasible or advantageous, or politically popular when critical choices were made.[7] To choose to do what is popular rather than unpopular, what has short-term rather than long-term advantages, what has a lower rather than a higher economic cost, is still to make a choice. The fact that the choice seems, in retrospect, natural or inevitable does not show that it was not a choice. Agents do make choices when they act in the international arena, just as they do in other contexts.

A third view is that the dogmatic intervention of moralizing people only serves to make international relations worse than they need to be.[8] Moral analysis is presumptuous in its assumption of an objective viewpoint from which things can correctly be appraised. It is just this kind of presumptuous thinking which leads to hostility, aggression, war, and destruction. Behind this criticism are important reminders. We cannot be sure our own ethical stance is the correct one. In international affairs, people have been too ready to defend a "morally correct" stance with horrifying means and disastrous results. Ultimately, though, the idea that the moral analysis of international relations will only make things worse and should not be pursued, is itself an expression of a moral position. The moral position is admirable in its advocacy of non-dogmatism, lack of presumption, and restraint in pursuit of our ends. It is, however, within morality and not outside it. As the expression of advice to remove moral talk from the international arena, the position is a moral one which is self-defeating.

There are moral arguments used in the discussion of foreign and defense policy, in Canada, as elsewhere, and these arguments are not beside the point. One prominent view in Canada seeks to derive obligations from benefits received – the obligation to test the cruise missile from the protection Canadians receive as they shelter under the American nuclear umbrella.

A first stage in reflecting on this argument is to examine the concept of the "nuclear umbrella." Obviously, this is highly metaphorical. It is also misleading and euphemistic – a comfortable, familiar word disguising an awesome and dangerous reality. A number of writers have commented on the bland, euphemistic nature of so much of the language of nuclear strategy and the nuclear debate.[9] To appreciate the general problem, think about the expression, "nuclear exchange." This sounds as though what is going on is something essentially civilized and polite, like an exchange of gifts. The term disguises the fact that millions would be vaporized, more millions cruelly burned, landscapes torn apart, and that thousands would die in agony without medical aid in such an "eventuality."

The expression "nuclear umbrella" sounds innocuous and familiar, sheltering, unthreatening, and comfortable. We have to stare at it, think about it, and force ourselves to think about what it means. It means that we owe our survival to the existence of 30,000 nuclear weapons in the American nuclear arsenal. Any single one of these weapons, if detonated on any targeted area, would cause hundreds of thousands of deaths and devastation of the environment. According to standard deterrence doctrine, we owe our survival in the nuclear age to our readiness to detonate those weapons on human beings in Russia – on innocent Russian men, women, and children. The umbrella which is said to protect us and our way of life, is a war machine of awesome potential, a war machine which could destroy our species if used. It is a war machine which human beings threaten to use and are prepared to use. To keep the nuclear umbrella in existence, thousands of human beings are trained to be prepared to kill millions of other human beings with a single push of a button. All around the world, such people combine an "ordinary life" with a job that involves continual preparedness to launch the apocalypse.

Having brought the euphemistic aspects of the term "umbrella" to the surface, we should explore the assumptions underlying its use. These are common wisdom within the nuclear establishment and too often escape analysis. These assumptions have to do with the protective nature of the umbrella. An umbrella, after all, keeps something from falling down upon us. The notion is that the nuclear umbrella keeps Russian missiles from falling down upon us. That is why it is a protective, sheltering umbrella. With it, we don't have Russian bombs exploding on our country, and without it we would – or could. The term "umbrella" encapsulates establishment thinking about nuclear deterrence. That is:

(*1*) Nuclear weapons have as their primary function the prevention of nuclear and major conventional war.[10]

(*2*) Nuclear weapons have performed this primary function, historically. Because we have had nuclear weapons since 1945, we have not had nuclear (or major conventional) war in that period.

(*3*) Nuclear weapons will continue to perform this function in the future. We will go on developing and maintaining nuclear weapons, and they will never be used in a nuclear war.[11]

(*4*) Maintaining a nuclear arsenal which we implicitly or explicitly threaten to use is the only way of preventing a nuclear war, and it is the best way of preventing a major conventional war.[12]

These assumptions are all a part of the metaphor of the nuclear umbrella. The first assumption spells out the common belief that the purpose of the American nuclear arsenal is entirely, or at least primarily, to serve a deterrent (protective) function. It exists to prevent a nuclear war, not to launch or fight one, and not to make nuclear threats against non-nuclear countries. The second stipulates that the arsenal has sheltered us in the past. This is the benefit which we have received from American defense activity, and the benefit which produces present obligations. The third assumption is that the umbrella is a safe, accident-proof protective device, which can be maintained forever without risk of misuse. The fourth is that there is no alternative to nuclear deterrence. We have "enemies" with nuclear weapons, they will always be there with their nuclear weapons, and the only way for us to prevent them from attacking us is to have nuclear weapons of our own. We might wish the world were otherwise, but wish is not reality.

All four assumptions are open to criticism. The first is historically false; the second is unverifiable, though it might be true; the third is unreasonably optimistic, unverifiable, and most likely not true. The fourth is the product of un-creative thinking about alternative arrangements and a failure to appreciate the very real disincentive to the use of nuclear weaponry which would continue to exist even if only one superpower possessed these weapons.[13] Casual use of the umbrella metaphor tends to inhibit us from reflecting on the assumptions, because we make them without even being aware that we are doing so.

The first assumption is undermined by a number of careful analyses of the nuclear age. From 1942 President Roosevelt regarded the atomic bomb as something with enormous "diplomatic potential" in the postwar world. (Note the euphemistic phrase.) He thought that with this ultimate weapon the United States would be able to dominate the postwar world. Clearly, this line of thinking embraced the use of tacit or explicit nuclear threats for limited strategic pur-poses. Nuclear threats have been made against non-nuclear countries (Russia in 1946; North Vietnam in 1969; China in 1958). Current policy embraces the use of tactical nuclear weapons in the context of disputes in the Third World. The idea that nuclear superiority is relevant to political "clout" around the world is pervasive. Nuclear weapons are part of an arsenal designed to protect American interests and have not been viewed solely as a means to preventing nuclear attack.[14] Daniel Ellsberg, formerly an insider in American defense plan-ning circles, has emphasized this point and, in a recent paper, points out that evidence for it that was not made public in previous decades is now available in diaries and memoirs of Eisenhower and other leaders.

Almost no one seems to be aware of this, but the fact is that every President in his term of office (except possibly Ford) has had occasion to consider the imminent use of nuclear weapons against, in almost every case, an opponent that did not have nuclear weapons. This was probably less dangerous than doing it against the Soviet Union. However, each of those opponents – the Koreans, the Indochinese, the Chinese – were allies or clients of the Soviet Union, so the problem remained one of preventing Soviet retaliation.[15]

The second assumption encompassed by the notion of a nuclear umbrella is unverifiable. To know that it is true, we would have to know that without nuclear weapons, there would have been a major conventional war involving Russia, the United States, Europe, and Canada after 1945. We would, that is, have to know something about an alternative world, a world missing a feature which is pervasive and deeply significant in our actual world. Nuclear weapons probably have served to make leaders more cautious but they have probably also served to make relations more hostile. Certainly Russian suspicions of the United States were greatly increased by the secretiveness of the Manhattan project and the sudden use of atomic weapons on Hiroshima and Nagasaki. Many Russian analysts believe that the primary reason for the bombings was not, as American officialdom has it, to end the war with Japan quickly but rather to terrify the Russians and bring them "in line."[16]

It is the third assumption, however, which is most crucial to the nuclear umbrella argument. If we are to benefit from the umbrella, it cannot explode into a fireball or a radioactive cloud. Even granting the first two assumptions, there is little benefit to the "nuclear umbrella" unless we assume that it will continue to ward off the attack. We are protected by the umbrella only insofar as it continues its "sheltering" function. The umbrella metaphor encourages us to ignore the many risks involved in nuclear deterrence. In a renewed Cold War atmosphere, with 50,000 nuclear weapons in the possession of the two superpowers, with a launch-to-detonation period of less than seven minutes for Pershing II missiles recently deployed in Europe, there are substantial risks in nuclear deterrence. Ever-more-accurate weapons are aimed at opponents' weapons, increasing the risk of preemptive first strikes. The development of "smaller," more flexible nuclear weapons makes it more likely that they will be used in a battlefield context, perhaps in a Third World dispute. With nuclear proliferation, and client states of the superpowers, such as Israel, having nuclear weapons,[17] disputes involving them could "go nuclear." There have been a number of close calls, and accidents continue to be possible, with the weapons' velocity making the detection of false alarms before response time all the more difficult.

For Canadians especially, a sober consideration of these risks will make the umbrella metaphor appear extremely inappropriate. Placed between the superpowers, Canadians would be devastated by a nuclear exchange between them. Missiles would be flying over our country; our airports and cities would in all likelihood be targeted due to our role in American defense systems and proximity to the United States. Analysts of the likely fate of Canada have said:

Any significant margin of survival after an exchange of nuclear weapons could easily constitute "victory," however hollow and short-lived such survival might be.

In these circumstances it is difficult to believe that military planners in the Soviet Union would try their utmost to destroy the United States while leaving on its northern border an intact ribbon of land that is rich in natural resources, energy (already being exported to the United States in large quantities), agriculture and industrial development which could give the American survivors a margin that could make the difference between such a "victory" and total annihilation.[18]

If, in some less-than-total scenario, Canadian cities and airports were not directly targeted, damage from fallout and other global effects of nuclear detonations would be considerable. The same may be said for other allied countries and, indeed, for all the nations of the Earth.

There is, of course, some possibility that the nuclear arms race will be unlike all other arms races and will not end in a war. We must earnestly hope that this is the case. Nuclear weapons are unique in their potential to destroy our globe. If leaders continue to perceive this uniqueness, it just might be that they can continue stockpiling these weapons indefinitely without ever again using them in war. However, it does not seem wise to stake our future on this hope. That the nuclear umbrella will continue to protect us from nuclear war is less likely than that it will explode in such a war – a war which its very existence has helped to bring about.

The fourth assumption, that the only way to prevent nuclear war is to continue our reliance on nuclear weapons, is just the kind of claim to which skepticism should be applied. There is very rarely only one way of doing something. Arrangements for joint security without nuclear weapons as a deterrent against war have not been seriously pursued by the superpowers since 1946.[19] It is premature to say in advance that no such arrangements would be possible. The possession of nuclear weapons by one superpower increases insecurity and hostility within the other, and propels the arms race leading in many cases to destabilizing technological developments. There would be very little incentive for one superpower to use weapons on another which had none, for global effects of fallout and damage to the earth's climate and the ozone layer would hurt the aggressor as well as the defender. In addition, world opinion would be overwhelmingly against the aggressor. The superpower contest is as much a contest for global influence as for control over territory. There would be no point in burning and radiating a territory one wished to control, in any case. Bilateral disarmament has never been seriously pursued as an approach to national security, and even unilateral disarmament probably brings with it less risk of nuclear war than the current situation. It is absolutely presumptuous to assume that our current system of nuclear deterrence based on a continuing arms race is the only way to prevent nuclear war.

If we return now to the argument that we benefit from the American nuclear umbrella and are therefore obligated to do our part in upholding American defense systems, we see that the opening premise is disputable in the extreme. Even if we agree that there have been some benefits in the past, it is very unlikely that the indefinite continuation of the system of nuclear deterrence will benefit us. If obligations to our allies come because we stand in a relationship in which we are receiving benefits, then perhaps we have no obligations after all.

There are however, several complicating factors here. One is that there is some case for claiming past benefits, even though that would be hard to demonstrate. Another, more important point is that Canadian and other allied leaders have obviously believed that there is a benefit in the nuclear umbrella. They have not seen the risks of nuclear deterrence as sufficient to warrant changing their defense system and have entered into alliances (in the case of Canada, NATO and NORAD) on the assumption that nuclear deterrence is the route to national security in the nuclear age. Perhaps perceived benefits generate obligations just as much as real benefits do, especially if agents enter into voluntary agreements pertinent to those perceived benefits. Perhaps for this reason, Canadians and other allies are obligated to participate in upholding the American defense establishment.

If an agent voluntarily accepts from another agent what he believes to be a good thing, then does he thereby acquire an obligation to assist that other agent, when called upon? There is a sense in which he does and a sense in which he does not, as we can see by exploring a simple parallel case. Suppose that Sam offers to protect Johnny against Ivan's dogs because he wants to keep the dogs out of their neighborhood. Johnny is happy enough to have Sam help him. So they build a massive fence, and for forty years, neither Sam nor Johnny encounters any of Ivan's dogs. Johnny has, so far as he knows, benefitted from Sam's help. (Neither Sam nor Johnny knows that any of Ivan's dogs were headed in their direction in the first place, but they do know that they haven't had any dogs around, and they assume that their fence kept the dogs away.) Now Sam thinks the fence needs strengthing and he asks Johnny to help him with some of the costs. But in the meantime, Johnny has started to worry about their situation. It seems that the material used for the fence is dangerous. It turns out that the construction materials contain a harmful substance, found to cause a debilitating disease which will show up after a long period. Eventually, everyone is likely to succumb to this disease unless the materials are removed from the neighborhood. Johnny hesitates about supplying the materials to Sam. Sam is furious. He tells Johnny that he has benefitted from Sam's help in the past and is therefore obliged to do something to assist him now. He accuses Johnny of hypocrisy and freeriding. He isn't asking much of Johnny – just a few materials – and now, after all he has done for Johnny, Johnny won't do anything for him.

Now Johnny does have some obligation to Sam in this case, clearly. He has had amicable relations with Sam in the past, and they have cooperated in an endeavor which both thought was beneficial, with Sam doing most of the work and supplying most of the money. Johnny should not simply turn his back on Sam and ignore the request. But is it his obligation to accede uncritically to Sam's request? Given what he believes about the construction materials, he should tell Sam the risks involved and try to establish a discussion in which they consider other means of protecting their property. In fact, for Johnny to accede uncritically to the request and supply material which he knows is dangerous is for him to ignore his benefactor's welfare as well as his own. He should communicate his concerns and try to bring about a change. If this fails, and Johnny remains convinced that their protective strategy is a dangerous one, he may withdraw from their arrangement. His obligation is to cooperate with his "benefactor" for their mutual good, as he best understands this. It is not to meet any and every request, regardless of whether he believes that his cooperation would endanger them both.

The benefit-obligation argument can be used to show that Canadians and other allies have obligations to the Americans. It cannot be used to show that they should unthinkingly meet every American request, nor that they should meet requests when they believe that the activity in question will increase their mutual danger. Those citizens of allied countries who sincerely believe that nuclear deterrence is an ever-more-risky system of national security have an obligation to consider the well-being of American citizens as well as their own. Their governments have voluntarily allied themselves with the American government and have perceived that alliance to be beneficial. Even if the system established were no longer beneficial, the previous cooperation and perceived benefits would establish a relationship in which future cooperation should be sought. Canadians and other allies should first try to work with Americans when they seek to lessen dependence on nuclear weapons and bring the dangerous arms race to a halt. Cooperating does not mean that they can only accede to American requests and must do what they are told without working for constructive change. Cooperation is not domination. It is not taking orders. Rather, it is working together, with all members thinking for themselves about what would be best for the group as a whole.

Whatever the morality of nuclear deterrence, it is a dangerous system in the long run. We have had nuclear weapons since 1945 without having had another nuclear war. This is no guarantee that nuclear war will never occur. The umbrella metaphor connotes safety in an unsafe situation. Our obligation is not to give whatever "aid" is requested, but to participate as thinking and concerned members of an alliance to work for global security. Contrary to the received wisdom in defense and foreign policy circles, nuclear deterrence is not, in the long run, the only route to global or national security. Nor is it even one such route. The obligation of citizens around the globe is to try to determine the best political strategy for departing from this risky situation and to work to make that strategy a political reality.   *University of Calgary*

NOTES

1 *Calgary Herald,* May 9, 1983. The open letter was reprinted in the *Bulletin of the Atomic Scientists* (October 1983, 2).
2 In Blake and Pole, pp. 157-78.
3 P. 176.
4 This is likely to be true in many circumstances; however it has been my experience that the moral argument does substantially affect the thinking of ordinary conscientious citizens, even though it is possible that astute politicians such as former Canadian Prime Minister Pierre Trudeau really use it as a cover-up for something else.
5 Cited by Ernie Regehr in "Canada and the US Nuclear Arsenal," in Regehr and Rosenblum, eds., pp. 10-12.
6 This view has been effectively argued by Bernstein in *The Atomic Bomb* and in a lecture presented to the Stanford University Alumni Society in August 1983 ("The Use of the Atomic Bomb: Politics, Ethics, and Impact on Western Culture," available on tape from the Stanford University Alumni Society).
7 Walzer.
8 Put to me in correspondence by Prof. S. Kounosu, Department of Physics, University of Lethbridge, Alberta. *In Just and Unjust Wars,* Walzer reports that a similar view was urged under the name of "realism" by people who thought wars regarded as moral crusades were likely to be even more ferocious and horrifying than those fought under nonmoral banners such as that of national interest.
9 See, for example, Hilgartner, Bell, and O'Connor; also Fox, "The Nuclear Mindset," this collection.
10 This presumption is relevant to the particular issue of cruise testing. Public officials defended the testing by discussing NATO and the role of the American nuclear arsenal, and the cruise as part of that arsenal, in defending Europe. In fact, the missile to be tested in Canada is the air-launched cruise, which plays a part not in Europe, but in American strategy in defending its interests around the globe – primarily in potential areas of conflict in the Third World.
11 Powers reports that the many military people he interviewed were unanimous in believing that nuclear weapons would always be necessary and would never be used.
12 This assumption is clearly at work in many circles. For just one example, see Morris.
13 See, for example, Lackey, "Missiles and Morals" and the subsequent discussion of his views by Hardin and Kavka.
14 I have argued this point in "Nuclear Illusion and Individual Obligations." Extensive historical documentation may be found in Sherwin, Chap. Nine; Herken, Chap. One; Jungk; and Ellsberg, "Nuclear Weapons." See also Ellsberg, "Confronting the Rising Risk of World War III," in Perry, ed.
15 Ellsberg, "Confronting," p. 257.
16 See Roy and Zhores Medvedev. The authors, prominent Soviet dissident scholars, say, "Soviet analysts – corroborated by not a few eminent Western historians – have generally viewed the American decision to destroy Hiroshima and Nagasaki with atomic bombs in August 1945, at a moment when the surrender of Japan was already

imminent, as a demonstration of force primarily designed to intimidate the USSR at this juncture."

17 According to Pringle and Spigelman, who present considerable documented evidence, Israel already possesses nuclear weapons. See Chaps. 17 and 18.

18 Bates et al., "What Would Happen to Canada in a Nuclear War?", in Regehr and Rosenblum, eds.

19 I give this date because 1946 was the year in which both the United States and the Soviet Union presented to the United Nations plans for the international control of atomic energy. Neither plan was approved by both powers, due largely to the US belief that its atomic monopoly was good for at least twenty years and to the developing Cold War atmosphere of the time.

Commentary: Alternatives to Acquiescence

FRANK CUNNINGHAM

Generally regarded Trudy Govier's conclusions are: (*a*) that countries in the orbit of one of the major nuclear powers have no obligation to acquiesce uncritically in its arms policy; and (*b*) that given the unsoundness of arguments for nuclear deterrence, small and great powers should cooperate for nuclear disarmament. In this commentary I shall suggest that Govier's conclusions can be strenghtened by clarifying the notion of obligation and by confronting the view that small powers may have no choice but to acquiesce – a view she sets aside.

Using the fence analogy Govier argues (*1*) that if Johnny (Canada) believes that the building of a fence (nuclear "umbrella") by Sam (the US) is a favor, then Johnny may have an obligation to help maintain the fence – and his obligation is independent of whether the building of the fence really was a favor – but that he has no obligation to help uncritically. The real-life situation being addressed here involves the most grave issues. For instance, "maintaining the fence" to date has meant supporting US refusal to declare a commitment not to use nuclear weapons first and its deployment of potential first strike weapons in Europe and elsewhere. The arguments of Govier and of the authors she cites, that neither Canadians nor anybody else has an obligation to support such policies, seem based on demonstrations that placing people under the nuclear "umbrella" is not in fact a favor. If this is the main argument against support, and I think it is a strong one, then whether there is even a presumption of obligation depends after all on the truth of a belief about whether a favor was done. Obligation about such things as favors is in this respect objective, for simply believing one has an obligation does not by itself decide the issue of whether one does. Recognition of this fact strengthens Govier's general position.

However, a proponent of a counter-position might produce a modified version in which obligation depends not on beliefs about international relations and the like but on *promises* made on the basis of such beliefs. Let us take version (2) of the analogy: Johnny believes the fence is necessary and as a result promises Sam to help maintain it. Given that there is some moral obligation to keep promises, then Johnny ought to help Sam even if he is wrong about the fence's necessity. This somewhat stronger version of the pro-support position links moral commitments to legal ones embodied in such things as treaties, but despite its popularity Govier's arguments tell against it also. In fact, they apply better to this view than to the one invoking favors. It makes sense to say that promising confers some obligation, but this does not commit one to doing what is promised unthinkingly irrespective of any new information one acquires or how circumstances change.

What is more, an argument based on promise-making may be seen to be increasingly weak the closer one gets to political reality. Consider these closer analogues: (2a) Johnny promises to help maintain a fence that he reasonably anticipates will be about six feet high, but Sam builds a fence thirty feet high that blocks the sun from Johnny's garden. Johnny can hardly be expected to let arguments of Sam that Ivan has a thirty-two foot fence or that no exact height was earlier discussed convince him that he is still obligated to keep his promise. No doubt he should carefully examine a claim of Sam's that Ivan has been breeding super jumping dogs, but even if he gave credence to this claim (and also agreed that there was no alternative to the fence) this would be a new agreement, based on newly perceived self-interest and not on the original promise. (2b) Johnny does not promise to maintain Sam's fence. Rather, Uncle Fred, a person chosen by Johnny's household to represent it in unspecified but various and sundry matters has made the promise, not having consulted other members of the household and in fact having rejected requests of Aunt Alice, Cousin Jane and others to hold a household vote or at least to vote on whether there should be such a vote. There does seem to be some measure of obligation here for Johnny to maintain the fence, though political philosophers are not in accord as to its exact source. What is clear is that this obligation is considerably weaker either than one where Johnny directly made the promise or where his representative had been more democratically responsive.

Situations (2a) and (2b) mirror the actual situation in Canada vis-à-vis us nuclear policy. Despite repeated protests, agreements like those to join NATO and NORAD and the Defense Production Sharing Agreement were made without direct input from the Canadian population and sometimes even without parliamentary consent. Indeed, the recent decision of the Canadian government to permit cruise missile testing was carried out against widespread opposition and opinion polls showing a clear majority against it. Nobody in the post-World War II years foresaw the present circumstance where the us and the USSR have giant overkill arsenals, where first strike weapons have been developed and deployed; where proliferation of nuclear weapons is putting them into more hands; where delivery time is too fast to allow for negotiation; and so on.

At this point a defender of cooperation with US policy might say that real politics demand that we drop an initial assumption of Govier's and entertain a third analogue: (3) Johnny thinks it imprudent not to help Sam with the fence. There are three ways that Johnny might reason: (3a) Johnny believes Ivan awaits a chance to turn his dogs loose on him and that Sam will let Ivan do this unless Johnny helps with the fence; (3b) Johnny thinks that Sam will himself retaliate, e.g., by foreclosing on his mortgage if he fails to cooperate; (3c) Johnny wants Sam and Ivan to patch things up, and believes that only by cooperating with the fence project can he gain sufficient confidence on Sam's part to influence him. This is not the place to discuss the prudential sides of the often-encountered political views for which these are models except to note regarding (3a) that even if this, what I take to be a Cold War, hysterical view, were accurate – indeed, especially if it were accurate – the US would hardly allow the Soviets to take over its northern neighbor whether Canada cooperated with the US or not. Regarding (3b) it is hard to think of worse US retaliation against Canada than destruction of the world in a nuclear war. Regarding (3c) it should be remarked that cooperating with US arms policy is itself a *source* of world tension, reinforcing a situation where each side tends to see the world entirely divided into two main enemies and their allies.

But is there room for moral debate if a 3-type situation is dominant? Govier suggests that this "might make any moral argument otiose." However, prudential and moral deliberations on the question at hand are closer to one another than many seem to think. First, it is almost never the case that there is no choice at all. Even if one's life is at stake, a choice can still be made to sacrifice oneself on moral grounds. It is unlikely that the US would threaten to annihilate Canada for non-cooperation in US foreign policy (its southern neighbor, Mexico, has more than once bucked this policy and still exists); rather, threatened or actual reprisals, if any, would be far short of this. Hence, it is possible, without supposing a country of saints, to contemplate possible risks of non-cooperation weighed against risks of war and to determine which of a range of morally relevant courses of action are feasible and which ought to be taken.

Second, given that the stakes are so high, there is a responsibility vigorously to explore ways to avoid being susceptible to coersion or alternate means to influence US policy. For example, successfully encouraging internationally inspected bilateral nuclear disarmament would lessen the risk of war without one's having to decide which, if either, of the main powers has noble or base intentions. An economic policy that made Canada less dependent on US trade and more in control of its own resources would protect its ability to make independent decisions. US policy might be influenced by direct appeal to US citizens. Canada's joining with unaligned nations would give this group important diplomatic clout. There are doubtless many other avenues to be explored.

Finally, when faced with a conflict between what is prudent and what is moral, it is often worth asking whether there is a flaw in the frame of reference in which the conflict appears. In the present case, I am thinking of some assumptions about what constitutes "national security." Thus, a case can be made that much international politics today is based on a concept inherited from a bygone feudal and immediate post-feudal era when autocratically governed states resorted to war to further often territorially related interests. A prominent national interest in this environment soon became the ability to launch war itself, and this concept has persisted to the present. An alternate perspective on national security links it to national self-determination and international cooperation. The secure nation on this view is one the members of which can determine their own destiny and who view and are viewed by the people of other nations as equal members of a world community deserving toleration and respect.

Is it realistic to strive to create national policies and international relations from this point of view? I suspect Trudy Govier and I agree that if the alternative is a continuing arms race, this is the only long-term option we have.

University of Toronto

Part II   Issues to Think About and Discuss

1 Wasserstrom argues that "there are many ... individuals in any country, no matter what its character as an aggressor, who have no [causal or closely analogous] connections [with its war effort]," and that therefore "the deliberate use of weapons of indiscriminate mass destruction against them is not and cannot be a part of an intelligible or defensible recourse to ideas of legitimate national defense." Do you agree or disagree? Why?

2 In McDonald's view, nuclear war, while "total" in one sense, is less "total" in another sense than conventional wars, even world wars. State and assess his argument on this score.

3 Nielsen contends that "Even if the most gulagish conception of Soviet world domination were accepted as plausible, that domination, that enslavement, could not last forever and would plainly be the lesser evil to the human destruction that would be unleashed by nuclear war." Critically evaluate this claim.

4 Does the "nuclear umbrella" argument establish Canada's obligation to permit us testing of the cruise missile over Canadian territory? Can you think of any other arguments that have a bearing on this issue? Explain carefully. (Refer to Govier's article.)

5 Cunningham argues that non-cooperation with us nuclear and foreign policy is Canada's only long-term option for both moral and prudential reasons. Do you agree or disagree? Defend your answer.

Part III The Environment

Nuclear Arms and Nuclear Power: Philosophical Connections

KRISTIN SHRADER-FRECHETTE

1 Introduction

In May 1974 India exploded an atomic bomb which it had built using plutonium acquired from a Canadian-supplied nuclear power plant. For many people, the Indian explosion illustrated a clear cause-effect relationship between the use of atomic energy and the construction of nuclear weapons. If one opposed the latter, one ought to oppose the former. Not all persons who are against commercial use of nuclear fission to generate electricity are against military production of nuclear warheads, however, and not all individuals who disagree with military production of nuclear warheads disagree with commercial use of fission. The purpose of this essay is to cast doubt on this "atomic asymmetry" and to argue that some of the same basic logical, epistemological, and ethical flaws are shared both by arguments in favor of commercial fission technology and by those for production of nuclear weapons. I argue that, at a minimum, if one is opposed to military uses of fission technology, then one also ought to reject its commercial employment for the generation of electricity.

2 Historical Links Between Reactors and Bombs

The story of the development of nuclear-fission technology, widely employed in medicine and in the generation of electricity, is in large part the story of the development of the atomic bomb. There appears to be little doubt that the US government initially pushed development of "Atoms for Peace" – commercial reactors for generating electricity – so that it could obtain the weapons-grade plutonium as a by-product.[1] During the postwar arms race, the US expended billions of dollars of research and development monies on water-cooled reactors because they were not complex to build and because their fuel was enriched uranium, already being used for making explosives. This is a critical point, because such reactors (unlike those of Canada, Britain, and the USSR) are faced with a much higher risk of "core meltdown," the chief potential cause of catastrophic reactor accidents.

To promote atomic energy in the US, private utilities were offered governmental subsidies to construct nuclear power plants, and in 1956 the US Atomic Energy Commission guaranteed that it would buy any plutonium generated by commerical reactors. Hence, at least in the US, fission generation of electricity began in large part both because it aided in the production of weapons, and because government provided industry with incentives ultimately directed at facilitating the military use of nuclear technology.[2]

3   Four Factual Links Between Reactors and Bombs

These historical links between nuclear weapons and commercial reactors were forged largely because there are four main factual links between reactors and bombs, and there are neither technical nor political ways of breaking any of them. *First,* because of laser separation technology, the fissionable material in any nuclear fuel cycle can be used to make weapons, either directly or after it is treated with equipment which is already available in commercial applications of nuclear technology. *Second,* most of the equipment used in the reactor business has a dual function: it is also useful for building bombs. *Third,* most of the knowledge and skills needed for a weapons program are also required for a commercial reactor program. Although important bomb-design information is classified, it is freely available in the reactor-safety literature. *Fourth,* the kinds of organizations needed to run something as complicated as a commercial reactor program are also very well suited to making weapons.[3]

4   Philosophical Links Between Reactors and Bombs

Because of these four intimate links between reactors and weapons, avoiding commercial generation of electricity by means of nuclear fission is a *necessary* condition for stopping the spread of atomic bombs. Although it is not, strictly speaking, a *sufficient* condition for ending proliferation of nuclear weapons, it comes very close to being one. This is because without commercial nuclear power, ingredients needed for bomb production would no longer be ordinary items of commerce, and therefore would be harder to obtain. They also would be more conspicuous and more costly, in a political sense, since their use would be unambiguously military. Bomb-producing countries could no longer say that their armaments programs were only innocent civilian vehicles for generating electricity needed for development.[4]

Other philosophical links between reactors and bombs exist because of the epistemological and ethical similarities in arguments used to defend both applications of fission technology. A review of some of the main arguments against commercial employment of atomic energy and some of the major objections to development of nuclear weapons will make it easier to see in what ways they differ and are similar. Investigating these similarities and differences, in turn, will enable us to understand why both proponents of commercial atomic energy and advocates of the production of nuclear armaments fall victim to some of the same philosophical fallacies.

4.1 Arguments Against Reactors. Although a great many arguments can be made against generation of electricity by means of nuclear fission, seven dominate the contemporary discussion. I shall examine these in turn.

4.11 The Argument from Due Process. The argument from due process, as its name suggests, focuses on the fact that, in the event of a catastrophic reactor accident, citizens are likely to collect only a fraction of the damages owed them. The maximum possible *property* damages from a major nuclear accident, according to US government estimates in the Brookhaven Report, are $17 *billion.* Yet, by the US Price-Anderson Act of 1957, citizens are prohibited by law from collecting more than $560 *million* in total damages (medical plus property losses), should such an accident occur. This means that, by law, citizens are guaranteed to receive less than 3 percent of their total losses, in the event of a catastrophic reactor accident.

According to proponents of the argument from due process, it is unethical to generate electricity by means of nuclear fission when there are such limits on public liability. (Without these limits, however, utilities have made it plain that they would not be willing to employ atomic energy, since the financial risks would be too great.) Considerations of due process demand that the rights of the minority (those likely to suffer losses as a result of a nuclear accident) ought not to be ignored in order to benefit the majority receiving nuclear-generated electricity. Proponents of the argument from due process claim, therefore, that to deny (for reasons of financial expediency) the rights of a minority to collect damages owed them is inequitable, unjust, arbitrary, and in violation of the Fifth and Fourteenth Amendments to the *US Constitution.*[5]

4.12 The Argument from Future Generations. The argument from future generations also focuses on ethical reasons for proposing that fission generation of electricity not be allowed. Each nuclear plant produces approximately 30 tons of radioactive wastes per year. Continuing to produce these carcinogenic, mutagenic, and teratogenic wastes, with no known method of successful storage for the millions of years required for them to decay, say proponents of this argument, is to threaten the health and well-being of future generations.[6] For this reason, many have argued that production of nuclear wastes, as a consequence of the generation of electricity, represents an inequitable burden imposed on future individuals without their consent, and is thus morally unacceptable.[7]

4.13   The Argument from Equity. The argument from equity focuses on the fact that it is unethical to impose radioactive risks on those now living when, without morally relevant reasons, those risks are inequitably distributed. Advocates of the argument from equity maintain both that current standards for low-level radioactive emissions are not strict enough, and that purely utilitarian considerations have induced reactor licensees and public policy-makers to deprive certain minorities of rights to equal protection in exchange for majority benefits of lower utility rates and cheaper energy production. They maintain that it is *prima facie* unethical to trade the health and welfare of the former for the economic well-being of the latter. They point out, for example, that if all the people within a 50-mile radius of a nuclear power plant receive the maximum allowable radiation dose from the reactor over its 30-year lifetime, then (according to government calculations) 3 percent of these people will produce children who will die from radiation-induced genetic deformities.[8] As this brief discussion indicates, most of the philosophical analyses used by proponents of the argument from equity rest upon explicit criticism both of risk-cost-benefit analysis and of utilitarian ethics.[9]

4.14   The Argument from Catastrophic Potential. The argument from catastrophic potential is that, in the event of a serious accident, a nuclear reactor poses enormous problems to human and environmental well-being; as a consequence, it should not be used to generate electricity. To substantiate their claims about safety, proponents of the argument from catastrophic potential point out that, for all commercial reactors in the US (now operating or under construction), the probability of a core-melt sometime during their generating lifetime (30 years) is approximately 1 in 4. They also note that even nuclear advocates admit that the chance of a Three Mile Island-type accident, somewhere in the US, could be as high as 1 in 2 annually.[10]

4.15   The Argument from Economics. According to proponents of the argument from economics, generating electricity by means of atomic energy is extremely costly and only appears to be economical because the government gives the nuclear industry enormous and disproportionate subsidies. They claim that hundreds of billions of tax dollars have supported fission research and development, waste storage, uranium enrichment, utility insurance, and fuel reprocessing. Were nuclear power to "pay its own way" (to the degree that other technologies like solar energy must do), fission would never have been used to generate electricity.

Amory Lovins points out that because of atomic energy, many utilities are already technically bankrupt and are using short-term loans to raise enough money to pay their unearned dividends. At present, says Lovins, nuclear power costs 50 percent more than coal-generated electricity, in terms of real capital cost per installed kilowatt, and the problem is not likely to get better. Largely because of these economic problems, he maintains, no new us commercial reactors have been ordered since 1978, and nuclear forecasts are plummeting worldwide. For example, a Canadian government committee said recently that it doubted whether the Canadian nuclear industry would survive the 1980s.[11] The only reason some nuclear plants are still being built outside the us, says Lovins, is that they are constructed in centrally planned economies, like France and the ussr, where subsidies for their construction generally exceed the total cost paid by the utilities purchasing them.[12]

4.16   The Argument from Alternatives. A sixth objection to commercial atomic power, often used in conjunction with one of the preceding lines of reasoning, is the argument from alternatives. Citing studies such as those done by the us Office of Technology Assessment and the Harvard Business School, proponents of this argument maintain that alternatives to nuclear fission, such as conservation and solar energy, are both more economical and environmentally desirable than atomic energy.

The Office of Technology Assessment concluded recently that "soft-path" energy technologies (solar, wind, geothermal, and conservation, as opposed to coal, fission, and oil) are capable of supplying, cost effectively, 40 percent of all us energy needs by 1985.[13] The authors of the Harvard study, *Energy Future,* concluded that conservation can enable the us to avoid any increased use of hard-path energy technologies until the soft path is able to supply, cost effectively, the remaining 60 percent.[14]

4.17   The Argument from Proliferation. Perhaps the most significant argument, in terms of its relevance to the issue of nuclear weapons, is the argument from proliferation. According to proponents of this approach, stopping the use of atomic energy to generate electricity is a necessary condition for slowing the arms race. They point out that even if one does not obtain weapons-grade plutonium from reprocessing spent reactor fuel, it is still possible to use the commercial nuclear cycle as part of a weapons effort.[15] For advocates of the argument from proliferation, those who supply nuclear reactors or uranium, like Canada and the us, encourage both *vertical* proliferation (accelerating competition for more devastating arms among existing nuclear powers) and *horizontal* proliferation (the spread of nuclear-weapons capability to more and more national and sub-national groups). Moreover, despite the negative civil-liberties impact of attempts to avoid nuclear proliferation,[16] it is generally admitted that no safeguards are foolproof. Supporters of the argument from proliferation point out that we have been unable to stop international heroin traffic, and that there is likewise no way, in principle, to stop commerce in weapons or to safeguard uranium and plutonium.

4.2 Arguments Against Producing Nuclear Weapons. As we have seen, economics and safety are two of the main concerns of those who oppose the generation of electricity from atomic energy. These two considerations also crop up in objections to production of nuclear arms. Let us briefly examine some of these arguments, with an eye to seeing the philosophical similarities and differences between debates regarding atomic energy and those concerning nuclear weapons.

4.21   The Welfare Argument. One of the most common objections to the production of nuclear weapons is what I call the welfare argument. Proponents of this line of reasoning maintain that the vast sums spent on armaments for the planet, $550 billion annually – over a million dollars per minute – could better be spent to enhance human welfare. They point out, for example, that over 450 million children die annually from starvation, that countless others succumb to disease, and that if only a fraction of expenditures on armaments, say $450 million, were spent to avert human sickness and death, then malaria could be wiped out completely. For much less than that amount, polio could be eliminated in Asia and Africa, where 500,000 children are annually crippled for life. As one person put it, money spent on arms is stolen from the poor.

4.22   The Argument from Human Error. Some hold, further, that because of their catastrophic potential and the propensity of humans to use them irrationally and erroneously, nuclear arms ought not to be created at all. I call this the argument from human error.

To substantiate their claim that nuclear holocaust by false judgment, sabotage, or terrorism is possible, proponents of the argument from human error point out both that detonation of only one percent of the world's arsenal of nuclear weapons would cause a "nuclear winter" and that thefts of nuclear arms have likely been attempted in Europe, where the US has about 7000 tactical weapons. They also reveal that US weapons controls, the best in the world, are not foolproof; in 1961, for example, the US Air Force "accidentally" dropped a 24-megaton bomb near Goldsboro, North Carolina. Only one of its six safety devices worked; had the sixth and last also failed, then the US would have been subjected to a single explosion larger than the cumulative total released in all wars in human history. In fact, US accidents, many of which were "near misses" because of faulty safety equipment, have dropped more thermonuclear weapons on the US than the Russians had mounted on all their ICBMs put together twenty years ago.[17] Because of the vast potential for human error, many experts maintain that the nuclear risk should not be taken; they claim that 300 million lives are too many to risk in pursuing the arms race and various deterrence strategies.

4.23   The Argument Against Negotiating Tools. A third objection to nuclear weapons is that they are not needed as bargaining chips, contrary to what is claimed by many of their proponents. I call this the argument against negotiating tools. The position of those who support military buildup is that if the leader of a nuclear nation is to negotiate effectively with other world powers in order to obtain arms reductions, then he must have many atomic weapons to back him up. By offering to eliminate production of these arms, he can give other nations an incentive for reducing their own weapons.

As John Holdren points out, however, this military argument is faulty: "in every past instance the continuing buildup of nuclear weapons during the process of negotiation has undermined the basis of these negotiations and has drastically reduced what they might have accomplished."[18] Moreover, when a government says that it needs to go beyond thousands of strategic tactical nuclear weapons to create a whole new generation of armaments and thereby attain the capacity to negotiate for peace, it is taking a highly implausible position: that one must make things more complicated in order to simplify them. A further point is that continuing the production of nuclear arms today means that nations continue to develop weapons that defy verification, like the ground-launched, sea-launched cruise missile. But if they defy verification, and if verification has always been a key element in arms-control agreements among the superpowers, then it is unlikely that arms-control agreements will ever come about.

4.24   The Argument Against Military Inferiority. Closely related to the preceding argument is the reasoning that continuing the arms buildup is necessary to avoid military inferiority. Proponents of this argument likely err, however, for a variety of reasons. *First,* both superpowers have the ability to destroy the other many times over, and neither side can deprive the other of this retaliatory capacity, even if there were an initial "sneak attack." Therefore, neither side can plausibly claim that avoiding military inferiority is the real reason for its arms buildup. *Second,* those who advocate pursuing a course of arms buildup in order to avoid alleged military inferiority subscribe to a self-defeating position, and they fall victim to what Holdren calls "the fallacy of the last move."[19] The nation over whom one gains alleged temporary superiority, in "the last move," is likely to follow the same strategy, causing a dangerous treadmill of escalation of weapons construction. *Third,* at least on the part of the us, military buildup to avert alleged inferiority is likely premised on the false assumption that the

US is militarily deficient, as compared to some other nation.[20] *Fourth,* the arms race cannot be defended on the grounds of avoiding military inferiority because most of the buildup, at least in this decade, has been for offensive and first strike weapons, rather than for defensive or retaliatory weapons.[21]

4.25   The Argument Against Deterrence. Of course, one might argue that offensive or first strike weapons are essential to avoid military inferiority, but this argument can only be made consistently on the grounds that development of atomic weapons is needed for deterrence. This brings us to a final objection to construction of nuclear arms, which I call the argument against deterrence. This line of reasoning is basically a response to those who claim that a nation ought to produce atomic weapons because they deter hostile acts of other nations.

Those who subscribe to the above argument believe that proponents of deterrence make a number of errors in their reasoning. *First,* they say, once a nation gets into the business of an escalating arms race, even on the grounds of deterrence, it all too easily slips from a defensive to a war-fighting posture which threatens world peace and thrusts all people to the brink of nuclear holocaust. *Second,* there are 50,000 nuclear weapons in the world. If only a few are capable of wiping out civilization as we know it, then how can producing even more of these arms deter nations from war? A *third* line of reasoning is that anonymous or unattributable threats or attacks cannot be deterred. If people can blow up cities without governments knowing who they are, then the whole basis of deterrence theory evaporates.[22] *Fourth,* as McGeorge Bundy, advisor on major elements of US foreign policy over the past twenty years, points out, the deterrence policies of Finland, Austria, Canada, and Mexico have worked as well; these nations have prevented the use of atomic weapons against them by pursuing a policy comprised of not building massive and sophisticated nuclear arsenals.[23] *Fifth,* even if deterrence were in itself a consistent and workable policy, it is often joined with other policies that make its realization impossible, e.g., the failure to pledge that one will not use nuclear weapons first. China and the Soviet Union have made such a pledge, but the US has not.[24]

In response to the argument that the absence of a no-first-use policy undercuts the goals of deterrence because nations will seek to use their weapons rather than lose them, proponents of deterrence point to the difference between a "counterforce" strategy, in which weapons are targeted against other weapons, and a "countervalue" strategy, in which warheads are directed at nonmilitary objectives. They maintain that although a counterforce strategy might not deter the first use of weapons, a countervalue strategy would be much more likely to do so, because both sides would then target civilian population centers and retaliation would be devastating. According to this view, a countervalue strategy raises the stakes of war, but because it does so, provides Mutual Assured Destruction or MAD as an effective deterrent.

The main problem with the countervalue strategy, however, is that, even if it is a stronger deterrent, it is likely much less morally acceptable than a counterforce strategy. In other words, just because something works does not mean that it is ethically permissible.

4.3   Arguments Supporting Both Uses of Nuclear Technology Often Share the Same Philosophical Flaws. One of the more interesting aspects of unsupported assumptions in the nuclear arms debate (e.g. the assumption that deterrence has "worked") is that they are not unique to arguments about weapons. Some of the same kinds of ethical, logical, and epistemological fallacies may be found both in arguments for commercial uses of fission technology and in those advocating construction and deployment of nuclear weapons. Two such fallacies may be found in what I call "the probability argument" and "the frequency argument."

4.31   The Probability Argument. The probability argument focuses on the allegedly small likelihood that undesirable consequences will occur as a result of either construction of nuclear weapons or generation of electricity by means of atomic energy. Arguing that "the bulk of disagreement" over nuclear power is over different beliefs about the probability of catastrophic accidents,[25] proponents of commercial fission typically err in ways similar to those who advocate construction of nuclear weapons. They assume that the probability of catastrophe, associated either with civilian uses of atomic energy or with nuclear weapons, is extremely small. They also assume that, apart from whether this judgment about probability is accurate, the improbability of a nuclear catastrophe would constitute sufficient grounds for dismissing worries about either a nuclear holocaust or a reactor accident.

To substantiate their assumption that the probability of a nuclear war is quite small, officials in the Pentagon have used game theory to draw the conclusion that the likelihood is one percent a year. Disarmament experts and mathematicians, such as Jeremy Stone and Arthur Westing, agree that they are "content with" this figure.[26] Likewise, to support their claims that the probability of a nuclear core-melt is small, energy experts, at least in the US, typically rely on the Rasmussen Report (WASH 1400) figure of a per-year, pre-reactor probability of core-melt of one in 17,000.[27] Since these probabilities appear quite small, both sets of proponents reason that nuclear generation of electricity and weapons production are unlikely to have serious consequences. However, there are a number of reasons for questioning this conclusion. For one thing, although the annual probabilities appear small, once one takes into account the long-term chances of a catastrophe, the numbers become much larger. Stone points out, for example, that the "one percent chance" of a nuclear war really "means that over the next fifty or a hundred years, we will have a nuclear war."[28] Likewise, if the probability of a reactor core-melt is 1 in 17,000, then for the 150 or so US reactors now in operation or under construction, there is a 1 in 4 probability of such a disaster sometime in their 30-year lifetime. This means that a nuclear core-melt is virtually guaranteed to occur somewhere in the US within the next 60 to 120 years.[29]

Another reason for believing that these probabilities need not be small is that they are based on a number of very theoretical and abstract calculations and extrapolations. As defense analyst Pierre Sprey says, "Strategic analysis is a dream world. It is the realm of data-free analysis. There's [sic] no test data, no combat data."[30] This means, of course, that various military probabilities, as estimated by the US Defense Department for example, vary by as much as 500 or 600 percent, or an order or two of magnitude, owing to a variety of highly variable assumptions.[31] It is not clear, moreover, how one estimates the probability of human error or sabotage; any assumptions about a nuclear holocaust are highly dependent upon human parameters which are next to impossible to estimate. If so, then Stone may be correct in his claim that the real danger is not that some allegedly small chance of disaster will be played out in the international political arena; rather, it is the war that nobody wants, a war thought to be avoidable because of unrealistic assumptions about human error and misunderstanding. Similar highly variable assumptions underlie calculations of core-melt probabilities, for similar reasons; there are no full-scale empirical data on core-melts, and the calculated probabilities are derived on the basis of a highly questionable method known as "fault-tree analysis."[32]

In addition to the highly theoretical nature of the calculations, another reason for believing that the probability of a nuclear holocaust or of a reactor core-melt is not small is that many of those informed about these chances believe that both catastrophes are quite probable. For example, despite the fact that a nuclear holocaust is said by US Defense Department analysts to be improbable, Switzerland has embarked on a costly program of building domestic bomb shelters. The Chinese likewise consider this threat to be quite real, and have dug hundreds of miles of tunnels under their cities.[33]

In the case of nuclear-generated electricity, the private insurance industry provides a correlative example of the fact that informed people consider a core-melt accident to be highly probable. Private insurers have always been unwilling to provide coverage for the nuclear industry at a price which makes fission-generated electricity cost-effective, and this explains, in part, why it has always been so heavily underwritten by government. As a matter of record, the utility industry was itself unwilling to get into the business of using atomic energy to produce electricity until the us government gave it a guaranteed liability limit.[34]

In addition to subscribing to the erroneous assumption that nuclear catastrophe, from either cause, is unlikely, those who accept the probability argument also err in presupposing that if both chances are small, it is reasonable to take both sorts of nuclear risk. However, in the case of using fission to generate electricity, extremely undesirable risks are often associated with allegedly low accident probabilities. Fischhoff and others who do psychometric studies of technological risks indicate that the level of probability is almost never a determinant in whether a risk is judged to be acceptable or perceived as safe enough to take. Rather, they note that allegedly improbable risks are perceived as unacceptable if they are unfamiliar, inequitably distributed, or likely to lead to catastrophic consequences. In fact, risk assessors have found that perceived risk can be predicted almost completely accurately, solely on the basis of the single variable, "severity of consequences," *even if* the probability of those consequences' occurring is quite small and is perceived as such.[35] But if this is true, then it is the *possible* consequences, not their perceived likelihood of occurrence, that is important in societal evaluation of the risk from nuclear weapons and atomic energy.

Perhaps one reason why assessors typically employ the probability argument, in assuming that likelihood of catastrophe is the single most important indicator of risk acceptability, is that the us Atomic Energy Commission, the us Nuclear Regulatory Commission, and courts have generally not attributed much importance to the values placed on consequences. Courts "have consistently taken the position that probabilities are determinative of risk, regardless of potential consequences."[36] Nuclear risk assessments in the us have also repeatedly adopted the nuisance rule that probabilities alone determine risk. The basis for this rule very likely has been society's interest in technological development.[37] There are, however, at least two reasons for arguing that, in certain cases, like atomic energy and nuclear weapons, the consequences are more important than the accident probabilities.

First, although assessors, government agencies, and the courts often define risks simply in terms of probabilities, such a definition fails to account for the greater social disruption arising from one massive accident as compared to the social disruption caused by many single-fatality accidents killing the same number of people. *Second,* the law of torts recognizes the heightened importance of high-consequence events, apart from their probability of occurrence, and it allows for application of the rule of strict liability for abnormally dangerous activities.[38] Part of the justification for this judicial emphasis on accident consequences is apparently the fact that the parties involved in litigation over catastrophic accidents – viz., the injured persons and the persons liable for the injury – are not equal in bargaining power. This is because the representative of some technological, industrial, or military interest usually has more clout than the person damaged by it. Because of the non-equivalence between parties in liability suits involving catastrophic technological accidents, laws sensitive to consequence magnitudes are needed to insure attention to serious public health effects and to provide limits to dangerous impacts not comparable to those in our previous experience.[39] For both these reasons, then, there appear to be grounds for denying that the allegedly low probabilities associated with a nuclear holocaust or a reactor accident are plausible reasons for accepting either type of nuclear risk.[40] In the case of using fission to generate electricity, for example, the consequences of a major accident could be catastrophic: 145,000 deaths, destruction of an area the size of Pennsylvania, and $17 billion in property damages alone, not counting medical costs. After only one year of operation, each commercial reactor has the potential for an accident causing destruction equivalent to that of 1000 Hiroshima bombs.[41]

Much the same situation occurs in the case of evaluating the risk of a planetary holocaust as a consequence of the production of nuclear arms: 160 million immediate deaths, irrevocable ecological damage, economic collapse, and the occurrence of a "nuclear winter" (with destruction of the ozone layer and creation of a situation in which no crops could grow), which could snuff out almost all remaining life on earth.[42] As former us President Eisenhower declared: "The alternative is so terrible that any risks there might be in advancing to disarmament are as nothing."[43]

4.32   The Frequency Argument. I now turn to an examination of the frequency argument. Proponents of this line of reasoning maintain that reactor accidents and misuses of atomic weapons are infrequent and that, so far, production of nuclear arms and fission generation of electricity have worked since there have been no serious consequences from either. Military advocates of this argument point out, for example, that we have had forty years without nuclear war. Those who support utilities' use of fission often make a similar point. They note, as does the us government, that except for the Three Mile Island incident, there have been "no nuclear accidents to date." Moreover, they point out that this 1979 episode was not serious, since "certainly not more than one or two persons could die as a result of that accident."[44]

Perhaps the most basic flaw in the frequency argument is that its proponents confuse frequency with probability. Simply because the *frequency* of a nuclear war or a commercial reactor accident is quite low does not mean that the *probability* of either occurring is small. On the one hand, very low values of an accident probability, per reactor-year, for example, are consistent with an assumed record of zero accidents or zero core melts in 17,000 reactor-years. On the other hand, a probability as high as 1 in 2000 reactor-years would be consistent with the observed nuclear-accident record. In other words, even though an accident record may be consistent with very small probability values, this frequency alone "does not prove that the values are low."[45] Moreover, since we have reliable and empirical probabilities for events that have had a long recorded history,[46] inductive use of historical risk data, whether for nuclear war or for commercial reactor accidents, appears to result in an underestimation of risk, because certain events may not have occurred between the inception of a technology and the end of the period for which the risk information has been compiled. Claims that a nuclear war has not occurred and that a catastrophic reactor core-melt has not taken place are both predicated on relatively sparse accident records for the new fission technology.[47] Further, because of factors such as sabotage, terrorism, and simple error, it is questionable whether the fact that "it hasn't happened yet" provides grounds for believing that a reactor accident or a nuclear war is unlikely.

Proponents of the frequency argument err not only in theory, but also in practice, because of their tendency to define accidents as non-accidents. For example, even though there were major releases of radiation to the atmosphere in the 1966 Detroit nuclear accident and the 1961 Idaho Falls accident, the us government declined to define these "incidents" as "nuclear accidents."[48] Since only the us Nuclear Regulatory Commission can *define* when an "extraordinary nuclear occurrence" has taken place, and since the armed forces can simply classify information about military nuclear blunders (recall the example in section 4.22), there is little practical assurance that often-cited data about reactor and military accident frequency are correct.

Put most simply, those who accept the underlying assumption of the frequency argument, whether on theoretical or practical grounds, are like the man who jumped off the Empire State Building. Someone waved at him as he passed the fortieth floor, and asked him how he was doing. As he whizzed by, the jumper shouted, "Just fine."

5 Conclusion

We have seen that there is indeed a set of crucial connections between the production of nuclear weapons and the generation of electricity by means of atomic energy. There are no "atoms for peace." Not only is nuclear power a necessary (and nearly sufficient) condition for the production of nuclear weapons, but also some of the same fallacious lines of reasoning appear in arguments for commercial fission technology and in those in support of the construction of nuclear weapons: the probability argument and the frequency argument. (Many other questionable approaches are shared by both military and commercial advocates of fission technology, but there is no space to discuss them here.)

Because there are both empirical and conceptual grounds for rejecting the "plutonium economy," citizens and policy-makers ought at least to give serious thought both to an immediate halt to weapons production and to an immediate end to construction of nuclear-power reactors. Once both these actions were accomplished, we could then devote our efforts to what Lovins calls a "Sunbeams for Peace" program, i.e. the development of safe, soft energy technologies which would significantly reduce both the threat of nuclear war and the risk of a catastrophic reactor accident.[49]

A "Sunbeams for Peace" program is essential not only for the preservation of the planet from nuclear war and from reactor-induced radioactive pollution, but also for the continuation of a democratic way of life.[50] This is because all-important decisions about nuclear war-fighting and reactor licensing are not subject to Congressional or parliamentary debate. Hence, even though average citizens are like front-line troops in the case of nuclear warfare or a reactor accident, they are really worse off than privates because they have no real control over either the conduct of war or the operation of a nuclear power plant. As a consequence, it could be argued, for example, that because nuclear war forecloses moral opportunities such as conscientious objection and democratic control, persons have a very strong claim to more power regarding decisions about production of nuclear arms. This being so, pursuing a "Sunbeams for Peace" program would do much to transfer public policy from the cabinets of the elite to the votes and voices of the common person. It would do much to bring control of citizens' daily lives and well-being back from the hands of "experts" plotting deterrence strategies and place it in the hands of those most likely to be their victims.   *University of Florida*

NOTES

1 Cited by Novick, pp. 32-33; see also p. 22 where Novick substantiates the claim that commercial nuclear fission was begun in the US for military reasons. The claim is corroborated by Willrich, pp. 5-6.

2 See Shrader-Frechette, *Nuclear Power and Public Policy* (hereafter *NPPP),* Chapters 1 and 4 for a discussion of the history of nuclear technology and for an analysis of core-melt and its consequences.

3 Amory Lovins, "Soft Energy: Links to Security," in Brouwer, ed., p. 62. See also Lovins and Lovins, Chapters 2-3; and Prins, ed., pp. 253-57 for a discussion of the links between reactors and weapons.

4 Lovins, p. 63; Lovins and Lovins, Chapters 2-4. Calder, p. 77 makes some of these same points.

5   For a discussion of the argument from due process, see Shrader-Frechette, *NPPP,* Chapter 4.

6   For verification of this information and citation of all the numerous environmental impact assessments and government documents from which it was taken, see Shrader-Frechette, *NPPP,* pp. 49-52.

7   For further discussion of the rights of future generations and the extent to which production of nuclear wastes violates these rights, see Callahan; Shrader-Frechette, "Technology Assessment, Future Generations, and the Social Contract"; Partridge; and Shrader-Frechette, *NPPP,* Chapter 3.

8   See Shrader-Frechette, *NPPP,* pp. 34-35 for this argument.

9   Many of the egalitarian criticisms of current emission standards rest upon the work of eminent philosophers such as Dworkin, Gewirth, and Rawls. For several versions of the argument from equity, see Shrader-Frechette, *NPPP,* Chapter 2; Shrader-Frechette, "Energy and Ethics," in Regan, ed., pp. 107-38.

10 For calculation of the core-melt probabilities and the Three Mile Island probabilities on the basis of the government's own data, see Shrader-Frechette, *NPPP,* pp. 84-85; for government-calculated data on the consequences of a catastrophic nuclear accident, see pp. 78-79. Both sets of data are taken from the Rasmussen Report and the Brookhaven Report commissioned by the US Atomic Energy Commission.

11 Gordon Edwards, "Canada's Nuclear Industry and the Myth of the Peaceful Atom," in Regehr and Rosenblum, eds., p. 148.

12 Lovins and Lovins, Chapter 5; Lovins, pp. 64-66. See also Shrader-Frechette, *NPPP,* pp. 54-60 and Chapter 5, where it is pointed out that once government subsidies are taken into account, nuclear fission turns out to be *more expensive* than other sources of energy.

13 US Office of Technology Assessment, *Application of Solar Technology to Today's Energy Needs,* Vol. 1, pp. 3, 18, 21.

14 Stobaugh and Yergin, eds. For more discussion of economical, soft-path alternatives to commercial nuclear fission, see Lovins and Lovins, Chapter 8.

15 Edwards, "Canada's Nuclear Industry," pp. 164-66.

16 See, for example, Ayres.

17 Lovins and Lovins, pp. 27-28 give abundant data on such domestic accidents with nuclear weapons and they also cite numerous government and scientific publications which document these accidents.

18 John Holdren, "Defusing the Arms Race," in Brouwer, ed., p. 129.

19 John Holdren, "Backing Away From the Brink," speech given at the University of California, Santa Barbara, May 24, 1984.

20 Linus Pauling, "Unilaterial Actions for World Peace," in Brouwer, ed., pp. 177-79. The myth of Russian superiority is also refuted in Aldridge, *The Counterforce Syndrome,* and Kaplan, *The Dubious Specter,* pp. 55 ff., 66 ff.

21 Gene LaRocque, "Monitoring the Military Buildup," in Brouwer, ed., p. 20.

22 Lovins, p. 61, makes this argument.

23 Mills, 3.

24 See Holdren, "Defusing the Arms Race," pp. 130-31.

25 Starr and Whipple, 1116.
26 Jeremy Stone, "The Causes of War," in Brouwer, ed., pp. 55-56.
27 For a discussion of the Rasmussen figures and an evaluation of their correctness, plus complete bibliographical information, see Shrader-Frechette, *NPPP,* pp. 82-90.
28 Stone, "The Causes of War," p. 56.
29 For calculation of these probabilities on the basis of data found in US government documents, especially the Rasmussen Report, see Shrader-Frechette, *NPPP,* pp. 84-85.
30 Cited by Kaplan, *The Dubious Specter,* p. 41. For another view of the uncertainties regarding nuclear war calculations, see Bunn and Tsipis.
31 See Calder, pp. 146-51.
32 See Shrader-Frechette, *NPPP,* pp. 83ff. for a discussion of fault-tree analysis.
33 Information on China and Switzerland is contained in Calder, pp. 54-55, 152-53.
34 See Shrader-Frechette, *NPPP,* pp. 8-12, 74-77 for a discussion of these points about insurance for the nuclear industry.
35 Fischhoff et al., 148-49; and H. Green, 909-10.
36 Yellin, 992.
37 *Ibid.,* 987.
38 *Ibid.,* 983-84.
39 *Ibid.,* 987-88.
40 See Shrader-Frechette, "Risk-Assessment Methodology and the Challenge of Jeffersonian Democracy," especially 36; Shrader-Frechette, "Economics, Risk-Cost-Benefit Analysis, and the Linearity Assumption," 222-23.
41 See note 10 and section 4.14 of this article.
42 Riordan; see especially pp. 33 and 130-32 for a bibliography on the effects of a nuclear war. See also Schell, *The Fate of the Earth*; and Ramberg.
43 Quoted in Calder, p. 158.
44 Subcommittee on Energy Research and Production, p. 68.
45 Fairley, p. 425.
46 Lowrance, p. 6.
47 See Shrader-Frechette, "Risk-Assessment Methodology and the Challenge to Jeffersonian Democracy"; Shrader-Frechette, "Economics, Risk-Cost-Benefit Analysis, and the Linearity Assumption"; and Shrader-Frechette, *Risk Analysis and Scientific Method,* especially Chapter 6.
48 See Shrader-Frechette, *NPPP,* pp. 96-101.
49 See Lovins, p. 66.
50 Although this remark opens up a whole set of questions which I cannot discuss here, see, for example, Ayres.

Commentary: Nuclear Weapons as a Threat to the Permanence of Life

JONATHAN BORDO

By drawing out the connections between arguments against nuclear weapons and arguments against nuclear power, Kristin Shrader-Frechette presents a disturbing and composite picture of the threat which nuclear energy poses to the environment. I wish to extend her picture by arguing that the threat posed to the environment by nuclear weapons comprises the deepest level of their indefensibility.

I

Any discussion of nuclear weapons must begin by noting that they have a special character which distinguishes them from "conventional" weapons. Two important ways of demarcating them are technico-scientific and moral-humanistic.

From a technico-scientific viewpoint, nuclear weapons are special because their all-pervasive destructiveness derives (*1*) from the release of large quantities of energy (much greater quantities than are possible through chemical processes); and (*2*) from the production, as a side effect, of large amounts of radiation. Primarily because of these two factors, the atomic physicists themselves have spoken of nuclear weapons as devices of a qualitatively different kind.[1]

From a moral-humanistic viewpoint, nuclear weapons are useless for furthering traditional political goals because the consequence of their massive use is collective destruction. Richard Wasserstrom has cogently shown how nuclear weapons cancel Clausewitz's dictum of war as an extension of politics by other means.[2] Nuclear weapons would destroy not only the usual human goods (property, free-standing structures, human beings) but the institutional supports for these goods as well as the very biophysical support systems for collective human life. It is in this latter sense that they represent a unique threat to the world's environment and the biotic conditions necessary for life. Cities have been rebuilt after wars, societies revived. After a climactic "nuclear winter" forecast recently by scientists,[3] what is to be rebuilt and by whom? The special character of nuclear weapons can be expressed in terms of an unbridgeable disproportion or *incommensurability* between the all-pervasive destructiveness stemming from their nature and the limited ends or goals which human beings would pursue with them as instruments.

To provide an assessment of nuclear weapons which takes into account their potential ecological consequences, I must first develop a notion of moral standing which conceptually represents the character of nuclear threats to the environment. Following Goodpaster, Regan, and others,[4] I begin with the conception of ourselves and other entities as worthy of moral consideration. A thing has moral standing if and only if we have to take into consideration the effect our action will have for it. Being alive is a plausible enough general criterion for identifying things as having moral standing. Thus, a few things which would be contained in a rather lengthy catalogue of living things having standing would include mammals, trees, biotic systems of all sorts (perhaps even micro as well as macro). In addition inorganic items such as air, soil, water, geological systems should be added to the list even though they are not alive, because their destruction instrumentally affects the survival of organic entities, systems, and processes. Thus all entities, systems, and processes which are alive or are necessary conditions for the support of life should have moral standing.

Now with respect to human beings (and to the higher forms of animal life), not only do the organic and the inorganic provide support structures for species' continuance but human evolution has yielded a highly complex cultural and intellectual apparatus. What is the status of artificial structures such as our systems of knowledge and their storage containers such as libraries? Of monuments of intellect such as architecture and art? The typical justification for a work of art is in terms of its intrinsic and aesthetic value. We partially justify the value of wilderness on these same grounds. We justify the preservation of wilderness in terms of its instrumental value as a natural resource for future human generations. Our justification of knowledge is typically both intrinsic and extrinsic. What unifies our commonplace justifications for these sorts of cultural artifacts, whether intrinsic or extrinsic, is that their value is relative to us as centers of value-ascription. From the object-based ecological account I am sketching, I want to suggest that cultural artifacts have another, deeper status upon which their subject-centered value depends, namely, that they are part and parcel of the support structure for what sustains, perhaps uniquely, human beings as the kind of living thing we are. We are history-makers carried by our history. It might be conjectured that the manner of cultural obliteration which would accompany a nuclear holocaust would result in biological devolution. It is important to mention this because defenders of nuclear survival often base their belief on some limited and peculiar sense of biological survival that assumes the almost surgical removability of culture. Would the nuclear winter survivors be recognizable as humans by any present human life form?

To sum up, there are two sorts of things having moral standing – living things and those structures, systems, and processes which support living things. These supports in turn can be divided into two kinds, natural and artificial. In light of the distinction developed so far, it should be apparent that the fundamental immorality of nuclear weapons stems not merely from their possible consequences for human continuance but from their consequences for the continuance of all things which have moral standing.

The notion of moral standing captures two aspects of what is profoundly unseemly about nuclear weapons. First, it captures the dimensions of the threat: a threat to the standing of x means a threat to the permanence of x. Threats to standing are then characteristically threats to classes, wholes, or types of things, not merely to individuals. Thus, with respect to threats to standing, the difference between nuclear energy and nuclear weapons (and here I slightly amend Shrader-Frechette's unified account of nuclear energy) is that nuclear weapons pose an all-pervasive, systematic, and calculated threat to standing, whereas nuclear power, like acid rain, poses threats to standing which are less inclusive, intermittent, and unpremeditated. With nuclear weapons, once used there is no significant tomorrow, at least not for us. Second, the concept of moral standing captures the restricted and impoverished character of our commonplace agent-centered, individualized, and anthropocentric moral scheme because it is built (in all its variations) upon the assumption of the permanence of life which nuclear weapons would destroy. We have invented these devices, militarily organized their deployment, articulated the rationale and circumstances for their possible use, and we now find that they not only threaten us with collective destruction but that their very existence has rendered obsolete our commonplace morality.

We can summarize the discussion so far in the following moral injunction. Since the use of nuclear weapons threatens the permanence of life, there is absolutely no moral justification for their use.

II

Despite the immorality of the use of nuclear weapons, it might still be said that they are needed to prevent their actual use and the ubiquitous destruction that would ensue. The idea of our having them in our possession as the best means of preventing their actual use is the keystone of the policy doctrine of deterrence which arose after the nuclear destruction of Hiroshima and Nagasaki[5] and the development of a nuclear capability by the Soviet Union in 1948. Now the doctrine of deterrence accepts as a historical and cultural *fait accompli* that we are stuck with them and that we can't disinvent them. Further, it accepts (belatedly) the absolutist moral prohibition against their ever being used (again). At the core of the doctrine is the idea that a kind of possession of them is the best way for preventing their actually being used. The crucial aspect of this kind of possession, what marks it as policy and doctrine, is that each nuclear weapons holder must threaten their use in order to demonstrate to other nuclear holders the apocalyptic consequences of their use. (Mutual Assured Destruction is prevented by threatening use.) Thus, in a word, the mutual-threatening-of-use-to-prevent-use is the essence of the policy doctrine of deterrence.[6]

Deterrence, its history, myth, and reality, cannot be documented here although others in the present volume have given it good coverage.[7] In casting doubt on the reliability of deterrence from an environmental perspective, I wish to make the following two points.

(*1*) The doctrine of deterrence harshly exemplifies the environmentalists' critique of the restrictively anthropocentric character of our commonplace moral outlook, what Routley and Routley call our "human chauvinism."[8] Deterrence, from this perspective, compresses threats to standing into dependent and highly particularistic human claims of rights – rights with respect to sovereignty, self-determination, acquisition, etc. – rights circumscribed by the nation-state. It treats the human claim to rights as equivalent and adequate representation of the environmental claim to standing. It treats as equivalent matters concerning the permanence of life and matters of the peculiar right of a particular form of life and its conception of the human individual. From the environmental perspective, no such equivalence is even *prima facie* plausible. Thus, there is no human good worth preserving to the extent that doing so would threaten the permanence of life.

What justifies the instrumental appropriation of nuclear devices by the State? What justifies our belief that deterrence is the best way to prevent collective self-destruction? The defenders of deterrence justify its rationality in terms of its effectiveness. It has preserved the peace (at least in Northern Europe). If deterrence turns out to be ineffective, that is, fails to provide a stable and enduring peace, then deterrence is immoral and irrational, and we will have to look elsewhere in order to understand why it is that the principal nuclear weapons holders, the US and the USSR, go on accumulating weapons and fine tuning their threats. We would then be wise to look elsewhere than to the nuclear states' *raison d'état* for our survival, a conclusion reached elsewhere in this volume by Kai Nielsen in his response to Wasserstrom and McDonald, via a different route.

(*2*) Here is not the place for refuting the effectiveness of deterrence except to make the following naive appraisal of the existing state of nuclear belligerence between the superpowers going back to World War II. Commencing with the competition over size and quality of weapons ("biggest bang for the buck"), we have witnessed competition over offensive delivery systems, and now over systems to counter offensive delivery systems. We are at the threshold of introducing outer space technology, having just recently put into place new offensive delivery technologies (MX, cruise, Pershing II) which severely reduce the capacities of the belligerents to calculate the opposing side's intentions. If stability were a criterion for effectiveness, then it would be hard on any definition to square with it what appears to be a hyperbolic arms race. To be sure we should be grateful that life as we know it continues for the moment but it requires an unwarranted leap of faith to believe that the future will conform to the past, that our survival is assured because of deterrence.

III

There seems to be little ground for belief in the rationality of deterrence, and the use of threats as instruments of policy when the contents of such threats are the most comprehensive and devastating weapons systems humanly available. I suggest that deterrence turns out to be not only irrational and immoral, but to be merely a mystification, a code word of the principal nuclear weapons holders to justify their continued possession.

But then there are no mitigating circumstances for threatening the permanence of life, since it will turn out, if deterrence is ineffective, that threatened use is not effective to thwart actual use. This leads to the conclusion that our very possession of nuclear weapons threatens the permanence of life, and hence continuing to hold them in the way that we have is absolutely without moral justification.[9]

According to the classical democratic theory of the State, the State's role is to assure the life, liberty, and well-being of its members. In that capacity, the State does not have the right to destroy itself by destroying the conditions upon which its legitimacy rests. The ecological character of nuclear threats thus exposes a profound crisis in the legitimacy of the nuclear state.[10]

University of Calgary

NOTES

1 For a recent scientific appraisal of the character and physical effects of nuclear weapons see Adams and Cullen, eds., especially section 3.

2 See Wasserstrom's essay in this volume. Also Glucksmann.

3 The ongoing debate concerning Sagan's climatic nuclear winter forecasts continue to unfold in *Nature* magazine.

4 Goodpaster, "On Being Morally Considerable"; Regan, especially Chapter 9; Attfield, Chapter 8; and Brennan.

5 For the physical, medical, and social effects of the use of atom bombs on Hiroshima and Nagasaki see Committee for the Compilation of Materials on Damage Caused by the Atomic Bombs. See also Schell, *The Abolition* for an interesting account of the origins of deterrence doctrine.

6 The importance of the prisoner's dilemma depends upon whether one considers deterrence effective. If considered effective, then the prisoner's dilemma is a positive conceptual device for representing the security of the prison. If considered ineffective, then prisoner's dilemma-type situations have a game-like property which bears little relation to the existing condition of conflict.

7 See especially Sherwin and Kennan.

8 R. and V. Routley, "Against the Inevitability of Human Chauvinism," in Goodpaster and Sayre, eds. Another term for this belief is *speciesism*.

9 If deterrence is but policy-makers' way of talking about the arms race, then any policy which proposes to reverse the direction of the arms race is positive. The proposed freeze is a minimal and even radical position given the momentum of the arms race and the commitment of the superpowers to maintaining their hegemony. Having shown that threatened use and actual use both comprise threats to standing, one's political position has the moral absolutist content of the basic position. It is a right to resistance.

10 The argument of this commentary owes much to discussion with Chris Hohenemser, David Miller, Kai Nielsen, Theo von Laue, and Hakan Widberg.

Commentary: The Unacceptable Gamble

Kristin Shrader-Frechette has drawn attention to and usefully classified the variety of specious arguments that are often used to support nuclear power and the production of nuclear weapons. In doing so, she has underscored many of the risks in both applications of atomic technology, showing the parallels between them, and has explained why the risks are far greater than has commonly been admitted. Jonathan Bordo has brought to the forefront one of the deepest objections to the arms race – that a nuclear confrontation threatens to damage irreparably the delicate ecological balance which sustains all life on our planet. I would like to develop both approaches a bit further.

One does not have to be a particularly shrewd observer of the present world political scene to note that though everyone's for peace (the leaders of the two nuclear superpowers above all), the arms race continues and accelerates. This manifest contradiction springs from complex and deep-seated sources, and attempts have been made elsewhere in this volume to probe them (by Gay, Govier, Hirschbein, Zimmerman, Santoni, Litke, Jaggar, Groarke, Brunk, and myself). In spite of the contradiction – or perhaps because it is so apparent – many "experts" in government and the military have sought to persuade us that the probability of nuclear war is very small, even negligible.[1] Shrader-Frechette, however, offers the rejoinder (in section 4.31 of her article) that even a "one percent chance" of a nuclear war translates statistically into a very high cumulative probability of its taking place within the next 50-100 years. While the "one percent chance" may have been arrived at by means of "a number of very theoretical and abstract calculations and extrapolations," as Shrader-Frechette alleges, the inexorable logic of statistical science shows that the ultimate likelihood of a nuclear war, given current trends, far from reinforcing complacency, ought instead to cause great alarm.

Consider now the facts of nuclear proliferation. According to the Cambridge

Seminar on Disarmament, "around forty countries are likely to have enough separated or separable plutonium to make at least a few bombs by 1985."[2] In addition to the six present members of the nuclear "club" (US, USSR, Great Britain, France, China, India), the following countries are thought to have or almost have the capacity to develop nuclear weapons, to be leaning in this direction, or to be potential nuclear powers if unfavorable political pressures exert themselves: Israel, South Africa, Argentina, Brazil, Pakistan, Egypt, Indonesia, Iran, Iraq, Libya, South Korea, Taiwan, Algeria, the Philippines, Nigeria, Zaire, Syria, Chile.[3] How much greater the risk of nuclear war must be with so many fingers on the infamous button one can only guess, but the prospect is truly frightening. We may derive some comfort from the circumstance that while many countries may soon have the bomb, very few as yet have a workable, let alone an intercontinental delivery system. But we must remember that we are living on borrowed time, and that low-yield nuclear devices may become so compact that they are fully transportable in a suitcase, a trunk or a small truck.

Bordo points out, following those scientists who have propounded the "nuclear winter" theory of environmental devastation to which a fateful confrontation between the superpowers could lead, that the biosphere as a whole is likely to be the greatest casualty of nuclear war conducted on *any* scale. "With nuclear weapons, once used," Bordo writes, "there is no significant tomorrow, at least not for us." Nor will there be for other forms of life on Earth in the opinion of many. These views may be mistaken; the nuclear winter prognostications may be inaccurate by so-and-so-many degrees of magnitude. But recall that the risk of putting such theories and counter-theories to the final, tragic test is high. Given that the risk is high, and likely to grow steadily higher through the process of proliferation, and given that the potential environmental impact is *at least possibly* catastrophic, can we afford to take the gamble? I think the answer must be no, and that is why I hold that *any probability of a nuclear war greater than zero is totally unacceptable.*

The jargon and techniques of risk assessment, like those of cost-benefit analysis, seem peculiarly out of place in the context of an event or set of events which could spell the end of life, not just "as we know it," but of life *period.* It is for this reason that Bordo labels both the use of nuclear weapons and the policy of nuclear deterrence irrational and immoral. For while the actual use of these weapons would threaten the permanence of life in a most obvious way, technology being what it is, the policy of deterrence seems to lead inevitably to escalation and an increased risk of a nuclear exchange. And for reasons stated elsewhere in this book (e.g. by Groarke and Werner), there are grounds for serious doubt that a nuclear war could ever remain "limited."

There are too many factors in the arms race that act to raise the risk of nuclear war. Some of the variables are known, some unknown. The web of life is frail. Once torn asunder it may not be mendable. It has been estimated that even a single megaton weapon, exploding over a major city, would cause as much devastation as "all the destruction which Britain suffered in the Second World War."[4] The genetic damage and human carnage caused by so "small" a blast, it is fair to assume, would be considerable. Since we are part of nature, these too would be "environmental consequences." While the effects of a global or all-out nuclear war would be an unparalleled ecological disaster,[5] a less than total nuclear exchange could also annihilate some species, poison ecosystems, decimate a region's natural resources, and render large areas uninhabitable for centuries. We should therefore use our creativity and ingenuity to pursue all initiatives that will reduce and eventually eliminate the risk of nuclear war. A necessary first step is to avoid being seduced by those who speak of acceptable levels of nuclear risk.   *Queen's University at Kingston*

NOTES

1 See President Reagan's remark cited at the beginning of section 3 of my article immediately following. Philosophers too, while hardly Establishment insiders, have made these claims. Examples were provided by Douglas Lackey and Terrance Tomkow at a recent conference on "Philosophy and Nuclear Arms," University of Waterloo, September 28-30, 1984.
2 Prins, ed., p. 215.
3 Walter Schütze, "A World of Many Nuclear Powers," in Griffiths and Polanyi, eds., p. 87.
4 Solly Zuckerman, p. 29.
5 See Peterson, ed.; Sagan; and two articles by Turco et al.

Part III   Issues to Think About and Discuss

1 Shrader-Frechette takes issue with the view that both nuclear deterrence and fission-generated electricity have "worked" or proven themselves, and that neither poses an unacceptable degree of risk. Take a position on these issues and defend it.

2 "There are no 'atoms for peace'." (Shrader-Frechette) Discuss this statement critically.

3 "There is no human good worth preserving to the extent that doing so would threaten the permanence of life." (Bordo) Discuss the implications of this claim.

4 Fox maintains that *"any probability of a nuclear war greater than zero is totally unacceptable."* Do you agree or disagree? Explain.

Part IV Conceptual and Psychological Dilemmas

The Nuclear Mindset:
Motivational Obstacles to Peace

MICHAEL ALLEN FOX

One of the paramount dangers of nuclear weapons, should they be used, will be the inevitable tonnage of fallout they will produce. There is, however, a sense in which we are already experiencing a kind of fallout, namely, "psychological fallout."[1] I am referring here to fear, gloom, despair, cynicism, fatalism, mean-inglessness, apathy, and related psychological aberrations and mental paralyses by means of which the arms race holds us hostage. Despite Edward Teller's avun-cular assurance that the radioactive fallout from a nuclear attack can simply be wiped or washed off our bodies and our food,[2] there is no tidy recipe for the elimination of psychological fallout, which takes its daily toil quite apart from the actual use of nuclear weapons.[3] In my view, the only way out of the present impasse is to look the causes of psychological fallout in the face and work our way through or past them, painful as it is to do so. To accomplish this effec-tively, however, we must be prepared to admit that we are all affected and in-fected, avoiding such simplistic generalizations as that ideological conflict is the "real" cause of the arms race; that this deadly contest can be attributed to the insane machinations of a small inner clique of political and military leaders; and the like.

The arms race, like any other set of deeply ingrained, pervasive and institu-tionalized behaviors, is highly complex and difficult to understand. I do not claim to be presenting the whole story, even from the psychological perspective. From the time of the Potsdam Conference in July 1945, where President Truman received the news of the first successful US detonation of an atomic bomb over the New Mexico desert, American administrations have used nuclear weapons threats – sometimes veiled, sometimes very overt – to attempt to bully and manipulate the Russians. (The Soviets, for their part, have also stated or im-plied their reliance on these weapons as an ultimate instrument of political sua-sion.) More recently, with the rise of right-wing influence in decision-making circles, the US has tried to force changes in internal Soviet and East Bloc politics in the same manner. Some commentators have even suggested that the US is simply attempting to bankrupt the Soviet economy by forcing the Russians to exhaust their resources striving to keep pace with their adversary's expenditures on armaments. There is no denying that raw power-seeking and aggressive (some would say "macho") posturing are important dynamics in the arms race. Other, less overt expressions of power and forms of pressure admittedly fuel and accelerate the arms race and appear to make it beyond control: rapid advances in technology; military, economic and other vested interests; public opinion molded by Cold War rhetoric; workers' resistance to peace initiatives which they see as job-threatening; to name a few. Nonetheless, I believe that psychological factors of the most basic sort are the primary causes of the arms race, and that chief among these is fear. Fear and, more specifically, our responses to it pose perhaps the greatest obstacle to peace. For they control our attitudes and modes of thinking about the world; and if we cannot change these things we can hope to change little else.

I think few of us will seriously question the assertion that fear has played a principal role in stimulating and driving the current arms race. I am referring here to fear of what the Soviet Union would or might do to us, which gives rise to the sense that whatever threat it might pose must be countered or held in check somehow.[4] If we go back in time still further, we find that the chief motive for the development of the first atomic bomb was also fear – fear that the Nazis would develop the weapon and use it on the Allies. It is equally arguable that the first and so far only use of nuclear weapons, against Japan, was motivated by fear – namely, the fear of the one million or so casualties that US strategists estimated would be suffered in a full-scale invasion of that enemy's territory.

Fear, which exists, as we say, "in the face of" some particular threatening situation, thing, person, or possible action, may also, if it persists long enough, generate anxiety, a generalized, often unrecognized mood of apprehension which may permeate one's consciousness, though one may know nothing of its cause. Fear of this kind, I should want to add, can be removed, if at all, only by identifying its source and then coming to terms with and overcoming the uneasiness we experience, which itself requires that we be able and willing to undergo certain fundamental changes in thinking, beliefs, attitudes, values, or the like. While both fear and anxiety may be emotionally draining or debilitating, anxiety is, as a rule, considerably more stressful, since it tends to be an ongoing state of unrest rather than a transitory emotion tied to a specific situation. We don't typically have the sense, when experiencing anxiety, that "this too will pass."

Just as fear may be aroused by something largely or even purely imaginary, so may anxiety. But if such a cause is not unearthed and recognized for what it is, we may find ourselves in an intensely difficult situation from which there is no exit. The perception that we are locked into a conflict which has no resolution will serve only to create in us a sense of hopelessness which in turn is bound to aggravate the sense of anxiety we have. But the worse our anxiety becomes, the less we are able to find a solution to our predicament, and the more inclined we are to seek relief in escapist diversions rather than in the task of destroying the illusions which enslave us. It is this sort of vicious spiral the arms race has produced.

In what follows I want to examine the arms race as something which is propelled by fear and anxiety – not just the fear and anxiety that are only too natural and reasonable in the face of our possible extermination, but the irrational fear and anxiety that distort our thinking, give rise to dangerous illusions, control our actions, and send us in pursuit of a degree of security we can never attain. I want to show as well how distorted thinking and conceptual confusion in turn exaggerate our nuclear fear and anxiety, for the connection between these factors is an intimate and philosophically interesting one.

1   Fear and Anxiety as Causes of the Arms Race

It is not my purpose here to provide a history of the arms race or of American-Soviet relations. This has been done very adequately and illuminatingly elsewhere and there is little point in rehashing what others have said so well.[5] I shall simply note that conflicting perceptions of international political realities and of each other's political systems and intentions, as well as perpetual uncertainties concerning each other's military and technological capabilities, have bedevilled US-Soviet relations throughout the period from 1917 to the present. Unclear thinking based upon misperceptions and limited information has led to dubious and risky policy-making on both sides. Except for a brief interlude during which the watchword was "peaceful coexistence," the two superpowers have placed their hopes on each other's collapse as a system from internal and external pressures, and have spared no efforts to bring this about.

Apart from power politics and xenophobia – the latter itself a form of unreasonable fear – relations between the two nuclear giants have been permeated and driven by fear, primarily the Russians' fear of encirclement and invasion, and the Americans' fear of Soviet "expansionism." In both cases the fear is in part rational, in the sense that more or less well-grounded inferences from what is known or observed underlie it. The Russians' experience of repeated invasion of their homeland over the past century or two is, for example, the foundation of a genuine fear that those hostile to their way of life or very existence may try again if the opportunity presents itself. They have been given additional cause for fear not just by the sophisticated and rapidly expanding Western and Chinese arsenals, but also by the harsh rhetoric and aggressive posturing of their principal adversaries. The Americans, for their part, have witnessed the absorption of several independent countries into the Soviet Union, its establishment of a sphere of European satellite states, and Soviet involvements in various regions of the world. They can also find in Marxism-Leninism a doctrine of global revolution, and are on the receiving end of equally harsh rhetoric – what former Canadian Prime Minister Pierre Trudeau has called "megaphone diplomacy" – and aggressive gestures. There is, in addition, each side's awareness of the other's very visible escalation and deployment of new weapons systems. In these factors one finds the breeding grounds for fear. I am not concerned here with examining the issue of whether these fears are exaggerated; suffice it to say that they do have real or objective grounds. Most important, we must realize that what is at stake for both sides today is, as they see it, *survival* – the survival of a way of life, a system of cherished beliefs and values, and now, in the nuclear age, survival *per se*.

Locked into the arms race as we are and have been for some decades now, we witness ourselves becoming, as a people, more and more preoccupied with the external "threat" posed by the Soviets.[6] Many North Americans and a substantial number of Europeans are also apprehensive concerning the very real threat to themselves posed by *our own* nuclear weapons – their sheer number and wide distribution, their ever more deadly accuracy and sophistication, the decentralization of command over them, and the seemingly reckless and irresponsible attitude toward their use on the part of our leaders and decision-makers.

2   *Deceiving Ourselves about the Arms Race*

It is a well-established psychological fact that when animals are cornered, in a life-and-death struggle, or in a situation perceived as such, their two possible responses are "fight or flight." When faced with an ultimate challenge the alternatives are either to stand and confront the would-be attacker in a death-or-surrender contest, or to run away and thereby avoid the possibility of annihilation altogether. Humans, being more complex creatures with a highly developed conscious life, are still animals, but we have discovered other ways of dealing with threats to our existence. While animals utilize elaborate instinctual displays of behavior to intimidate their foes, we may try to browbeat them with harsh words. When we find this fails to do the job, or succeeds only to some measure, we become more creative and devious. In addition to fighting and fleeing, we practice what is known in psychiatry as *denial,* a defense mechanism designed to neutralize a perceived or real threat by pretending it does not exist. We practice denial simply because a high level of anxiety is extremely stressful – psycho-

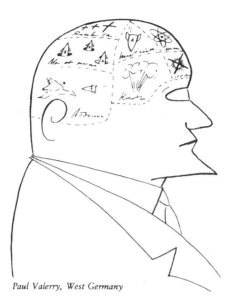

Paul Valerry, West Germany

logically painful – and denial is a way of coping with this stress. A 1963 US public opinion poll showed that "persons who are very anxious about nuclear destruction ... avoid relevant information and remain badly informed."[7] Not much had changed by 1981 when in a *Newsweek* poll "nearly *half* the Americans surveyed checked a box that read 'I am concerned about the chances of nuclear war, but I try not to think about it'."[8] Denial is a (pseudo) solution we resort to when reality cannot be faced and dealt with in a more straightforward way.

But isn't there a contradiction here? How can we be preoccupied with the Soviet threat and absorbed in making our own counter-threats while at the same time refusing to face the Soviet threat honestly and realistically? Of course there *is* a contradiction. How can it be explained? The easy answer is that like all defense mechanisms denial is not a very adaptive form of behavior; it is only a compromise, only partially effective, since reality impinges upon us even against our will. The more complex answer is that we endeavor in many ways to disguise the truth from ourselves, engaging in self-deception, in this way pretending to deal with something other than we are really dealing with, or that we can resolve our nuclear extinction anxiety in some way other than by confronting it directly and honestly.

The psychodynamic processes by means of which we delude ourselves concerning the nature of the arms race are so many ways of coping (however inadequately) with the stresses arising from the ever-present possibility of our nuclear annihilation. These processes are, in addition, ways of rationalizing the profound moral conflict we experience concerning the prospect of the actual use of nuclear weapons, acting to transform our ambivalence into an amoralism that makes their use not only more acceptable, but more probable. There is, as I indicated earlier, a genuine basis for fear and anxiety in the nuclear age. There really *is* a threat to fear and a possibility of extinction to be anxious over, though we have avoided coming to terms with it sensibly and rationally, opting instead for dealing with it at the level of fantasy, aided by distortions of language and thinking.

Robert W. Gardiner has discussed the distortions perpetrated by the threat of nuclear war:

The nature of mass-destruction weapons generates a kind of semantic disorder, reflected in radically distorted relationships between language and reality. This distortion is not simply verbal. The structure of language reflects the structure of thought. Hence any serious pathology in the realm of *meanings* is more than a problem of language; it is a problem of *consciousness.* [9]

The essential problem Gardiner has in mind is the debasement of language in our talk about nuclear weapons and nuclear war, and corresponding corruptions in consciousness itself. Whereas these processes may be initiated by our leaders and continued by the media (which in turn pass them on to the public at large like a contagion) it is fair to say that we are *all* responsible for being drawn into this network of self-deceit and obfuscation.

How does this debasement of language and consciousness occur? Gardiner makes the following observation.

The essential function of language is to reveal reality. Language functioning properly does this. ... But language often functions in just the opposite fashion, by serving as an instrument of falsehood and self-deception. It may do this in a number of ways: for example, through misstatement of fact; through interpretations or theories that distort the relationships and the implications of facts; through reifying the symbolic constructions of imagination, as if they had an objective existence of their own; through language whose primary associations are radically incongruent with the realities designated. [10]

We need not look far afield for examples of what Gardiner is referring to. It is not too much to say that all the rhetoric and jargon of the arms race has beguiled us into pondering apocalyptic scenarios in ways that make no sense. It has led us to entertain bizarre and irrational concepts, to give credence to the incredible, and to think the unthinkable, as when we ponder ideas of "survivable" all-out nuclear war in which our side "prevails."

The first stage in this process, in my view, is the depiction of our adversary as some sort of larger-than-life monster about to consume us whole. In all periods of history human beings have endowed their enemies with mythical and magical qualities, seen them as inhuman or subhuman, labelled them irredeemably evil, and so on. These acts are evidently designed to explain the enemy's mysterious power, its determination and opposition to a way of life it threatens; but they also serve the purpose of mobilizing the collective will to stand against the enemy. To a great extent these notions flow from the very concept of an enemy itself: an implacable foe, a treacherous and hostile adversary who wills our failure as we will its, who hates and seeks to injure us and our interests (or our nation and its national interests) at every opportunity. Needless to say, we can always attribute the worst intentions to an enemy, for after all what can we expect of it other than enemy-type behavior? Further, the ideologists and image-makers of the day can keep before our imaginations a steady succession of worst-case scenarios in order to serve their own ends. There would seem to be little room for common humanity here, for trust or for the ability to distinguish between governments and their policies on the one hand and the people they represent on the other. (Remarkably, such a distinction *is* often made by average individuals, though those in power usually do everything possible to thwart it.)

More specifically, let us look at the image of our actual "enemy," the Soviet Union. The Russians are seen as "the focus of evil," "rapaciously lusting after power and world dominance," "opportunistic," "manipulative," "aggressive," "bent on exporting revolution," "Godless Communists," "callously disregarding human rights," "fomenting trouble," "ruthless," "untrustworthy," "treaty breakers," and the like. Communism is typically seen by those who formulate US policy as a monolithic, USSR-based conspiracy in which other countries friendly to the Soviet Union are mere "pawns," "clients," "proxies," or "surrogates." (The official Soviet image of the US is of course similar or symmetrical in most respects.)

How far-reaching and durable these perceptions of the enemy are can be better appreciated in the light of observations by those who have studied the phenomenon carefully. Ralph K. White, a psychologist and specialist in Sino-Soviet studies, has, for example, stated that

Given an image of the self as wholly peaceful, the power-oriented actions of the opponent cannot be perceived as anything but aggressive, and given an image of the opponent as aggressive, the power-oriented actions of the self are perceived as defensive and entirely consistent with peacefulness. The two images, peaceful self and aggressive enemy, are mutually complimentary and thoroughly interdependent. [11]

Urie Bronfenbrenner, a child psychologist who has been a lifelong student of Soviet society, found that when he asked American fifth- and six. -graders why the Russians lined their roads with trees (as shown by photographs), typical responses were: "So that people won't be able to see what is going on beyond the road" and "It's to make work for the prisoners." When asked why American roads were tree-lined, the answer was "for shade" or "to keep the dust down."[12] White's and Bronfenbrenner's analyses suggest that every unflattering portrayal of the enemy and every arms escalation engaged in can be *rationalized* by appeal to the basic image-asymmetry maintained by each side. An enemy such as this serves the additional useful function of being a scapegoat for our problems, for we can *project* onto it our own worst traits, assigning it our share of blame for the world's ills as well as its own. The problem with doing this systematically and over a long period of time is that the image we imprint on the enemy not only obstructs any realistic dealings we might have with it, but also tends to transform our foe into what we imagine it to be. (This self-fulfilling prophecy, I believe, has been experienced by the US in both Vietnam and Latin America, to take just two recent examples.)

It is most important for the preservation of this kind of image and in order to insure its continuing efficacy in controlling our ways of thinking and acting that a hypocritical and myopic one-sidedness be maintained at all times. In this effort, the media are infinitely obliging. Thus, when the US began to move cruise and Pershing II missiles into Europe late in 1983, it was just stepping up NATO defenses according to a prearranged plan; but when the Russians logically replied by increasing nuclear submarine patrols off US shores, one newspaper's headline read, "More Soviet subs menace US coasts."[13] A recent survey of Toronto's three daily newspapers over a six-month period netted a total of 922 items on the Soviet Union. Analysis of these revealed a virtually unremitting torrent of journalistic hostility directed at the Russians. Not one editorial expressed a positive opinion about the Soviet Union or its people, and of a mere 21 articles about daily life in the USSR, only one could be identified as not being anti-Soviet.[14] (A survey of the US media reveals an equally dismal level of reportage.[15])

The next stage in the process of self-delusion comes with the introduction of "doublethink," at which our age is particularly skilled. We are told, for example, that nuclear weapons are not really weapons but "deterrents," that they "exist only in order not to be used," or alternatively, in the words of President Reagan's Secretary of the Navy, John Lehman, that their "sole purpose is to defend our values and way of life."[16] Who could conceivably object to something so innocuous, so positively patriotic and beneficial? It is by means of such descriptions that we seek to hide from ourselves the awful fact that nuclear weapons are made to be used, as is or was every weapon ever manufactured. They are, moreover, *intended* to be used in the sense that even when sitting idle, they signify the ability to carry out a threat that has been seriously made. (These weapons are, if you like, the physical embodiment of the intention to annihilate the enemy under certain conditions.) It may be observed, then, that we hold reality at bay by conceiving of the conflict between the US and the USSR in the strongest black-and-white terms, and by trying to convince ourselves that hideous weapons of mass destruction and agony are something other than they are – that they may even be benign friends.

The process we have traced thus far continues into a third stage, which is the proliferation of jargon and catch-phrases – what Gardiner refers to as "the semantics of megadeath"[17] – that can be used to befuddle, sooth or arouse a gullible public, as circumstances require. Language here functions on a plane that is detached from everyday meanings and emotions; it takes on a tone of pseudo-objectivity and apparent high-tech precision. Some expressions aim to "sanitize" nuclear war or give it homey, familiar, comforting associations: hence we hear talk of "clean bombs" (neutron bombs), "bonuses" (the destruction of secondary, unintended targets, such as population areas), "nuclear umbrellas," "Minuteman" missiles, "the Peacekeeper" (the MX missile), and so on.

There are other terms and expressions which are elements of the peculiar, obfuscating jargon spawned by the arms race. Some have perhaps less to do with sanitizing nuclear war than with obscuring and blunting our grasp of what is really being talked about: hence we hear talk of "countervalue" strikes (attacks on population centers), "retaliatory capability" (the ability to destroy the other side's total social fabric), "tactical weapons" (nuclear warheads that can be used to vaporize enemy forces in a battlefield setting), "acceptable risk" (low probability of starting World War III), etc. And finally, there are the plain red herrings, which have even been effective in the winning of US presidential elections: hence we hear of the "window of vulnerability," the "military spending gap," "vital interests," "negotiating out of weakness," "limited nuclear war," "protracted nuclear war," "winnable nuclear war," and the like. These terms and phrases illustrate forcefully the truth of George Orwell's contention that "political language has to consist largely of euphemisms, question-begging and sheer cloudy vagueness. ... Such phraseology is needed if one wants to name things without calling up mental pictures of them."[18] (Mental pictures, after all, may be difficult to handle; they could even be the catalyst to mobilize voters into a movement that demands genuine disarmament.) We may reflect here too on the keen insight contained in E.P. Thompson's remark that: "Wars commence in our culture first of all, and we kill each other in euphemisms and abstractions long before the first ... missiles have been launched. ... The deformed human mind is the ultimate doomsday weapon. ..."[19]

When we allow ourselves to employ and become accustomed to such usages as those already mentioned, we not only screen off from view the significance of nuclear weapons systems and the contemplation of their use, but also the effects nuclear explosions are known only too well to produce. There seem to be two complex processes at work here. The first combines what Jerome Frank, an American psychiatrist, calls *adaptation* and *assimilation*.[20] The existence of nuclear weapons and talk about their possible use are accepted as features of normal everyday life today; we simply adapt our responses according to what is demanded of us. Thus, as Frank notes, "Today the massive and growing stockpiles of nuclear weapons elicit only perfunctory reactions, if any."[21] But further, we attempt, by devising appropriate terms and concepts, to integrate the unfamiliar and strange – in this case nuclear weapons – into our ordinary world-outlook, thereby reducing it to the familiar, assimilating it, mentally digesting it, so as to deal with it in terms of what we know we can handle. This tendency may be seen at work in the linguistic usages noted earlier, but also in the predominant view, in Western military circles at least, that nuclear weapons are not qualitatively different from preceding kinds of weapons from either a strategic or a moral viewpoint. The US strategy of "flexible response" to Soviet acts of "aggression," wherein nuclear weapons could be introduced into a conflict at numerous stages and levels of destructive power, epitomizes this latter mode of thinking.

The second process that occurs when we slide into nuclear jargon and corresponding thought constructions is a profound *alienation* which takes place between humans as knowing, caring, deciding, responsible beings and the products and consequences of their activities. This alienation may be referred to as *distancing,* that is, the deliberate or semi-deliberate separation in thought of our acts from their consequences, or of contemplated acts from their possible or likely consequences. In a now famous experiment, social psychologist Stanley Milgram found that his subjects' willingness to administer what they fully believed were painful, unavoidable shocks to other subjects varied inversely with the degree of contact the agents had with the effects of their behavior. In general, people could be induced to do what they would normally regard as morally reprehensible if sufficient physical and psychological distancing took place.[22] The same danger exists in the linguistic and conceptual insulation of nuclear weapons from the potential consequences of their use.

Two examples may illustrate how cool, detached intellectualization works against the expression of normal, healthy responses. In 1981 a group of individuals known as the "Ploughshares Eight" were tried for illegally entering a General Electric plant in King of Prussia, Pennsylvania, damaging missile nose cones and defacing company records with human blood. When a GE official was called upon to testify concerning the nature of a "re-entry vehicle" (read: nuclear-tipped missile) brought into the courtroom as an exhibit, he referred to the object in question only as "the product." In like manner, the explosive load carried by such "products"–in this case a possible ten warheads, each equivalent to seventeen Hiroshima bombs–is called by those in industry "the physics package."[23] The second example is the well-known response of military men who have been carefully groomed to implement the actual firing plans for nuclear missiles if and when the time comes: when asked how they feel about their responsibility, they reply that they don't really think about it very much; they only think about doing their job right when asked to do so.[24]

I have had occasion to indicate that the psychological dynamics of the nuclear age are not just complex but contradictory. This is apparent in a countervailing tendency to those just discussed, what I shall label *negativism*. We do flee from the nuclear threat through euphemisms, the niceties of inappropriately applied everyday language, adaptation, assimilation, and alienation or distancing, but many of us also flee in the opposite direction through a fatalistic withdrawal. Three decades ago Viktor Frankl, a psychiatrist who has devoted his career to studying the "will to meaning" as a fundamental drive in human life, characterized this attitude as follows: "Today the average man says: 'Why should I act, why should I plan? Sooner or later the atom bomb will come and wipe out everything.' And thus he slides into the attitude of: 'Après moi, la bombe atomique!'"[25] I think this observation exceedingly prescient, for a major cause of the disillusionment and sense of purposelessness so widespread among well-informed and thoughtful young people is anxiety over nuclear extinction.[26] This sense of the inability to do anything, of powerlessness to affect decisions or the flow of events, is characteristic of the modern sociopolitical context, in which so many of us feel ineffectual, but is exacerbated to a high degree by the threat of nuclear war. The great danger inherent in this way of thinking, of course, is that it will become a self-fulfilling prophecy. As Martin Buber once said, "Nothing can doom man but the belief in doom, for this prevents the movement of return."[27] Another form of fatalistic withdrawal is of course the self-centered complacency of the status quo: business as usual, the comfortable, consumption-oriented lifestyle. Many of us take this route, choosing not to think, or at any rate not enough to upset us very much: we simply *repress* ideas and images of nuclear war, excluding them from our awareness.

As Jerome Frank has suggested, the magnitude and immediacy of nuclear devastation are so great and so far exceed our comprehension that we are unable to deal with them on an emotional level. The nuclear threat, according to his view, is "psychologically unreal" in this sense.[28] Unlike Frank, who argues that nuclear weapons are unreal to us because we lack experiential categories adequate to grasp their power and effects, I believe they are unreal primarily because of the anxiety which forces us to reel away from the inescapable confrontation

Paul Valerry, West Germany

with the threat of our own extinction.

We have examined various psychological maneuvers by means of which we seek to escape from this confrontation. These range from the detached, super-objective jargon-mongering of technocrats and industrialists who set an example of how to compartmentalize our consciousness and hold consequences of acts, moral judgments and normal emotional responses at arm's length, to the self-lobotomizing behavior of the negativist. What is common to all these cases is that they exhibit what psychiatrist Robert Jay Lifton calls *psychic numbing* or mental paralysis.[29] Hence each mode of reaction to the threat of nuclear annihilation manifests distortions in language and thought, denial of reality, suppression of normal feelings (lack of affect), rigidity and narrowness of vision, and the inability to identify and do anything effective about the fundamental cause of fear and anxiety. Rather, each of these responses to the nuclear threat serves as an example of what Freud labelled "the psychopathology of everyday life" – each seeks to disguise the threat, to represent it in some form that spares us from confronting it in its full dimensions and in realistic terms. What we have before us, then, are the variegated phenomena of denial, aided by repression, projection, and other defense mechanisms.

3   Fear, Anxiety, and Security

If the principal source of fear and anxiety in the nuclear age is the threat of extinction, often dressed up as "the Soviet threat," then the rational response would be to try to reduce or defuse this threat. US defense policy, on the other hand, appears dedicated to the search for some ultimate and impregnable condition of total "security." (It isn't clear what goal the Soviets are pursuing, though in developing weaponry they invariably follow suit.) According to this view, "security" is fully attained when and only when the threat posed by the other side has been stymied and thus eliminated. Integral to this position is the belief that insecurity has a specific, eliminable cause the neutralization of which is not only feasible but will abolish our unpleasant state of consciousness. Let us see how this thought-process unfolds in actual practice.

In January 1984 President Reagan, in an address intended to counter claims that the prospects of nuclear war are imminent, remarked that "We have never been as far removed from that possibility as we have in the past several years." He continued by declaring that the "deterrent power" of the US is what keeps the risk of war at a low point.[30] We see here that deterrence appears as something that can be *quantified,* as something we can, in some straightforward sense, have more or less of, and of which it would obviously be better to have more than less.[31] Not only this, but more deterrence is a direct function of more weapons. The more weapons we have, the more secure we are. "Deterrent power" is the means for obtaining this goal of "security." (I have simplified the reasoning involved here, such as it is, but not by much.) I don't propose to consider all the flaws in this line of thinking or to analyze the deficiencies in the concept of deterrence, of which there are many, but want instead to focus on the quantitative aspect of the preceding formulation.

There is an obsession on both the Soviet and the American sides over the numbers of weapons, modernization of weapons and the relationship between these factors and those of balance and superiority. Some proponents of the current US military buildup contend that the US can only effectively deter Soviet "aggression" if and when it has a clearly superior nuclear force. Opponents of the continuing buildup often play the same numbers game, asserting that contrary to official administration views, the US already has an insurmountable superiority and that there's no evidence that the Soviets are striving for superiority. This claim is in turn countered by those who cite "evidence" that the US is behind the USSR in every weapons category, and is threatened by "Soviet adventurism" as long as this continues. Spokespersons for both the US and the USSR never tire of laying charges and counter-charges concerning each other's government's intentions, lacing their tirades with statistics about weapons buildups and imbalances.[32]

Many sensible critics of the two superpowers have maintained that technological advances in weapons design and sheer buildups in numbers cannot and do not bring security, that the problem of security is not one that is amenable to a technological solution in terms of modernization and greater mass production. Unfortunately, however, the prevailing view today is that national security is a "good product," a commodity that economic allotments by a dedicated society can *purchase,* just like food, clothing, housing, and transportation.[33] From this perspective, spiralling expenditures on armaments are not wasteful and unproductive, but rather costs that, no matter how high, are justified in terms of the basic social good they can procure (security), upon which the enjoyment of all other goods is predicated. I don't believe this kind of thinking is so very different, however, from the reasoning that has stimulated US nuclear spending for decades. Security has always been "just around the corner" if only more tax dollars would be pumped into the military R & D budget. The atomic bomb failed as the supposedly ultimate guarantor of peace and security when the Russians broke the American monopoly in 1949. Then it was the hydrogen bomb, antiballistic missile systems and now laser-powered space battle stations that served or serve as the emblems of final security.

There are two points that must be made about all of this. The first is that the attempt to buy security is a product of wishful thinking: the view that if you neutralize the apparent immediate cause of insecurity, you neutralize the insecurity itself. But the elimination or reduction of the fear and anxiety which we call insecurity can come, if at all, only from addressing the much deeper and more complex causes of mistrust and animosity among nations. The second point is that the search for security (or "national security") is itself an entire edifice of self-deception, for it was the US nuclear monopoly in the 40's that provoked the USSR – presumably because of *its* feelings of insecurity – to enter the arms race, increasing the level of insecurity on our side, and so on. Moreover, so far as how people feel (as opposed to how they're told they are or ought to feel) is concerned, most of us experience greater insecurity with every new development in the arms race. So far from its being the case that security is acquired when we buy greater "deterrent power," the opposite seems closer to the truth.

4   Conclusion: Fear, Anxiety, Security, and Hope

The quest for ultimate security is in vain; security cannot be bought even by the wealthiest of nations. Every system of defense that exists or is likely to be devised is vulnerable or penetrable, hence fallible; and, given the nature of modern weapons, the effects of their failure is almost certain to be fatal. Richard Nixon seems to have realized this when he floated the desperate idea in private, before his trusted advisor H.R. Haldeman, that he ought to pose as a madman, so the Russians could never be sure when or under what arbitrary set of circumstances he might push the button.[34] The problem with this strategy is that irrational actions are needed to give it credibility. Moreover, when the time comes to reason together no sane adversary will seek out the company of a bankrupt madman who seeks security through sheer intimidation. At that point the strategy will find its bluff called. Nor can we rid ourselves of the conditions that cause the unique fear and anxiety of the nuclear age. It is unlikely that the bomb will go away, and even if it does, the knowledge of how to make it won't; nor will the Russians disappear.

There remains but one choice: we must seek a reduction of world tensions, mutual trust, disarmament, and peace.[35] Security is not the *absence* of fear and anxiety, but a degree of stress and uncertainty with which we can cope and remain mentally healthy. For security, understood in this way, to become a feature of our lives, we must admit our nuclear fear and anxiety and identify the mechanisms that dull or mask our emotional and other responses. It is necessary to realize that we cannot entrust security to ourselves, but, strange as it seems and however difficult to accept, must entrust it to our adversary. Just as the safety and security of each of us, as individuals, depends upon the good will of every other, any one of whom could harm us at any moment, so the security of nations finally depends upon the good will of other nations, whether or not we willingly accept this fact.

The disease for which we must find the cure also requires that we continually come face to face with the unthinkable in image and thought and recoil from it.[36] In this manner we can break its hold over us and free ourselves to begin new initiatives. As Robert Jay Lifton points out, "confronting massive death" helps us bring ourselves "more in touch with what we care most about in life. We [will then] find ourselves in no way on a death trip, but rather responding to a call for personal and professional actions and commitments on behalf of that wondrous and fragile entity we know as human life."[37]

I have tried to show what we are up against. The first step toward change is to know what constraints are acting on us and to isolate those within our control because they are of our own making. Awareness of these conditions is often the road to their transcendence.   *Queen's University at Kingston*

1 The term was, so far as I know, coined by Carey.

2 Teller.

3 See Beardsley and Mack; Carey; Sibylle Escalona, "Growing Up With the Threat of Nuclear War: Some Indirect Effects on Personality Development," in Goldman and Greenberg, eds.; Milton Schwebel, "Effects of the Nuclear War Threat on Children and Teenagers: Implications for Professionals," in Goldman and Greenberg, eds.; and Yudkin. See also "Fear of nuclear war creates selfish generation, says psychiatrist," Kingston *Whig-Standard* (Canadian Press service), October 12, 1984, 4, where it is reported that a recent Gallup poll found that "38 per cent of [US] voting-age residents expect a nuclear war within a year."

4 When I say "us" I generally mean the US and its closest allies, such as Canada. How nuclear weapons are thought about and talked about in Canada, for example, is difficult to distinguish from those modes of thinking and talking that prevail in the US at any given moment. In any event, for better or worse, many countries' nuclear fate is wedded to that of the US.

5 See, for example, Russett; and Holloway.

6 See Wolfe.

7 Modgliani.

8 Cited by Ground Zero, *Hope,* p. 109 (Ground Zero's emphasis).

9 Gardiner, p. 67 (Gardiner's emphasis).

10 *Ibid.,* pp. 71-2. For more on this, plus many excellent examples, see Hilgartner, Bell, and O'Connor, Part VIII and Index of Nukespeak Words.

11 White, "Images in the Context of International Conflict," p. 249.

12 Bronfenbrenner, 96.

13 William Lowther, "More Soviet subs menace US coasts," *Toronto Star,* January 28, 1984, A1.

14 Zwicker, "Our Portrayal of the Soviet Union Dooms Ourselves."

15 Zwicker, "Study of Coverage of USSR in US Media."

16 John Lehman, "Nuclear Weapons Defend Judeo-Christian Civilization," in Bender, ed., p. 95.

17 Gardiner, p. 67.

18 George Orwell, "Politics and the English Language," in *Collected Essays;* cited by Gardiner, p. 74.

19 E.P. Thompson, cited by Zwicker, "Journalism and the Bomb," 7.

20 Frank, "The Nuclear Arms Race: Sociopsychological Aspects."

21 *Ibid.,* 951.

22 Milgram.

23 Zwicker, "Inside the Mushroom Cloud," 168.

24 Pringle and Arkin, p. 168; Howard Blum, "US gunner on nuclear-armed fighter is on alert for flight to 'Armageddon'," Kingston *Whig-Standard* (*New York Times* service), March 6, 1984, 11; Frank, "The Nuclear Arms Race: Sociopsychological Aspects," 951.

25 Frankl, p. xvi.
26 See Yudkin. Many, of course, like their adult counterparts, just don't know or to know about the nuclear threat. But this posture too, unless it is simple naiveté, is a mode of escapism or denial (willful ignorance).
27 Buber, p. 107.
28 Frank, "The Nuclear Arms Race: Sociopsychological Aspects," 951.
29 Lifton and Falk, pp. 100-10.
30 "us 'never further from war': Reagan," *Toronto Star,* January 14, 1984, A12.
31 The notion that deterrence is something that can be quantified is widely held. One nonpartisan study of the arms race states, for example: "the basic question of deterrence is – 'How much deterrence is enough?'..." (Ground Zero, *Nuclear War: What's In It For You?,* p. 173.)
32 Good examples of these views can be found in Bender, ed., Chaps. 1 and 2.
33 Committee on the Present Danger, "The Case for Increased Defense Expenditures," in *ibid.,* p. 78.
34 Shawcross, p. 90. Nixon *publicly* maintained that "the real possibility of irrational us action is essential to the us-Soviet relationship."
35 It is worth noting, in this connection, that our poor image of the Soviets, which governs our relations with them so completely, *can* nonetheless change relatively swiftly. Frank offers the cynical yet hopeful observation that in less than four decades "in American eyes the bloodthirsty, cruel, treacherous, slant-eyed, buck-toothed little Japs of the Second World War have become a highly cultivated, charming, industrious, and thoroughly attractive people." (Frank, *Sanity and Survival,* p. 135.) Frank documents a no less dramatic alteration in our image of the Germans.
36 This is the essential message conveyed by the controversial 1983 TV movie *The Day After* and by Schell's book *The Fate of the Earth.*
37 Lifton and Falk, p. 125.

Commentary: Atomic Cultism

RON HIRSCHBEIN

Michael Fox has discussed the psychological dimensions of the arms race. I wish to consider a possibility he does not discuss. Taking a fresh look at American nuclear endeavors, two profoundly disturbing facts emerge. (*1*) The nuclear arms race appears irrational. We live in an age of more than mutually assured destruction, yet more weapons are built every day. (*2*) Still worse, every American administration in the nuclear age has seriously considered using such weapons.[1] In fact – as the Cuban Missile Crisis illustrated – American policy-makers are prepared to risk everything in a confrontation with the Soviet Union.[2]

What makes the men[3] who control the us nuclear arsenal tick? The facts don't speak for themselves. When I first began to dig beneath the surface I saw that the irrationality inherent in nuclear weapons development cannot be understood without assigning an appropriate place to the dynamics of the group that controls the means of destruction. My thesis is that a strange cabal has recently intruded in history – the Atomic Cult. It acts like a lens refracting all the usual sources of perfidy. It lends a distinctly nihilistic – indeed, surrealistic – coloration to ancient sources of human destructiveness. It exhibits the fundamental characteristic of all cults: group-induced regression to a more primitive, pathological mentality, and corresponding forms of behavior.

I arrived at this conclusion in the following way. I first examined critically the position I call "Nuclear Rationalism": the claim that the nuclear arms race is instrumental in attaining realistic objectives, such as deterrence, nuclear warfighting capacity, or corporate profit. However, these explanations are plainly inadequate. As many former government insiders have stated,[4] the requirements of deterrence[5] were met and exceeded with the advent of nuclear submarines twenty years ago. Yet escalation continues unabated, suggesting that something other than strategic requirements drives the arms race.

When all is said and done, us theorizing about nuclear war-fighting lends itself to only two possible interpretations: (*1*) The President's advisors are actually planning for an apocalyptic battle with the USSR. If this is so, such folly demands a deeper explanation. How is it possible for policy-makers who – as individuals – seem intelligent and decent to harbor such fantasies? (*2*) The apocalyptic vision of nuclear triumph currently in vogue is merely an "in house" rationalization for the addiction to nuclear weapons. But if this is true, we once again remain in the dark about the forces impelling nuclear endeavors. Finally, even if we assume that the arms race is economically determined, that corporate profiteering calls the tune, this does not explain why the arms race is a *nuclear* arms race. It is conceivable that defense contractors might profit as much – or more – by building conventional weapons. Why, then, the infatuation with things nuclear, especially when a nuclear war would create a decidedly unfavorable business climate? Once more we are at a loss in seeking for an ultimate explanation.

While a definitive account of the forces that produced the Atomic Cult is beyond the scope of this essay, it is possible to consider several ways in which the nuclear enterprise possesses a distinctively cultist structure. Thus, the nuclear brotherhood has many of the structural features associated with cults: it is a small, secret society marked by arcane knowledge, millennarian visions, and messianic devotion. So it has been since the Manhattan Project was launched in 1942. Yet these structural features are necessary but not sufficient for inducing a cultist mentality. The Franciscans have many of these features, yet they are hardly cultists.

Curiously, the regression to a cult mentality is, as Freud and others have noted, situational. Cultists are akin to victims of post-hypnotic suggestion: beyond the pale of the group they are thoughtful, compassionate, and restrained; immersed in group ritual they regress to a collective consciousness (or unconsciousness) marked by cognitive impairments, diminished capacity to empathize with outsiders, and the inability to resist malign authority.

Freud marvelled at how readily the hard-won gains of civilization could be swallowed up by the primitive group mentality.[6] It has taken perhaps sixty centuries to produce an individuated ego capable of resisting group pressures through autonomous thought, morality, and restraint. However, the anxiety engendered by confronting the world as an isolated, autonomous individual can be unbearable. When the world is perceived as falling apart, civilized individuals readily surrender their identity and seek asylum in the mass psychology of peculiar groups. This surrender of identity initiates a process which ultimately leads to the most disturbing feature of cult mentality – the destruction of the self characterized by affective, cognitive, and behavioral characteristics which seem endemic to American nuclear endeavors.

As the bonds of brotherhood are cemented men deny their sensitivity, compassion, and willingness to compromise and negotiate. Psychiatrist Joel Kovel suggests[7] that membership in rigidly hierarchical, martial groups may be so emasculating that men feel the need to overcompensate by acting out *machismo* parodies. Primal instincts are mobilized and magnified as cultists displace their love from the self to the group and its "glorious" ideal. Like any lover, the cultist devalues himself while deifying the object of his love. More disturbing, cults have the power to unleash intoxicating, destructive urges brewed in the dankness of the unconscious. These aggressive designs are denied by projecting them onto the despised out-group. Overwhelmed by the unleashed powers of the unconscious, cultists quickly lose their cognitive acuity as reason becomes subservient to the group mind. Thought processes are reduced to instruments for rationalizing group-induced compulsions; these rationalizations quickly turn to delusions which are blended into a disconfirmable, dogmatic doctrine. Even able scientists fall prey to this influence.

From time immemorial cultists have sought refuge from the complexities of reality in a Manichaean morality play which pits good against evil. The group idol appears as a magical, cosmic power – a messiah – which will enable the faithful to immortalize themselves by working wonders in history. This is the ultimate, driving vision of the cultists – the seizing of control over life and death. It is no coincidence that the early patriarchs of the Atomic Cult entertained such visions, or that the cosmic struggle between good and evil figures so prominently in today's Cold War rhetoric. Unable to bring about the millennium, and threatened by outsiders, cultists attempt to perpetuate their world by redoubling their devotion to the group ideal. This gives rise to the myth that only ritualistic, cultist devotion preserves the world. Just as Aztec priests insisted that only human sacrifices kept the world from ending, today's national security managers convince the faithful that only more nuclear weapons can preserve the peace. Unflinching obedience to malign authority, a feature of many cults, is equally evident in the American nuclear enterprise. We could be the last generation of humans because our leaders have a disposition to act out their nuclear delusions while their subordinates reflexively follow orders – even at the cost of destroying themselves and everything they cherish.

The Cult of the Atom, so far as it affects not only those within ruling circles but the citizenry as a whole, tends to paralyze our most basic survival instincts and exact our ultimate devotion to an ideology dedicated to perfecting the means of massive self-annihilation. This is the ultimate menace posed by cultism, and we must hope that reason, however frail a flame, will in the end assert itself and prevail. In highlighting some of the characteristics of cults and some respects in which the nuclear endeavor resembles a cult, I hope I have made a contribution to initiating this process.   *California State University, Chico*

NOTES

1 Daniel Ellsberg, "A Call to Mutiny," in Thompson and Smith, eds., pp. v-vi.
2 It was John Somerville who first called my attention to the significance of the Cuban Missile Crisis. See his *The Peace Revolution* and his dramatization of this episode in *The Crisis*.
3 The Nuclear arms race is virtually an all-male endeavor. See Easlea for a fuller treatment of this topic, and also the articles by Litke and Jaggar in this collection.
4 For example Rickover, p. 12.
5 These are: (*1*) A second strike capacity which is reliable, undetectable, and invulnerable to enemy attack; (*2*) The ability to fire unstoppable warheads; (*3*) The capacity to damage the Soviet Union to such a degree that they could not conceivably profit from aggression. See Wieseltier; and Mandelbaum, Chap. 4. The earliest rationale for deterrence is found in the writings of Bernard Brodie (see his "War in the Atomic Age," in Brodie, ed.).
6 Freud, p. 4.
7 Kovel, p. 139.

Anthropocentric Humanism and the Arms Race

MICHAEL E. ZIMMERMAN

We live in an age of crisis. Crises threaten to destroy established states of affairs, but crises are also opportunities for creating something novel and beautiful. At first glance, it would appear that the nuclear arms race is the most pressing crisis facing us. Surely if this arms race ends like those before it, we will destroy much of humanity as well as many other forms of life that share the Earth with us. The nuclear arms race, however, as I shall argue in the following essay, may only be a symptom of a deeper crisis that has been developing for many centuries. This crisis has to do with how we understand ourselves as human beings. Today, human beings in the so-called developed countries regard humankind as the center of reality, the source of all meaning, and the only beings with intrinsic value. I shall use the term "anthropocentric humanism" to refer to this way of understanding who we are. The dark side of humanism is often ignored in favor of the positive dimension of humanism with which we are more familiar. The positive thrust of humanism includes its recognition of the importance of individual human freedom and its affirmation of the dignity of humankind. The dark side of humanism involves an arrogant human-centeredness that reduces the nonhuman world to the status of a commodity whose only value lies in its usefulness for human purposes. According to the German philosopher Martin Heidegger, conceiving of ourselves as masters of all beings, we adopt a false sense of superiority that undermines our true humanity. In the following essay, which will make use of some of Heidegger's thoughts about human existence in the nuclear age, I argue that this same drive to dominate the natural world is present in the armed struggle between nations. The current nuclear arms race can be interpreted as a conflict between two great representatives of anthropocentric humanism, the United States and the Soviet Union. Strangely, each nation is prepared to annihilate the other side in order to defend the principles of "true humanism." Marxists and capitalists alike regard their way of life as the only legitimate fulfillment of the Enlightenment ideal of human progress and freedom. But to a large extent, both superpowers are guided by anthropocentric humanism, whose highest aim is power and security. Hence, neither superpower can rest content until the other side is eliminated or at least neutralized. Paradoxically, the quest for total security leads to total insecurity, as we are finding out now that the nuclear arms race is moving to even more threatening levels. In my view, the danger of nuclear war will not be eliminated, even though some arms controls might be successfully negotiated, until there occurs a basic shift in our understanding of what it means to be human. The positive side of humanism, which has some insight into what it means to be fully human, points in the right direction, but the dark or anthropocentric side predominates today. Let us consider for a moment Heidegger's view that anthropocentric humanism is the underlying disorder, of which the nuclear arms race is but a particularly dangerous symptom.[1]

1   Heidegger's Critique of Anthropocentric Humanism

Most of us have been raised in a humanistic culture, so we take its values almost for granted. Heidegger would agree with some of the ideals of the Renaissance and Enlightenment humanists, who proclaimed that for human beings to flourish, they must not be governed by prejudice and ignorance. He would also agree with the humanistic doctrine that humankind is unique, that we have been endowed with unusual capacities that – so far as we know – distinguish us from other forms of life. But he would not agree with the idea that our remarkable attributes give us the right to dominate all other beings. The anthropocentric dimension of humanism arose at the time Europeans were throwing off the burden of medieval authority – religious, political, economic, scholarly, and social. In their haste to free themselves from bondage, however, these daring men began speaking as if there were in fact nothing higher or more important than human beings. They declared that human reason and not divine Revelation was the source for determining the truth about reality and also for establishing what is good and evil. Supposedly, Enlightenment humanists rid themselves of the doctrine of traditional religions, including the notion of a transcendent God. Yet while insisting that there is not a supernatural world, but instead only the natural one, anthropocentric humanists smuggled in a new God: the human being. Human self-worship is a key ingredient in the dark side of humanism. The great wisdom traditions, including Christianity, acknowledge that there is a divine aspect to human beings, but these traditions warn that this divine aspect is realized through service, not through domination. Anthropocentric humanists secularize the claim of Genesis that humankind was given "dominion" over the Earth.[2] Fundamentalist Christians who rail against secular humanism are often unwittingly in league with it. Thus we have the specter of a former Secretary of the Interior who urged total economic development of American natural resources in order to fulfill the New Testament command that we not let our talents remain idle. A secularized version of this Protestant Ethic is embodied in the anthropocentric doctrine that it is humanity's right and even its duty to exploit Nature for human purposes.

Anthropocentric humanism, then, provided a new way for humankind to understand its relationship to the natural world. While in the Middle Ages, the natural world appeared to be a creature testifying to God's handiwork, in the modern era the natural world appears to be primarily a stockpile of raw materials without intrinsic value. Hence, there are no limits to what we can do with any nonhuman being. Modern science and technology have been brought to bear with ever greater efficacy to transform Nature into products for the material benefit of humanity, or at least certain portions of humanity. But science also claimed that human beings were really only highly intelligent animals sharing the Earth with many other forms of life. One might suppose that this view of humanity would have promoted a certain humility with respect to our relation to the rest of life on Earth. But when allied with anthropocentric humanism, the "naturalistic" view of humanity only helped to justify our domination of Nature. If we are animals, and if the primary goal of animals is to survive, then we can do anything we choose to survive in competition with the other animals and plants. This naturalistic license to dominate the natural world fitted in well with the anthropocentric view of humankind as the lord of Nature.

Both Marxism and democratic capitalism portray themselves as the only way humankind can attain the goals of freedom and security. Let me acknowledge from the outset that I believe there are very serious deficiencies in Marxist-dominated societies that are not present in the industrialized West. Marxist humanism appears to have problems, including authoritarian tendencies, over and above its anthropocentrism. The most obvious shortcoming is the lack of political and economic liberty for individuals. It is necessary for us, however, to be willing to take a critical look at our own society as well, in order to ascertain the extent to which our views are an expression of anthropocentric humanism. Such humanism cannot imagine a higher goal for humanity than survival with a maximum gratification of human desires. But survival cannot be guaranteed without security, and security requires power, economic as well as military. The present arms race can be seen, from Heidegger's point of view, as the inevitable tendency of national powers whose highest goal is the total appropriation and control of the Earth–for the sake of humanity! Both the capitalist West and the socialist East are preparing to eradicate the other side not simply because the "enemy" has nuclear weapons, but because the very existence of the enemy is a threat to its security. Moreover, the enemy's power stands in the way of attaining the goal of survival with maximum gratification. As long as we have not made the entire Earth our property, it would appear, we cannot have maximum security and gratification.

Serious problems arise from seeing the Earth only as property and from seeing ourselves primarily as security-craving consumers of that property. For instance, warfare and preparation for war turn out to be very efficient ways not only of consuming property but also of providing "security" against enemy threats. It is widely acknowledged that World War II helped end the Great Depression. And "priming the economic pump" through "defense" spending has been a common practice since then. But a former student of Heidegger's, Hannah Arendt, points out that the interlocking drive for security and for consumable property has a self-destructive logic. *Destroying* things is one way of denying their appropriation and use by the enemy; and such destruction is a perverse form of consuming what we insist belongs to us alone:

Property by itself ... is subject to consumption and therefore diminishes constantly. The most radical and only secure form of possession is destruction, for only what we have destroyed is safely and forever ours. ... A social system based essentially on property cannot possibly proceed toward anything but the final destruction of all property. ...[3]

If the capitalist West or its alleged opposite the socialist East cannot acquire the Earth through political or economic means, either side may try to "acquire" it by destroying it in a nuclear war. While there are significant differences between the United States and the Soviet Union, both of them seem to share the presupposition of anthropocentric humanism that the Earth is simply a commodity to be possessed by human beings – privately under capitalism, collectively under socialism. This desire to possess things and to destroy enemies has characterized human behavior for many centuries. Such behavior stems at least in part from conceiving of ourselves as separate egos that need security and gratification. The sense of separateness spawns isolation, fear, insecurity, and a craving for things that are apparently other than the ego. Heidegger argues that although people in previous cultures fought each other and also at times abused the Earth, they did not conceive of themselves as the source of all value, meaning, and purpose in the universe. Their egocentrism was tempered somewhat by recognition of a transcendent order of which human beings are but a part. But anthropocentric humanism declares that humanity is the source of all value – and that there are no limits to what we can do. Nationalism is one form that such humanism takes.[4]

Today, of course, each superpower depicts itself as the true embodiment of the humanistic value of promoting all human life, but "human life" usually turns out to mean only the lives of the people in the nation in question. Other people can then be viewed as obstacles to the fulfillment of our version of humanism. The rhetorical practice here is to denounce the enemy *government* as anti-humanistic, while portraying the enemy government's *people* as unfortunate dupes or slaves of the evil ideology. By this practice, preparation for destroying the opposing nation can be justified more readily as protecting ourselves against the threatening designs of the opposing government. Yet nuclear weapons cannot discriminate between government officials and the people. In today's world, of course, the enemy superpower does in fact possess thousands of nuclear weapons that are aimed at our nation. But this fact does not deny the role our own way of thinking and behaving plays in fostering the arms race that produces such weapons on both sides.

For nationalistic humanism, international "justice" is whatever one side declares is needed to protect its values and security. About the time Hitler ordered the invasion of Poland for the sake of Germany's "national security," Heidegger remarked that "when the English thoroughly blasted the French fleet anchored in the harbor of Oran, this was from THEIR power-standpoint wholly 'justified'; for 'justified' means only: what is useful for power enhancement."[5] War becomes the way to appropriate things completely, for war destroys what is produced. Thermonuclear war would be the highpoint of the dark human drive to dominate and appropriate the Earth, for at that point we would have expressed the highest and most perverse form of the will to power: the will to annihilate. Heidegger remarks that:

The consumption of beings is as such and in its course determined by armament in the metaphysical sense, through which man makes himself the "master" of what is elemental. The consumption includes the ordered use of beings which become the opportunity and the material for feats and their escalation. This use is employed in the utility of armaments. ... [The World Wars] press toward a guarantee of the stability of a constant form of using things up. ... The world wars are the antecedent form of the removal of the difference between war and peace. ... War has become a distortion of the consumption of beings which is continued in peace. Contending with a long war is only the already outdated form in which what is new about the age of consumption is acknowledged. This long war [World War II] in its length slowly eventuated not in a peace of a traditional kind, but rather in a condition in which warlike characteristics are no longer experienced as such at all and peaceful characteristics have become meaningless and without content.[6]

Heidegger is suggesting that the distinction between war and peace has been absorbed into the ongoing conflict of superpowers striving to appropriate the Earth. What is called the "Cold War," and what Orwell described as the constant state of war/peace in *Nineteen Eighty-Four,* point to what Heidegger is talking about here. Many modern writers have commented that the twentieth century has been an age of incredible inhumanity of one group of humans against another, despite the fact that we seem so committed to the ideals of humanism. Heidegger maintains, however, that the humanism currently operative is largely anthropocentric. What we need is a more profound humanism, even more profound than the positive dimension of the humanism that arose in the Enlightenment. Enlightenment humanism emphasized the importance of humanity and promoted human freedom, but neglected to consider that human life may be fulfilled through a kind of service that Enlightenment humanism omits. A profounder humanism would acknowledge our uniqueness but would also reveal that the aim of human life is not to dominate all beings, but in some sense to serve them by letting them be manifest as what they are. Such service can be understood as tolerance and love. We serve others by respecting them, which means in part giving them the freedom to act as they see fit for themselves, so long as they respect this freedom in other people as well. We respect ourselves by allowing our own talents to express themselves. But can we restrict such tolerance, love, and service to human beings alone? Can we be fulfilled as a species while all other species are turned into raw material for our needs? Must not an adequate vision of human life include the notion that nonhuman beings are intrinsically valuable and have their own appropriate place on Earth? According to Heidegger, even if we avoid nuclear war, we may still lose our humanity. By conceiving of ourselves as clever animals with divine rights, we forget that there should be limits to our behavior toward entities. Hence, "Man enters into insurrection. ... The Earth can only show itself as the object of assault. ... Nature appears everywhere as the object of technology."[7] Most threatening to our true humanity is the unchained will to power:

What is deadly is not the much-discussed atomic bomb as this particular death-dealing machine. What has long since been threatening man with death, and indeed with the death of his own nature, is the unconditional character of mere willing in the sense of purposeful self-assertion in everything. What threatens man in his very nature is the willed view that man, by the peaceful release, transformation, storage, and channeling of the energies of physical nature, could render the human condition, man's Being, tolerable for everybody and happy in all respects. But the peace of this peacefulness is merely the undisturbed continuing relentlessness of the fury of self-assertion which is absolutely self-reliant.[8]

A more profound humanism must take account of our obligations as human beings. We will move toward this deeper conception of humanism in the next part of this essay, where we consider how anthropocentric humanism evolved from a certain way of understanding what it means to be human.

2   *The Ontological Origins of Humanism*

If Heidegger is right, the current arms race as well as the environmental crisis result from important changes in the way we understand who we are. Currently, we think of ourselves as independent, God-like ego-subjects for whom the natural world is an object to be dominated. As long as someone stands in the way of attaining total control of the Earth, we feel insecure. Heidegger argues that people have not always thought of themselves as ego-subjects for whom all things are objects to be used. Our understanding of who we are and what other beings are changes through history. Heidegger's view here is controversial. Many people argue that fear and aggression have been part of human conduct for thousands of years, so that the present arms race is simply a repetition of a tragic, but ancient pattern. Yet Heidegger argues that there is something different about the modern industrial age with its world-scale violence. Whether he is right or not, his view is sufficiently provocative to be worth serious consideration. Before discussing his claim that our current international situation stems from a change in our understanding of what things *are,* let us pause briefly to consider what he means by "Being."

For Heidegger, "Being" does not mean a supreme entity (such as God), nor does it mean the material stuff that constitutes physical nature. Instead, "Being" means the presencing or self-manifesting of entities. An entity "is" insofar as it reveals itself. And humans are the "clearing" or "opening" in which this revelation can occur. Heidegger is not saying, with Bishop Berkeley, that "to be is to be perceived." Whether or not human beings are around, the planets and stars will continue to whirl through space. But the fact that they *are* at all will be concealed and hidden. Human existence enables entities to announce *that* and *what* they are. Here Heidegger is close to Hegel's notion that human beings allow the universe to become aware of itself. Emerson also suggested that human beings are "transparent eyeballs"in which Nature sees itself. Human beings are "transparent" in the sense that their awareness is not itself a thing, but instead the opening in which things can present themselves or "be." Paradoxically, just as the eye cannot see itself, so too human awareness cannot become directly aware of itself without turning itself into a thing.

As heirs of the Cartesian tradition, we often tend to think of ourselves dualistically, that is, as composed of bodies and minds. Heidegger claims, however, that such dualism does not offer an adequate account of human existence. The body is an entity that appears *within* the "clearing" or awareness of human existence. Moreover, the contents of the mind – such as judgments, evaluations, memories, and so on – are also entities that appear within the clearing. Normally, we identify ourselves closely with the voice in our heads that makes judgments and plans. Yet Heidegger suggests that we are not the voice, but instead the awareness in which the voice can appear as such. By identifying ourselves with some thing or other, especially the mind or ego, we experience ourselves as separate from everything else. All entities other than us either appear as potentially threatening objects that must be controlled, or else as potentially gratifying objects to be devoured to satisfy some desire of the subject. The great wisdom traditions tell us that our confusion and suffering arises from thinking we are some sort of thing, and that life is about nothing more than defending this "thing" (the ego, for example). Liberation or enlightenment, then, involves recognizing that we are not things at all but instead the open awareness in which things can appear or "be."

Anthropocentric humanism can be understood as a large-scale expression of this subject-object dualism. For such humanism, the "subject" is not merely the personal ego but the nation-state; the "object" is the threatening enemy, on the one hand, and the Earth as a totality of raw materials to be consumed, on the other. The current preoccupation with "national security" and our craving to possess and consume things betrays the deep sense of separateness and isolation bred by the subject-object dualism. We speak in ways that make potential adversaries seem even more threatening than they already are. By doing so, we behave in a threatening manner that makes the adversary respond in kind. This leads to the vicious circle called the arms race. Heidegger maintains that the subject-object dualism that now pervades Western civilization results in part from a decline in the power of language. Especially in his later writing, Heidegger claims that the human openness for the Being of entities is organized by language. As language changes, so does the way in which entities can show themselves to us. As language becomes abused and worn out, as it seems to be today, entities can only show themselves in a constricted and narrow way – as objects for domination, for example. While we may have progressed in terms of technological power, Heidegger suggests that we have declined in terms of our humanity since the great age of the Greeks. For the Greeks, "to be" meant to stand forth into presence from nothingness; for medieval people, "to be" meant to be present as a creature of the self-presenting God; for modern humanity, "to be" means to be an object that is utilized and represented by and for the human subject.

Heidegger, like many other German philosophers, may have romanticized the ancient Greek world, but he is not alone in suggesting that a change came over people in the early modern era. The noted political philosopher C.B. Macpherson also argues that in recent centuries a shift gradually occurred in the way Western people think about themselves.[9] With the growth of early forms of capitalism, people began defining themselves not as immortal souls hoping to attain salvation in the afterlife, but instead as beings of infinite desires that could be satisfied through the acquisition of wealth. Western people began seeing themselves as consumers and appropriators. Walter Weisskopf adds that Western thought defines all economic activity in terms of the quasi-psychological drive of "need satisfaction."[10] For thousands of years, the great wisdom traditions have told us that life is not fulfilled simply by quenching such desires, but instead by submitting to the natural or transcendent cosmic order. But people have always resisted this outlook, and today more than ever we seem bent on forcing the cosmos to submit to our desires, instead of curbing our desires in order to conform to cosmic law. Put in other words, today we identify ourselves with our desires, including bodily cravings as well as the ego's desire for recognition and esteem.

In the largely secularized modern world, we have abandoned the transcendent God (or, as some suggest, God has abandoned us). Now we attempt to be gods ourselves. But mortal gods are an unhappy lot. We desperately strive to avoid death and obliteration by making and building things that appear to be permanent. We try to establish something partial and limited, the human ego, as the eternal and infinite – clearly an impossible mission. Anxious about death, we project our mortality onto the enemy. By preparing to fight the enemy, we delude ourselves into thinking we are preparing to conquer death itself.[11] Almost like compulsive personalities, nation-states try to control everything, for they reflect the fears of their citizens. Acting in light of our fears, nation-states erect ever more powerful systems of destruction – called systems of "national defense" – that ultimately undermine the very security we are supposedly seeking. Any talk of alternative ways of behaving is perceived as a threat to the laboriously constructed defense system.

Could our preoccupation with the arms race lead us to overlook the very source of that race, so that the more we work to end the race, the more it is fueled by the hidden cause that we overlook?[12] Can we really expect so-called arms control negotiations to have any long-term impact if the states of mind of the parties involved remain hostile, suspicious, frightened, and acquisitive? I suspect that as long as we experience ourselves as separate beings who need to defend ourselves against others "out there," we will have to contend with the problem of arms races. Given the fact that the secret to making nuclear weapons is now out in the open, we are faced with the need to bring about a shift in the way we understand ourselves and our place in the cosmos. Heidegger would say that instead of thinking of ourselves as things, we need to recollect that we are the temporal-historical clearing in which things can appear. These "things" would include our own personalities and bodies, as well as the totality of natural beings. Our open awareness does not create things, but instead lets them manifest themselves as they are. When our awareness is constricted, however, entities can only manifest themselves in a partial way, for example, as commodities. We tend to think that we fulfill our highest possibility by turning the Earth into an object to be devoured for human ends. But could this process, which harms the fabric of life on Earth, not only threaten our survival as a species but also undermine our integrity as well? In other words, could we gain consumer satisfaction for all, while at the same time turning the Earth into a wasteland and ourselves into mere consumer-machines? Heidegger notes that "The devastation of the Earth can easily go hand in hand with a guaranteed supreme living standard for man, and just as easily with the organized establishment of a uniform state of happiness for all."[13] We could turn the planet into a gigantic factory, but something essential about us and the Earth would have been lost as a result.

According to Heidegger, our highest possibility is not to dominate things, but instead to care for them and to let them be. For action-oriented humanists, such talk of "letting beings be" seems frivolous, especially when so much remains to be done to alleviate human suffering. By "letting beings be," however, Heidegger does not mean to imply passive acceptance of evil and destructiveness. He urges us to do what we can to improve the world within the limits of the existing humanistic paradigm. Letting beings be entails loving behavior guided by profound awareness of what beings are. I cannot let a plant *be* a plant, that is, help provide the conditions needed for it to grow and flourish, if I am ignorant of its need for water and sunlight. Letting something be can involve decisive action and speech, but such action and speech must be rooted in an understanding of what the thing is to begin with. Letting human beings be does not mean sitting by and watching us blow ourselves up with nuclear weapons. But it does mean taking action that arises from a vision that transcends the usual "us *vs.* them" mentality that governs not only the arms race but also aspects of the "peace" movement. By depicting military people and government leaders as evil and wrong, peace workers sometimes tend to polarize the situation. So while working for alternatives to those presented by people from the opposing point of view, peace workers would do well to avoid turning the opponents into yet another "enemy." Those behind the war machine believe that they are working to prevent war and to provide security. They do not perceive themselves as evil. "Letting beings be," then, is not a justification for doing nothing, but instead a summons to let a deeper understanding of things and ourselves come upon us.

We are so influenced by anthropocentric humanism, however, that we remain stuck in it even when we try to find our way beyond it. In his moving book, *The Fate of the Earth*, for example, Jonathan Schell appeals to us to end the nuclear arms race in order to avert not only the destruction of human life, but of other life forms as well. Yet his attempt to shift our concern beyond the human is impeded by remnants of anthropocentrism, especially with regard to the origin of value. For example, Schell tells us that

Human beings have a worth – a worth that is sacred. But it is for human beings that they have that sacred worth, and for them that the other things in the creation have their worth. ... To borrow elementary philosophical language, as objects the members of the [human] species are among many things in existence that have worth in human eyes, but as the sum of all possible human subjects the species comprises all those "eyes" and in that sense is the sole originator of all worth as it is given to us to be aware of it.[14]

Is it "for us" that nonhuman beings have their worth? Or should we say that entities display their intrinsic worth *through* us? How can we be the "sole originators" of worth if such worth is "given to us to be aware of it"? Schell is groping for an alternative to the notion that entities are valuable only insofar as they promote human power, but he continues to speak of humankind in a way that overestimates our role in the origin of values. If the wisdom traditions are right, the cosmos has intrinsic value quite apart from our apprehension of that value. On the other hand, these same traditions suggest that there is something unique about human existence insofar as we apprehend not only the creatures of the world but also the very *presence* of those creatures. Heidegger calls this presencing "Being." We are human, so he argues, only insofar as we apprehend that things *are* at all. Hence, Heidegger states that "no catastrophe that could break out over the planet could be compared to this ..., that from man the relation to 'is' suddenly gets taken away."[15] We can recognize that presencing only insofar as we recall our own absencing or openness. And such recalling reminds us of the ego's mortality.

We can approach this issue of presencing from a religious perspective. When the Judeo-Christian tradition informs us that we are made "in the image of God," we might take this to mean that God is pure no-thingness, pure awareness, in which the whole creation can present itself – and that human beings are like God insofar as they share in this awareness and can thus "let beings be." From this viewpoint, neither God nor humans are things. One writer argues that idolatry means worshipping any sort of thing, including our egos and bodies, and even including a thing-like God. Idolatry arises when we worship our egos, instead of appreciating that we are the pure beholding in which all things – including the ego – can appear.[16] We might interpret the arms race as a symptom of such idolatry. Having identified ourselves with our minds and bodies, we direct toward these finite entities the reverence that can find proper fulfillment only in what transcends any thing. Little wonder that there is such dissatisfaction in our lives, despite an abundance of consumer goods. If we are most fundamentally openness and love but gradually forget this fact, nothing can satisfy us until we accomplish what Plato encouraged us to do: recollect what we have forgotten. Such recollection is impeded by our craving for pleasure. One scholar notes the following:

That purely physical and sensual pleasure requires ever more excitation and titillation, tension, and pain, was known not only to the Hindus and Buddhists, but also to the Greek philosophers of the Periclean and Hellenistic periods. It was, of course, known to Christian thought from the Fathers of the Church to the Middle Ages. All these cultures saw virtue in balance and moderation, or even in restraint and negation of desires. Modern civilization, however, has elevated the continuous creation of tension for the sake of pleasurable "satisfaction" to the dignity of an ultimate goal.[17]

Sensual gratification is a particularly absorbing type of distraction. And we seek such distraction because of our anxiety about death. Yet only by being willing to let anxiety come over us can we encounter the truth about who we really are. In the meditation traditions, anxiety constitutes the "guardians at the gates" who deny enlightenment to the faint-hearted. If someone wishes to wake up, he or she must be willing to recognize the finitude and mortality of the persona or ego. Anxiety, then, is not a negative phenomenon, but is instead the way in which we summon ourselves back to being open and alive, instead of contracted into the shell of the ego and its past. Note that anxiety differs from fear. Fear is always fear about something or other, but anxiety is anxious precisely about no-thing at all. Hence, we have the tendency to try to convert anxiety into fear, so that we can have the illusion of there being something out there against which we can defend ourselves.[18] In the face of mortality, however, there can ultimately be no defense. The ego and body must perish, but the open awareness in which they appear does not. This is the insight of all the great wisdom traditions. Now that we have examined how the arms race might have resulted from a failure to understand who we really are, let us consider what possibilities are open to us in coming years.

3   The Possibility for a Change in Human Self-Understanding

Today there seems to be dawning a kind of planetary or species-level anxiety. We are confronted as never before in history with the possibility that we can destroy the human race through our own deeds. Because the human race is one way in which the cosmos is aware of itself, extinguishing ourselves would be a very serious matter, one that would have cosmic, not merely human implications. Could this planetary anxiety call us forth into a new way of understanding ourselves, just as personal anxiety invites an individual to let go of old, destructive patterns and turn to new possibilities? Could such a new understanding eliminate the motive for the nuclear arms race? Heidegger once said that

"Things that really matter ... even when they come very late come at the right time."[19] Fear motivates much of the current movement to end the arms race, but anxiety is growing. Fear wants to do something about things – such as nuclear weapons – but anxiety reveals that such weapons arise from the attempt to deny and escape our mortality. So while we must accomplish what is possible as a result of fear-motivated actions, such as negotiating arms control treaties, there is a more difficult but also more profound way that calls to us. This way requires much of us, nothing less than following the teachings of the great wisdom traditions in light of the exigencies of our own epoch.

Finding an alternative to the present anthropocentric self-understanding does not require that we abandon technical knowledge and skills; there is no "going back" to some pristine pre-technological era. What we need is to go forward in a way consistent with our deepest teachings, philosophical and religious. We must not be misled by the fact that terrible wars have been fought by people claiming to follow the precepts of some religion or other. Such deeds speak ill not so much of the great religious traditions as of their alleged practitioners. The answer we seek lies not in installing a priest or preacher as head of state, for modern churches reflect many of the anthropocentric ideals that are the real source of our problems. We must be cautious about our tendency to want to do something, to act decisively in the face of the current threat, because so many of our actions are influenced by the very anthropocentric leanings that pervade so many of our institutions. Heidegger himself suggests that all we can do is prepare for a possible shift in our self-understanding, a shift that cannot come as a result of our will but only as a result of a destiny that transcends our control. Unfortunately, he does not discuss in much detail what form such "preparation" might take.

I have argued that the nuclear arms race is a symptom of a deep misunderstanding of who we are. Today, our highest possibilities go unfulfilled because of fear, craving, aversion, and ignorance. Murray Bookchin has observed that "a humanity unfulfilled is more fearsome than any living being, for it has enough of that mentality called mere 'intelligence' to assemble all the conditions for the destruction of life on the planet."[20] Anthropocentric humanism fails to fulfill human life because it forgets that there is a higher possibility for us than surviving with maximum gratification. This higher possibility has to do with bearing witness to the miraculous presencing of all beings. Caring for beings – including ourselves as well as non-human beings – might be called "love." Human beings, as Heidegger explained in *Being and Time,* are essentially this concernful, loving care.

Love involves a creative openness that we might label "vision." Vision is expressed in language through philosophy and poetry. Profound declarations can also be expressions of vision. Declarations bring forth possibilities that were not previously available. Moreover, declarations are often not consistent with given facts or evidence. When our Founding Fathers, and the women who supported them, declared that they were going to establish a new society in North America, many people regarded them as foolish. Everyone knew that the British army and navy were the strongest in the world. Moreover, even if the colonists somehow managed to defeat the British, many people had little faith in the possibility of establishing a viable democratic social order. All of the facts and evidence spoke against the possibility that the Declaration of Independence could really change the status quo. But we know that this change did come about.

Today, we are faced with facts and evidence about the nuclear arms race that counsel despair. What can an individual do in the face of such weapons in the hands of the superpowers? Each of us is called on to do at least this: to be willing to experience the anxiety that is the gateway to vision and declaration. Only when we have gone through that gateway can we make the declarations that open up the realm for an alternative to the given. We need to let language speak through us in a new way. Further, we must be willing for the worst to occur: all-out nuclear war. We must not be governed by fear; as long as we resist and deny the possibility of nuclear war, that possibility will persist and grow stronger. So long as we cling to whatever exists, including the order of things that now prevails, we cannot be open for alternatives that do not yet exist. When enough of us choose to be open for vision, the needed shift in human awareness may occur. Perhaps we will then be able to create a world beyond the old dichotomy of war and peace. Perhaps we will be able to create a new game for humanity, one in which we fulfill our highest possibility of bearing witness to the presence of all beings. In learning to dwell in harmony with all beings, human and nonhuman, we will become mature daughters and sons of the Earth – co-creators of the cosmic order. In the meantime, of course, while preparing ourselves for this paradigm shift in human history, we must be responsible politically within the existing paradigm.[21] We must find ways of easing tensions and reducing the tempo of the arms race. But we must also go about the silent work of re-creating politics by initiating a new way of life on Earth, a way that will let ourselves and other beings be.   *Newcomb College, Tulane University*

NOTES

1 Heidegger's most important discussions of anthropocentrism, technology, and the atomic age are: "The Question Concerning Technology" and "Letter on Humanism," in Heidegger, *Basic Writings; What Is Called Thinking?; The End of Philosophy; An Introduction to Metaphysics*. Cf. also the following works by the present author: "Humanism, Ontology, and the Nuclear Arms Race"; "Beyond Humanism: Heidegger's Understanding of Technology"; *Eclipse of the Self*.

2 On this topic, cf. Lynn White's now-classic essay, "The Historical Roots of our Ecologic Crisis"; Wilkinson; Crownfield; Rifkin, with Howard; Passmore.

3 Arendt, p. 145. Abridged from *The Origins of Totalitarianism*, copyright 1951 by Hannah Arendt; renewed 1979 by Mary McCarthy West. Reprinted by permission of Harcourt Brace Jovanovich, Inc.

4 Heidegger, "Letter on Humanism," p. 221.

5 Heidegger, *Nietzsche, II*, p. 198.

6 Heidegger, "The End of Philosophy," pp. 104-5.

7 Heidegger, "The Question Concerning Technology," p. 100.

8 Heidegger, "What Are Poets For?", in Heidegger, *Poetry, Language, Thought*, p. 116.

9 C.B. Macpherson, "Democratic Theory: Ontology and Technology," in Mitcham and Mackey, eds., pp. 161-70.

10 Walter Weisskopf, "Alienation and Economics," in Truitt and Solomons, eds.

11 On the topic of war and murder as outcomes of anxiety and death-projection, cf. Wilber's outstanding book, *Up From Eden:* and also Wilber's *The Atman Project*.

12 Cf. Herbert Marcuse's remark on the very first page of his *One-Dimensional Man*: "Does not the threat of an atomic catastrophe which could wipe out the human race also serve to protect the very forces which perpetuate this danger? The efforts to prevent such a catastrophe overshadow the search for its potential causes in contemporary industrial society. These causes remain unidentified, unexposed, unattacked by the public because they recede before the all too obvious threat from without – to the West from the East, to the East from the West."

13 Heidegger, *What Is Called Thinking?*, p. 30.

14 Schell, *The Fate of the Earth*, p. 127.

15 Heidegger, *Heraklit*.

16 For more on this topic, cf. Deikman.

17 Weisskopf, "Alienation and Economics," p. 43.

18 For more on fear and anxiety, see the essay by Fox in this collection.

19 Heidegger, "Letter on Humanism," p. 223.

20 Bookchin.

21 On the topic that we are undergoing a paradigm shift into a new form of consciousness, cf. Berman; Capra; Ferguson.

Commentary: On Psychological Diversions and Ontological Distortions

RONALD E. SANTONI

For many of us, the arms race, or the continuation of the arms race, may, without exaggeration, be viewed as a form of madness.[1] There seems no other way to understand the superpowers' feverish competition to build the most threatening and horrendous arsenals of nuclear weaponry imaginable, or their individual efforts to secure peace through senseless commitments to excessively destructive power and endless refinements in strategies and armaments of "overkill." For many of us it is virtually a truism that if this madness is not cured and the nuclear arms race brought to a halt, a nuclear "war" will eventually happen, leaving not only holocaustal results, but the possibility of continued life on this planet a question mark.

One need not share this precise perception or judgment to recognize the peril posed by the nuclear arms race and to ask *why*, in the context of this unprecedented possibility for planetary nuclear destruction, the governments of the two major superpowers – and many of their citizens – continue to support an arms race which involves each side's preparation for an act of genocide on the other. Why this competition that courts "multiple genocide"?[2] What are the factors that keep it going? Have our thoughts, concerns and sensitivities become so perverse, our self-understanding and ideological commitments so unquestioning, that we no longer care whether our distortions lead to the annihilation of a vast part, or all, of life on this planet?

One of the traditional roles of philosophy is to raise and address the question "why?" to try to explain what is not readily explainable, to lay bare what is presupposed by widely held views and behaviors. There is no question that Michael Fox and Michael Zimmerman address these philosophical concerns, among others. The titles of their papers may suggest otherwise, but both attempt to diagnose the underlying factors which propel the arms race, and, in light of these, suggest ways in which we can curb the vicious spiral of arms acquisition and liberate ourselves from the worldwide, potentially terminal plague of our time. And although their articles betray the inevitable differences which emerge from a predominantly psychological focus (Fox) and one that is predominantly ontological/existential (Zimmerman), it is important to note that they are often in agreement about the forms – if not the content – of the misperceptions that sustain or intensify the arms race. Distorted preoccupation with the threat posed by the Other; distorted conceptions of what constitutes a "threat," "the enemy," "security"; distortions in our understanding of and attitudes towards fear and anxiety; distortion, detachment, and debasement of our language; a delusive failure to cope with our own death anxiety and mortality, or to confront genuine threats of nuclear extinction; the psychical distancing of ourselves from nuclear "reality"; radical self-deception in the face of fear – these are for both Fox and Zimmerman (as for other analysts and critics of the nuclear arms race[3]) among the many "breeding grounds" of the United States' and the USSR's frenetic build-up of genocidal weapons. For both writers, the arms race symbolizes each nation's drive for total security – born in self-deceptive attempts to evade insecurity but destined to effect radical insecurity. Yet this hardly means that Fox and Zimmerman are in fundamental agreement concerning either the origins of the current nuclear impasse or the substance of their proposals and solutions for overcoming it.

For Fox, who appears strongly influenced by psychiatrists Jerome Frank and Robert Lifton,[4] among others, "psychological factors of the most basic sort are the primary causes of the arms race." Fear and anxiety are "the chief among these" and play the "principal role" in generating and fueling the arms race. American fear of "the Russians," Soviet fear of "the Americans," American fear of expansionism, Soviet fear of encirclement, the mutual fear of extinction, and other variegated forms of fear drive the arms race, paralyze us psychically and pose the major obstacle to peace. Overcome by the threat of nuclear annihilation, we seek to conceal our fear and anxiety from ourselves through diversionary mechanisms of psychological escape, "psychological maneuvers" of "self-deceit and obfuscation," which we design in order to elude inevitable confrontation with our own extinction. We "deny" reality, create "enemies," nurture images of "the enemy," and falsify language for the sake of hiding our most basic fears and giving ourselves a contrived sense of "security." But security is an "edifice of self-deception," what Lifton calls the "ultimate psychologism."[5] The way out of the fears that fuel the arms race is not a futile quest for ultimate nuclear security but an admission of our basic fear and anxiety, and an identification and acknowledgment of the psychological masks and aberrations which we (and our governments) have chosen in order to hide our basic malaise. By "de-numbing ourselves," by acknowledging and coming face to face with the possibility of the nuclear death of our planet (or "omnicide"), we liberate ourselves to pursue creative initiatives to keep our threatened planet alive.

In contrast, Zimmerman, who essentially restates the position of the German existentialist Martin Heidegger, argues that the origins of the arms race are deeper than psychological. Thus, the arms race is rooted in a radical misunderstanding of who we are as human beings, and is also a particularly dangerous symptom of "anthropocentric humanism" – an idolatrous modern humanism which, among other defects, both self-centeredly views the human being as the only being which possesses any intrinsic worth or value *and* understands human beings as things, e.g., as their "egos," bodies, or "personae." Adherents to two competing views of anthropocentric humanism, the two nuclear giants vie to secure the Earth and all of its commodities. Each regards its own version of humanism as the "true" embodiment of it, seeing the "other" as a threat to its individual goals of power, security and domination of the Earth. Each prepares to annihilate the other for the sake of its own idolatrous, self-destructive ends. Psychological insecurity is ultimately grounded in an ontological misunderstanding of both human and nonhuman being (the latter perceived as "raw material to be consumed by humankind"). Our craving to consume things betrays insecurity and expresses the sense of ontological isolation we experience as a result of anthropocentric humanism's subject-object dualism. Our distorted images and anxieties about "the enemy" stem in part from the arrogant view that *other* people, advocating a divergent ideology and a different form of humanism, must stand as obstacles to our controlling or appropriating the world.[6] Each side's preparations for nuclear war epitomize the "dark side" of modern humanism – its distorted drive to dominate the Earth at any cost to life. So steeped are we in this ego-centered humanism that we remain anchored to it as we try to find our way beyond it. It accounts for our resort to the psychological maneuvers which Fox discusses, not the other way round.

Given this analysis, what is needed to liberate us from the spiral of the arms race is no less than a "paradigm shift" in our understanding of what it means to be a human being. We need a "more profound humanism" that both acknowledges the uniqueness of the human being (we are not things but the "awareness" or "opening" in which things manifest themselves) and recognizes that the "highest human possibility" is not to dominate other beings but to serve them by letting them reveal themselves as they are. As Zimmerman and Heidegger put it, we must "let beings be." We must take on the anxiety that reveals to us the facticity of our death, that returns us to the truth of who we are, that summons us to relinquish old destructive patterns and adopt new creative ways. Only when we accept the creative disclosures of anxiety, "recollect what we have forgotten," refuse to be controlled by fear, and understand our being in terms of "open awareness" and love will we eliminate the threat of the Other and the motive for the arms race. Although Zimmerman appears to agree with Fox concerning our need to admit to ourselves our anxiety and fear, and to see through our self-deceptive efforts to evade the possibility of our extinction, it is clear that for Zimmerman the cure for our contemporary malady demands *first and foremost* a correction in our ontology – in our understanding of and attitude toward being – rather than a correction of our psychology. Coming to understand who we are in relation to the rest of being is a prerequisite to understanding and overcoming the psychological aberrations that spawn, nourish and hold us hostage to the arms race. Trying to own up to fear and anxiety without succumbing to delusive defense mechanisms – in the manner that Fox prescribes – requires, for Zimmerman, addressing our self-understanding and approach to all beings: only then will language be able "to speak through us in a new way"; only then will we be more open to serve than to dominate.

I agree with Zimmerman that the underlying causes of the arms race are deeper than psychological, that the psychological fears and distortions which heat the arms race are an outcome of our idolatrous attitude to ourselves and our exploitative attitude to other beings. I believe that the problem of what constitutes a person represents the fundamental philosophical issue of the twentieth century, and that it is in our confusions about and failures to discern the distinguishing ontological features of a human being that we find the bases of vexing contemporary problems of violence and dehumanization. These problems reflect the ways in which we *violate* the dignity, freedom and autonomy of human reality, in which we treat persons as things. The Zimmerman-Heidegger analysis serves to underscore my conviction that our present preoccupations with violence and preparations for nuclear "war" reveal a distorted existential perspective on all being, not just *human* being. We objectify human reality and are quite ready to devour the rest of Being for our human "ends," even if that process means the extinction of all life.

This is not to underrate, but rather to re-position, the psychological factors which Fox attempts to delineate so thoroughly. Although I am reluctant to call fear and anxiety, for instance, "primary causes" of the arms race (even Fox is interested in locating the causes, or what he calls "breeding grounds" and "sources" of these causes), I have no hesitation in recognizing the crucial part that his "psychological factors" (including our "responses" to fear and anxiety) play in continuing, fueling, perpetuating, even "motivating" the arms race, and in inhibiting any significant progress toward peace and disarmament. But being "propelled" (Fox's word) by fear and anxiety is simply not the same as being *caused* by them, although the cause(s) may well be served by the "propelling" conditions. To be sure, Fox has, in isolating and discussing the origin and role that "enemy images," "psychic numbing," and other forms of "psychic distancing" play in maintaining and intensifying the arms race, the results of some of the most reliable psychological and/or philosophical studies of the topic on his side. Related works of J. Glenn Gray – whose phenomenological study of "the warrior" offers a pivotal and unexcelled philosophical account of the origins of demonic "images of the enemy" – Frank,[7] and Lifton – who has called "psychic numbing" "one of the great problems of our age"[8] – directly or indirectly corroborate Fox's analysis of the "psychological forces" that feed and keep us trapped in a spiralling arms race. They appear to agree that self-delusion in the face of the "psychological unreality"[9] of the nuclear threat, and the maladaptive dehumanization[10] of those whom we deceptively project as the main "threat" to our "security," are intense contributing factors to the continuation of the arms race. From this concurrence, one may, however, hardly conclude that one has isolated the "primary causes" of the arms race. Zimmerman's account of Heidegger's analysis lacks connections at points, yet it offers important pointers to these "causes."

In passing, I want to say, first, that I regard most, if not all, of the "escapist diversions" (or "psychological aberrations") of which Fox speaks in relation to the arms race as part of what I call "nuclear insanity." The denial, pretense, and evasional mechanisms which he describes – and to which in a number of cases, Zimmerman also refers – manifest precisely the kind of psychic break or "rupture" with nuclear reality that I find in nuclear insanity. On my analysis, this incapacity to cope with the realities of a nuclear age – made evident in the tendency to behave as though one were still living in a pre-atomic age – often involves a "delusional remolding of reality" in which the victim "stagnates" the world according to his or her own wishes, and substitutes secure fantasies for lucid recognition of the perils of today's nuclear world. So much of the thinking and behaviors of the superpowers – of their governments and, too often, their citizens – betray this type of schizoid break with reality or with the consequences of their nuclear initiatives. The arms race itself is a macrocosmic instance of this nuclear insanity. Instances of nuclear insanity *within* the arms race only exacerbate the insanity of the arms race at large.[11]

Second, I need only mention that there are diversions other than the deceptions Fox discusses that stand as obstacles to our breaking the "nuclear mindset." Outdated myths and anachronistic habits of thinking continue to stand in our way and to heat the arms race. The myth of nationalism and national superiority; the habit of identifying patriotism with uncritical allegiance to one's own government; the myths that the superpowers' "balancing of terror" will deter a nuclear war, that violence can put an end to violence, that superpowers can make peace by preparing for war, that security can come through acquiring larger arsenals of weapons, that nuclear war is winnable, that it is better to be dead than red – these are but a few illustration of such antiquated patterns of thought. Until these myths and *pre-nuclear* modes of thinking are identified, recognized for what they are, suspended, and overcome, they will continue to stimulate the mad cycle of the arms race.[12]

To be sure, Fox sees the need for our undergoing "certain fundamental changes" in our "thinking, beliefs, attitudes, values" and Zimmerman calls for a "paradigm shift" in our thinking about ourselves, others, and the Earth. But it is not so clear that what either offers as suggestions for what we can, must, or should do in the face of a runaway arms race are sufficient to "wind down" the arms race *before* it leads to omnicide. In spite of the importance of Fox's analysis and reminders it is not clear that "admitting our (nuclear) fear and anxiety" to ourselves and "identifying the mechanisms that dull or mask our emotional and other responses" represent much more than examples of basic, often-stated principles of psychotherapy. Being aware of the psychological maneuvers that keep us numb to nuclear reality may well be the road to transcending them, but it must only be a "first step" (as Fox acknowledges), during which we simultaneously *act* to eliminate nuclear threats, break our complicity with the arms race, get rid of arsenals of genocidal weaponry, and create conditions for international goodwill, mutual trust, and creative interdependence.

Similarly in respect to Zimmerman: in spite of the challenging Heideggerian insights he brings out regarding what motivates the arms race, many questions may be raised about his prescribed "solutions." Given our need for a paradigm shift in our (distorted) understanding of ourselves and the rest of being, are we merely left "to *prepare* for a possible shift in our self-understanding" (italics mine)? Is this "all we can do"? Is it necessarily the case that such a shift "cannot come as a result of our own will" – and work – but only from "a destiny outside our control?" Does this mean that we leave to God the matter of bringing about a paradigm shift? Granted our fears and the importance of not being controlled by fears, as well as our "anthropocentric leanings," should we be as cautious as Zimmerman suggests about our disposition "to want to do something" or "to act decisively in the face of the current threat?" In spite of the.importance of our taking on the anxiety of our finitude and our present situation, does it follow that "we should be willing for the worst [i.e. an all-out nuclear war] to occur"? Zimmerman wrongly, I contend, equates "resistance" with "denial" when he says that "as long as we resist and deny the possibility of nuclear war, that possibility will persist and grow stronger." He also wrongly perceives "resistance" as presupposing a clinging to the "order of things that now prevails." Resistance connotes opposing, and striving to defeat, a prevailing state of affairs that would allow or encourage the "worst to occur." I submit, against

Zimmerman, that we should *not,* in any sense, be willing for nuclear war or omnicide to occur. (This is *not* to suggest that we should be numb to the possibility of its occurrence.) Despite Zimmerman's elaborations and refinements his Heideggerian notion of "letting beings be" continues to be too permissive in this regard.

In my judgment, an individual's decision *not* to act against and resist his or her government's preparations for nuclear holocaust is, as I have argued elsewhere,[13] to be an early accomplice to the most horrendous crime against life imaginable – its annihilation. The Nuremberg tradition calls not only for a new way of thinking, a "new internationalism" in which we all become co-nurturers of the whole planet, but for resolute actions that will sever our complicity with nuclear criminality and the genocidal arms race, and work to achieve a future which we can no longer assume. We must not only "come face to face with the unthinkable in image and thought" (Fox) but must act *now* – with a "new consciousness" and conscience – to prevent the unthinkable, by cleansing the earth of nuclear weaponry. Only when that is achieved will ultimate violence be removed as the final arbiter of our planet's fate.[14]   *Denison University*

NOTES

1 See, e.g., Ronald E. Santoni, "Nuclear Insanity and Multiple Genocide," in Charney, ed. See also Caldicott, *Nuclear Madness.*
2 I employ this expression in the article cited in note 1.
3 See, for example, Frank, *Sanity and Survival in the Nuclear Age;* Lifton and Falk; Kennan; and Schell, *The Fate of the Earth.*
4 See, in particular, Frank, *Sanity and Survival,* and Lifton and Falk.
5 Lifton and Falk, p. 83, for example.
6 Of course, Zimmerman, following Heidegger, also says that "Anxious about death, we project our mortality out unto the enemy."
7 Frank, *Sanity and Survival.*
8 Lifton, p. 509
9 This is Frank's term; *Sanity and Survival,* p. 7. It should be noted that "unreality" here connotes, among other things, the inability, psychologically, to acknowledge the reality of the nuclear threat. The Frank reference in the preceding sentence is taken from p. 3.
10 For a comparison between the *maladaptive* and *adaptive* functions of dehumanization and psychic numbing, I refer the reader to Lifton, pp. 500-10. It is of interest to note that Fox, understandably, tends to slight the psychologically adaptive functions of psychic numbing.
11 I refer the reader to Aronson's discussion of "Technological Madness."
12 For a development of this theme, see my "Omnicide and the Problem of Belief."

13 Santoni, "The Arms Race, Genocidal Intent, and Individual Responsibility."
14 Sentiments of Schell and Frank have, I'm confident, influenced me in these last two sentences.

Consciousness, Gender, and Nuclear Politics

ROBERT LITKE

The splitting of the atom has changed everything save our mode of thinking, and thus we drift toward unparalleled catastrophe.   Albert Einstein

I

We now stand at the threshold of Einstein's catastrophe. Responsible professionals of diverse kinds and millions of ordinary people appreciate our predicament. The task therefore, is to discover or create the new modes of thinking to which Einstein refers.

This is difficult. Ordinarily we do our thinking within well established modes. We observe, analyze, explain, argue, anticipate, debate, predict, forecast, set goals, plan strategies, etc. without regard for the frameworks within which this is done. We play the games: we do not reflect on their rules. Still less do we investigate the deeper reasons and feelings which lead us to create these games and spend our lives playing them. Now, however, the games are very dangerous: it is time we looked into them. This paper provides *one* way of doing this. It offers a perspective on the nuclear situation, on the forms of thinking which have led us to our current state.

II

I begin with the view of Brooke Medicine Eagle and a vision which occurred to her in a quest in South Dakota. Part of the vision was a meeting with the Rainbow Woman who described problems with the land.

She said to me that the earth is in trouble, that the land is in trouble, and that here on this land, this Turtle Island, this North American land, what needs to happen is a balancing. She said that the thrusting, aggressive, analytic, intellectual, building, making-it-happen energy has very much overbalanced the feminine, receptive, allowing, surrendering energy. She said that what needs to happen is an uplifting and a balancing. And because we are out of balance, we need to put more emphasis on surrendering, being receptive, allowing, nurturing. She was speaking to me as a woman, and I was to carry this message to women specifically. But not only do women need to become strong in this way; we all need to do this, men and women alike. [1]

Medicine Eagle's vision reminds us that there is strength in receptivity as well as aggressiveness – a fact celebrated in Taoist thought and martial arts for centuries. These are, moreover, complementary strengths, not antagonistic forces. A balance between them is essential for our livelihood.

The importance of a balance between receptivity and aggressiveness is reflected in a variety of current trends. It is, for example, at the heart of current attempts to divest ourselves of sex-role stereotypes. Hence men and women are rejecting the view that they should live out only half of their humanity, molded by exaggerated male aggressiveness or excessive female passivity. Other examples come from medicine. The chronically aggressive die younger. Too much "making it happen" energy can result in hypertension and heart disease. [2] Too much receptivity is equally destructive. Addiction to tranquillizers is epidemic in our society.

What is true of our bodies and our sexuality may also be true for the planet. Since Hiroshima, patterns of imbalance have become more evident. On the one hand, aggressive technological expansion in weaponry means less security not more. Never has all life on the planet been at risk because of human creativity. On the other hand, our tendency to tranquillize ourselves with the denial of nuclear facts is equally dangerous. The plain fact is that we threaten ourselves with self-destruction, continuously and at an accelerating pace. For most of us, this is too much to face and we distract ourselves with various forms of denial: apocalyptic visions of inevitable holocaust; "rational" arguments that nuclear war is winnable; fond wishes that nuclear weapons are safe because their use is unthinkable, etc. I take all of these to be ways of lulling ourselves into finding our current situation acceptable and distracting ourselves from the fact that we have created a catastrophic situation and have the power and responsibility to uncreate it. It is time to be aggressive in new directions: it is time to be receptive to new possibilities.

That we need balance between assertiveness and receptivity at all levels of human functioning is the central claim of the perspective which this essay offers. To see the implications this has for the nuclear question, I shall spell out some details and apply them to three distinct alternatives to present attitudes and policies.

III

The psychologist Arthur Deikman distinguishes between *object* and *receptive* modes of consciousness.[3] The purpose of the object mode is to act on the environment and control it. Such a mode is necessary for physical as well as psychological survival; according to Deikman, it is well established for most of us by three years of age. Subsequent experience and education amplify the powers inherent in it and it has become the primary way of functioning in our culture.

The object mode emphasizes "the perception of differences and boundaries, the structuring of diffuse stimuli into manipulable entities."[4] This is the heart of our intellectual grasp of things. It yields an integrated and comprehensive way of perceiving reality; the self and most things in the world are taken to be discrete objects, localized in space and time and subject to linear causality.

For example, in trying to obtain food by hunting (or driving a taxicab), one needs sharply focused vision; consciousness must include a clear sense of past, present, and future; planning, remembering, and calculating must take place. The self in such a mode of consciousness is an object, just as a deer or automobiles are objects; the self of ordinary experience, finite and distinct from other entities, makes up that world. In this way, the object mode enables the organism to act on the environment and thus to survive. Self-preservation and acquisition are the primary motives of the object self, and these motives both serve the object self and reinforce it. Thus, the way we perceive the world, our mode of consciousness, is a function of our purpose. The type of self we experience is integral to that mode, calling it forth and being sustained by it.[5]

Thus, according to Deikman, what we want, what we take ourselves to be, how we find the world, how we think we should act, are of a piece. We create and live out a kind of order, an order in which we exercise control, make things happen, and maintain a clear focus on our separateness from the world and each other. There is no question that this is an important part of who we are. A powerful expression of it occurs in contemporary science and technology.

The purpose of the receptive mode is to receive the environment: it requires allowing-it-to-happen rather than making-it-happen:

In contrast, the intention to receive from the environment (as in listening to music), rather than to act on it, as the hunter must, requires a different mode of consciousness, one that diminishes the sense of boundaries and permits the experience of merging with the environment. This "receptive mode" is associated with a different sense of self than the hunter's or taxi driver's, one less discrete, less prominent; past and future drop away and sensual attributes dominate over the perception of form and verbal meaning. Analytic thought tends to cease; attention becomes diffused and boundaries blur. The separate self dissolves, permitting the experience of connection or merging into the environment.[6]

Whereas the object mode requires us to see ourselves as separate, the receptive mode emphasizes "connectedness." Rather than adopt an arm's length relationship to activities and processes, we participate in them. Clear examples are the losing of self-consciousness in conversation, complete absorption in some activity, and experiences of communion, fellowship or solidarity with others. We are refreshed by such occurrences and enlivened by them.

The receptive mode is dominant at birth according to Deikman, but soon eclipsed by the object mode. Minimal access to it is necessary for bare survival, yet it seems evident that full and fluctuating access to both modes is needed for a balanced and satisfying life. Human relationships are, for example, a mere shadow of their possibilities if conducted solely in the object mode of consciousness. What Deikman says of sexual intercourse is metaphoric for the full range of human interaction: "if lovers treat each other like objects, attempting to control their partners and maintaining a clear and separate sense of self, they are likely to experience 'screwing' rather than 'making love'."[7] Beyond that, it seems that both modes are required for creative problem-solving, which, according to Deikman, involves two phases. "The first phase requires the object mode, with its active, vigorous, controlled thinking: assembling data, examining logical relationships, striving toward a resolution of the difficulty."[8] This is making-it-happen energy at work; it functions in accord with established forms of thinking. Assuming these routines of thinking to be adequate, there is no problem to be solved creatively. One simply works it through. We find ourselves at an impasse, however, when established routines are inadequate. In these circumstances, more effort along the same lines is simply more of the same; it cannot advance us. What is required is a shift to the receptive mode, to a willingness to receive what is needed. This may come in the form of subtle information from the environment which has not been noticed or as a new way of organizing information, a new mode of thinking. In either case, the shift to the receptive mode "permits a synthesis, a merging of what [the] object mode had kept separate."[9] Any new synthesis must, of course, be scrutinized and tested (active mode), though it still requires a basis in the receptive mode. It is in this way that the balance between the modes is a matter of moving between them in appropriate ways.

We may approach life in a variety of ways. We may take ourselves, human relations and the world at large as encompassed by our routines. This leaves the impression that life/reality is or should be entirely controllable and the promise is that the well-controlled life is the life well-lived. On such a view, the active mode must be dominant. We may, however, take life to be only partially known and only modestly controllable. This leaves the impression that life/reality may require us to explore past the edge of what we know, even beyond established *ways* of knowing. Given such a view, we need not be embarrassed when we admit that we don't know how to think or what to do; we need not be dismayed when life leads us into deep receptivity; we may be open to more than well-known modes of functioning. We can flow between "know" and "don't know," between controlling and allowing.

I turn now to another body of considerations. In some ways they are closer to the surface of human behavior and more immediately recognizable. Certainly they stem from an entirely different kind of investigation than the one that Deikman undertakes. If I am not mistaken, the results are nonetheless continuous with Deikman's.

The developmental psychologist Carol Gilligan has recently argued that the moral life gives rise to two distinct modes of thinking.[10] One she calls the *ethics of justice*, the other the *ethics of care*. Each mode springs from one facet of human experience and both are required for moral maturity: "These disparate visions in their tension reflect the paradoxical truths of human experience – that we know ourselves as separate only insofar as we live in connection with others, and that we experience relationships only insofar as we differentiate other from self."[11] The ethics of justice celebrates the primacy of the individual and separateness. Its ideal is autonomy; the mature individual identifies himself/herself in terms of individual achievement.[12] In contrast, the ethics of care focuses on the primacy of relationships and connectedness. The moral ideal is responsiveness to human needs; the mature individual identifies herself/himself in terms of the fluctuating requirements of relationship.[13] Gilligan insists that these two modes are characterized by theme and not by gender,[14] though she finds that men typically view matters from the perspective of the ethics of justice, while women often adopt an outlook founded on the ethics of care. My view is that balanced individuals are sensitive to both points of view.

The moral life seeks to do good and avoid harm. As Gilligan points out, there are complementary ways of doing this. The ethics of justice focuses on rules, principles, and procedures for the control of the moral life. In practical circumstances, we try to find the relevant rules; in our theoretical endeavors we attempt to formulate them into a coherent, efficacious, and complete moral system which has appropriate foundations. In all of this there is a deep assumption/conviction that impartiality is an essential feature of the moral life and that formulated rules and procedures serve the interests of impartiality.

The ethics of justice can be seen as a natural development of certain familiar childhood patterns of behavior: "Thus Lever extends and corroborates the observations of Piaget in his study of the rules of the game, where he finds boys becoming through childhood increasingly fascinated with the legal elaboration of rules and the development of fair procedures for adjudicating conflicts, a fascination that, he notes, does not hold for girls."[15] I see no harm in a fascination with the development of rules and procedures. It is a legitimate and powerful way of bringing order into our lives. Harm does arise, however, if our fascination becomes an obsession which eclipses other equally authentic ways of functioning.

In marked contrast to the masculine focus on rules and procedures, research indicates that girls tend to engage in games in which the adjudication of disputes is less likely to arise. When conflict does arise they are more likely to avoid it rather than settle it: "In fact, most of the girls whom Lever interviewed claimed that when a quarrel broke out, they ended the game. Rather than elaborating a system of rules for resolving disputes, girls subordinated the continuation of the game to the continuation of relationships."[16] It is in view of this that the ethics of care does not focus on formal rules for the resolution of competing rights or conflicts of interest. Rather, it attends to what Gilligan calls "the psychological logic of relationships."[17] Contextual relativism is emphasized, not impartiality: the concern is on how best to care for oneself and others in the matrix of constantly changing relationships. When functioning in this mode one does not have formulated rules and routines; one draws on the cumulative experience of what human relationships require and the ways they unfold.

Let me summarize our discussion so far. The ethics of justice is formal and stable: it gives us a way of controlling our moral situation through the use of established and impartial forms. In my view, this is an authentic and valuable expression of who and what we are. The object mode of consciousness is dominant in such matters. In contrast, the ethics of care is contextual and fluctuating: it gives us a way of living through our moral situation; it requires that we be sensitive and receptive to the nuances of relationships. It is, surely, an equally valuable and authentic expression of who we are, though it requires a great openness to the receptive mode of consciousness. Before moving on, I want to insist that we do not have to choose between these two modalities. Humans require both separateness and connection; we desire both justice and care; we want independence blended with empathy; compassion with autonomy. We can have it both ways for we contain both within us. We can assert control when it is appropriate and can accept the way that things unfold when that is called for.

The fact is that our culture (our philosophy, our morality, our history, our politics, our economy, etc.) overvalues one modality and thereby diminishes the other. It is this that the research of Deikman and Gilligan suggests. This view is further corroborated by Brian Easlea's discussion of science and nuclear technology in *Fathering the Unthinkable*.[18] He shows that science is marked by the unbalanced assertiveness characteristic of our culture. This is evident in its philosophical beginnings and its current practice.

Easlea weaves a complex story to support his view that the arms race, together with its associated science and technology, is the result of an overly masculine, exaggeratedly aggressive orientation. I wish to limit myself to two of the least controversial features of his position, features which transparently illustrate the perspective I have been developing with the help of Deikman and Gilligan.

One expression of our exaggerated assertiveness is a singleminded and obsessive drive towards control:

Twentieth-century science and in particular the nuclear arms race are obviously phenomena of an industrialized and industrialising world in which the masculine objective of ever-increasing power over nature has been its seemingly inexorable driving force. The ongoing achievement, however, of such ever-greater domination over nature, exacts, as we have seen, a very heavy penalty on its proponents and practitioners. ... The heavy price, of course, that masculine men have to pay for ever-increasing domination of nature is their own self-mutilation as they necessarily proceed to subjugate and conquer the feminine within themselves, such as the need to relate, to enter into dialogue and, above all, to be receptive. What remains after such masculine subjugation and conquest of the feminine is ... the ideal of ever-more powerful masculine mind in ever-increasing control of the rest of the cosmos.[19]

I take Easlea to be drawing our attention to the obvious. The dream of rational control has become a nightmare in a variety of domains. The arms race is but one. Our culture has become so fascinated with the possibilities of scientific control and technical manipulation that we have all but lost grip on the fact that balancing control with receptivity is desirable and possible.

A second indicator of the unbalanced assertiveness characteristic of science is its competitiveness:

I wish to underline the ... remark that it was scarcely in a spirit of co-operation with each other that physicists planned and carried out their attacks on the atomic nucleus but rather in a spirit of intense, competitive rivalry – rivalry for fame, rivalry for the funding that successful achievement helps to attract, and rivalry for the institutional power over other human beings that accompanies the control of resources. The demands of such rivalry allowed little time for physicists to reflect on the wider human significance of their work but rather dictated that the maximum possible working time be spent in attempting to outdistance rivals and so establish a commanding lead in the race to be the first to make that historic breakthrough and to communicate it in print to rivals, colleagues, and the world. The historian of science Spencer R. Weart has summed up this aspect of the matter admirably: "The point of science is to discover things, and it means little to be the second to make a discovery; by universal agreement among scientists the first to publish is the first and often the only one to get credit, so in a fast-moving field much can depend on speed of publication."[20]

It has been said that the pursuit of knowledge often appears secondary to winning the race. Easlea gives several examples from the recent history of science, and the reader may refer to his book for a discussion of them.

I have chosen these two elements of Easlea's discussion because I take them to be integral to the pursuit of science and the development of technology and a natural expression of the object mode of consciousness. The desire for control and a love of competition are not harmful in themselves, but it is evident upon a moment's reflection that exaggerated forms of these may be unfortunate for the individual. We are beginning to realize that when they dominate an entire culture they may spell catastrophe.

Easlea makes a strong case for the view that the unbalanced assertiveness of science reaches its ultimate expression in weaponry that can devastate the planet. It is the story of Frankenstein: the creation destroys the creator. I said above that our culture overvalues assertiveness and diminishes receptivity. But the culture *is* us: Plato would say it is the soul writ large. It is we who threaten ourselves with unbalanced assertiveness. It is we who can avert catastrophe by recovering our balance.

IV

Staggering amounts of money, human energy and human life have been and continue to be dedicated to deterrence. Apparently, it is thought of as a rational way to deal with potential conflict. Now we play the game with nuclear weapons: some are designed for first strike capability, others are retaliatory, and each side plays with enough weaponry to destroy all life on the planet many times over. It is clear that deterrence has become an extraordinary kind of "Russian" roulette – what John Somerville calls omnicide.[21] We hold a revolver to our own and everyone else's head (including that of our opponent) as a way of deterring the other side: justified self-defense transmutes into justified omnidestruction. This does not seem rational. Rather, it seems psychotic, unbalanced.

From time to time we read of analogous things in newspapers. Crazed individuals threaten and sometimes kill themselves along with unjust employers, unfaithful spouses, or ungrateful families in a final fit of fury. We are not tempted to view such individuals as rational or even sane. Suppose now that they threatened to kill all unjust employers, all unfaithful spouses, etc. along with themselves. The greater the numbers the more crazy the behavior seems. Now imagine a counter-threat made by the class comprising all potentially unjust employers, all possibly unfaithful spouses, etc. against all potentially unbalanced individuals. We see here on a smaller scale how bizarre threats made in the name of deterrence really are. If this is the soul writ large, the soul has gone awry, however much politicians, bureaucrats and generals propose it as the epitomy of reason.

Let us leave the matter of *nuclear* deterrence for a moment. What of the basic game itself: is deterrence rational? Social psychologist R. Fisher suggests it as the crudest form of behavior control.

The essence of deterrence – manipulation via threat – is a primitive approach to social relationships. ... It is most easily invoked when we see our opponents as unreasonable, or barbaric, or simple-minded, or as less than human. We resort to threat and punishment with children, animals, criminals, or other creatures who only appear to understand force and violence.[22]

Deterrence is an expression of the least of who we are. It should be our last resort. However, current levels of defense spending in the world indicate that it is given priority.

Worse than its crudity is the efficacy of deterrence – the way it often works out. When I feel seriously threatened, for example, I typically focus on defense. I do not seek improved relationships; I do not seek effective communication; I do not try to solve problems creatively. I react in primitive ways and devote myself to one thing: my defense. This may take many forms but it often includes counter-threats which are likely to primitivize my opponent. As Fisher writes:

The simple point is that threats are typically invoked and responded to in ways that further aggravate the situation. Threats are used when one assumes that the adversary is untrustworthy and hostile. Not only does the threat communicate this, but it may easily invoke the self-fulfilling prophecy that leads the adversary to behave and be perceived in ways that are indeed hostile. The inevitable result is that the adversaries become locked into a vicious and self-generating conflict spiral of hostility and violence.[23]

Threats lead to counter-threats: deterrence leads to mutual deterrence which often leads to violence. This is a mainstream in the recorded history of the human race. The behavior of political leaders recapitulates that of squabbling children.

Against the background of the perspective we developed earlier, we can readily see that the difficulty with deterrence is that it is all give and no take: it is a dramatic and dangerous form of imbalance in the direction of assertiveness and aggressiveness. Recently, this has been coupled with another powerful expression of assertiveness: the aggressive expansion of nuclear arsenals. The logical outcome of this combination of tendencies has been described by Nigel Calder:

When both superpowers are armed to the teeth with "counterforce" nuclear weapons, the danger is not that either side is tempted in cold blood to make his strike, but that both are driven towards it by mutual fear. There may come a moment when, without any malice in your heart, you have frightened your opponent so badly you must hit him before he hits you. [24]

As a short-run, last-resort measure, threats can (as we all know from personal experience) be useful. Deterrence is not, however, a game which can be played for very much longer in the international setting. We must shift our minds to other ways of dealing with each other.

An alternative to the exclusive reliance on deterrence is GRIT or *Graduated Reciprocation in Tension Reduction.* [25] Charles Osgoode proposed GRIT in 1962 as an alternative to unilateral disarmament. Fisher summarizes GRIT as follows:

GRIT is simple and straightforward, and it does not create the vulnerability of complete or major unilateral disarmament. A series of unilateral reductions are planned and announced; these steps are then open to international verification. The steps are graduated, beginning with lower-risk moves; further moves become increasingly significant. However, the initial moves must be reciprocated by some equivalent steps by the other side in order for the sequence to continue. At the same time, the initiator maintains an adequate deterrent and makes it clear that it will defend its national sovereignty and international interest. The initiatives are taken with clear communication and within a considerable time period so as to increase the probability of a positive response from the adversary. [26]

As Fisher points out, such an alternative was successfully pursued by the Kennedy administration in 1963 and resulted in the present ban on atmospheric testing. Social research conducted since that time shows that GRIT is a feasible technique for reducing tension and increasing trust, precisely the opposite effect of a steadfast reliance on deterrence. Fisher recounts some of this research.

GRIT turns on reciprocity: on giving *and* taking: on alternating between assertiveness and receptivity. The genius of GRIT is that it does not require a trust in one's opponent, only openness to the possibility that one's opponent *may be found trustworthy.* It does not require advance agreement on anything. Rather, one undertakes unilateral action to reduce tension and waits for a response. It requires that one flow between "know" and "don't know," between controlling and allowing. In the process, one must suspend the aggressive mindset of deterrence, namely the view that one's opponent is barbaric and criminal, beyond the reach of intelligent and human reciprocity. GRIT is a gesture towards balance, an opening to one's opponent to see if it too is prepared for greater balance in human affairs. To the extent that we are invested in the mindset of deterrence we are committed to our own unbalance. To that extent the enemy is us. GRIT is one concrete way of trying to extricate ourselves from this form of imprisonment.

A more radical alternative to current forms of imbalance is offered by Gandhi's philosophy, in particular, the practice of *satyagraha*. The basis of Gandhi's approach is two fundamental values: *satya* or truth, and *ahimsā* or nonviolence.[27] It is the former I wish to consider. The *satyagrahi* is one who tries to grasp the truth – an attempt which requires, according to Gandhi, an intensive investigation of how to flow between assertion and receptivity in politically demanding circumstances.

The easiest way to understand the significance of Gandhi's views is to contrast them with the way conflict is ordinarily perceived. According to the predominant view, conflict should be *managed*. To do this properly one needs a clear knowledge of one's goal. Secondly, one should be assured that one's goal is justifiable (morally, legally, etc.). In the third place, one seeks clarity about effective means to one's end. Finally the means should also be justifiable in the relevant ways. The central point I want to make is that such a view places a very high premium on *knowing* and managing the conflict from the perspective of what one knows. The second point is that one is prepared to be more or less coercive in the pursuit of one's goal. Since you *know* what you are doing and you *know* that you are justified you must be prepared to press for what you want. Within appropriate limits you must coerce your opponent through argumentation, sanctions, threats, etc., on up to psychological and physical violence. The ideal is to approach the conflict with a great deal of assertiveness grounded on a thorough knowledge of one's own justified position. One knows what one wants and is prepared to "fight for it." It is clear that our culture approves such an attitude and admires those who are successful in executing it. We reward them with positions of great power in all domains – economic, political and military. It may be true that such assertiveness is a natural expression of who we are. However, there are other ways of being and other ideals available as more positive models of human behavior.

According to the perspective of *satyagraha,* conflict should be investigated, not assertively managed from an established perspective. The main concern is to learn the truth about the conflict, something one probably does not have. Indeed, the fundamental assumption is that the conflict itself is evidence that the truth is not fully known. Added to this is the working assumption that one may require the cooperation of one's opponent to fully grasp the truth about the human needs which form the context of the conflict. The presumption is that each side will most likely have precise and elaborate information about their interests – information determined by their beliefs, values, etc. Much of the *satyagrahi's* effort is, consequently, devoted to bringing about the required cooperative investigation. At the heart of this perspective is a deep acceptance and conscientious honoring of the fact that there may be much that one does not know when one is in conflict.

At the same time, there is much that the *satyagrahi* does know. If the conflict is a substantial one and one has been conscientious in examining one's own side of it, one knows that one has legitimate concerns which are being thwarted, that justice is not being done, and that one is justified in pressing for change. To practice *satyagraha,* one must flow between "know" and "don't know." One knows that things are not right and one is prepared to be assertive in one's demand for change (as exemplified by Gandhi's part in history). On the other hand, one doesn't know precisely what will make things right; one is required to be deeply receptive to the information that may be needed to resolve the conflict in a way that will do justice to all relevant human needs.

Horsburgh has captured the complementary attitudes that *satyagraha* requires:

> The Gandhian attitude to conflict is very different [from our normal one]. The *satyagrahi* holds fast to his demands while he believes them to be just. But their justice is not taken for granted or held to have been established. He remains open to persuasion from his opponent, and can even be said to appeal to him to confirm the moral acceptability of what the *satyagrahi* demands. ... The surface rigidity and the underlying flexibility are two aspects of the same unremitting search for truth. ...[28]

According to the perspective already suggested, one must be balanced; one must flow between assertiveness and receptivity. To do this, however, requires a major shift from the mindset of deterrence to that of *satyagraha.* In the case of the former, we see our opponent as barbaric, simple, or unreasonable, as receptive only to threats or violence. In the case of the latter, we appreciate our common humanity. We assume that our opponent has an intelligent and sensitive grasp of its side of the matrix of interests and needs, out of which the conflict arises, as we have of our side. In other words, *satyagraha* requires that we respect our opponent as roughly equivalent to ourselves.

There is still another, more strenuous, requirement for *satyagraha* – the requirement that we respect the truth. In science we have the view that the truth will win out. It is understood that intellectual politics, personal vanity, vested interest, reputation and other things distort the process but "the facts" will eventually resolve conflicts between competing hypotheses and theories. *Satyagraha* shares in this ideology. It holds that the views we have of things, and the underlying beliefs and values, are approximations which may have to be surrendered or transcended in the face of new information – information which is actively sought by investigating the conflict with our opponent. Without this overriding concern for uncovering the truth, *satyagraha* would be just a manipulative technique for getting what one wants. (Nonviolence is often used in precisely this way.) What this means is that one's most cherished convictions may have to be abandoned in the course of the investigation. *Satyagraha* requires great openness of mind – deep receptivity; it also requires that one be highly assertive in conducting the investigation, ruthless even in one's respect for the truth as it unfolds. It invites us to experiment with both parts of who we are and offers us a way out of our current imbalance.

v

In her research, Carol Gilligan finds two visions in the hearts and minds of human beings. One perspective suggests that human relationships are essentially problematic, even dangerous. What is precious, what must be protected, is separateness: personal autonomy and national sovereignty. We protect ourselves from the encroachment of others through various security measures: rules and rights, treaties and arsenals, procedures and agreements. Connection with others always carries with it the possibility of entrapment or betrayal, even loss of identity. One is preeminently safe only when secure *from* others. Affiliation is dangerous; isolation safe. The image here is that of the self as a fortress.

The other perspective is a mirror opposite. Isolation is problematic, often dangerous. What is valuable, what must be attended to, is human affiliation: "The ideal of care is thus an activity of relationship, of seeing and responding to need, taking care of the world by sustaining the web of connection so that no one is left alone."[29] According to this perspective, the central human responsibility is to prevent and to repair tears in the fabric of connectedness. Separation from others always carries with it the possibility of aggression, helplessness, loss of identity. One is preeminently safe only when woven into a web of relationships.

These views call us in opposite directions. Each fits some of the facts of our lives. Our task is not to choose one and diminish the other; the challenge is to work imaginatively with their complementarity. The danger of these times demands an intensive investigation of more of our possibilities. In particular, we must learn more about how we can live together – or we shall extinguish ourselves. We are the crucible in which the stuff of larger life is first worked out. We are the souls which are being written upon the planet at large. We have this kind of creative power. We have this kind of global responsibility.

Wilfrid Laurier University

NOTES

1 Halifax, p. 89.
2 Benson; and Friedman and Rosenman.
3 Deikman.
4 *Ibid.,* p. 70.
5 *Ibid.,* pp. 70-71.
6 *Ibid.,* p. 71.
7 *Ibid.,* p. 73.
8 *Ibid.*
9 *Ibid.*
10 See Gilligan.
11 Gilligan, p. 63.
12 *Ibid.,* p. 163.
13 *Ibid.,* p. 160.
14 *Ibid.,* p. 2.
15 *Ibid.,* p. 10.
16 *Ibid.,* p. 11.
17 *Ibid.,* p. 73.
18 Easlea.
19 See Easlea, pp. 145-46.
20 *Ibid.,* p. 69.
21 See the article by Somerville in this book.
22 Fisher, p. 493.
23 *Ibid.,* pp. 494-95.
24 Nigel Calder as quoted in Regehr and Rosenblum, eds., p. 18.
25 See C.E. Osgood.
26 Fisher, p. 497.
27 Horsburgh, p. 239.
28 *Ibid.,* p. 240.
29 Gilligan, p. 62.

Commentary: Gendered Thinking and Nuclear Politics

ALISON M. JAGGAR

I share Robert Litke's view of the futility of the arms race and agree that both GRIT and *satyagraha* are preferred alternatives to it. I also endorse at least part of Litke's critique of the contemporary science that has developed nuclear technology. I believe that averting nuclear catastrophe requires entirely new ways of conceptualizing and acting on reality, however – ways that must go beyond those endorsed by Litke.

Litke's conceptual framework is conspicuously dichotomous. He presents realities and options in terms of paired opposites: aggression/receptivity; activity/passivity; separation/connection; isolation/affiliation; justice/care; control/sedation; competition/cooperation. The first term in each pair is identified as masculine, the second as feminine. Such categorizations of reality in terms of polar opposites are a common conceptual strategy. They are characteristic not only of the Western philosophical tradition, which opposes mind to body, thought to action, and reason to emotion, but (as Litke notes) are also found in much Oriental thinking. In particular, the Oriental concepts of yin and yang, together with their many correlates (light and dark, dry and wet, and of course masculine and feminine), have become part of the popular counter-culture. An oppositional mode of conceptualization is thus employed by many critics of the status quo, including advocates of some alternative forms of therapy and some approaches to feminism.

Despite the diversity of those who employ such modes of conceptualization, there is considerable overlap between their lists of opposites. Invariably, they separate male from female and masculine from feminine, and list mind, reason, action, culture, and light in the masculine category and body, emotion, passion, nature, and darkness on the feminine side.

Although they conceptualize reality in basically similar ways, practitioners of oppositional thinking disagree in their practical recommendations. Some groups, including so-called cultural feminists, recommend the substitution of "feminine" for "masculine" values:[1] they advocate "returning to nature," "getting in touch with" one's body or one's feelings, "going with the flow," etc. Other groups, including those who have been influenced by Oriental thinking, argue in favor of a "balance" between the qualities and values embedded in the two lists, claiming that each pole in the paired sets is complementary to its opposite. Feminists who advocate androgyny[2] adopt this second position, and so does Litke. He wants us to alternate activity with passivity, aggression with vulnerability, separation with connectedness, and justice with care.

Dichotomous modes of conceptualization have been so fundamental to Western thought that it is often difficult to realize that there are alternative ways of conceiving reality. Even so, some past philosophers have challenged prevailing dichotomies and in recent times such challenges are becoming increasingly frequent. A number of philosophers, for instance, have argued that the mind-body problem is quite insoluble so long as it is framed in the terms of traditional Cartesian dualism, with mind and body construed as completely contrasting entities.[3] Other philosophers have claimed that it is misleading to oppose reason to emotion or thought to feeling, arguing that emotion necessarily involves certain cognitive judgments about the world and that emotional responses motivate and inform our rational understanding.[4]

An uncritical acceptance of prevailing dichotomies has a number of unfortunate consequences. Most obviously, insofar as the paired opposites are gender-linked, it perpetuates stereotypical views of women and men. Typically, for instance, femaleness or femininity is linked with nature, body, feeling, passivity, and a lack of separate individuality. In addition, and on a deeper level, many familiar dichotomies point to generalities which mislead us about the nature of reality. In doing so, they also deceive us about the political possibilities that are available.

Litke's paper, as I have noted earlier, is structured around a copious list of opposites. In my opinion, many of these need to be subjected to critical examination. I cannot do so in detail here, however, and shall conclude with just a few suggestions about places a critical inquiry might begin.

One of the most important contrasts that needs to be investigated is that between the "object" and the "receptive" modes of consciousness. Litke takes this distinction from psychologist Arthur Deikman and employs it in the formulation of his central thesis. A number of questions immediately arise, however. Why, for instance, is conceptual synthesis, which could well be taken as the paradigm of intellectual activity, assigned to the receptive mode of consciousness? (Because it proceeds intuitively rather than deductively?) Why is the assertiveness of object mode thinking identified with aggression and receptivity equated with passivity and even sedation? Although some feminists might be willing to accept the need for a "balance" between receptive and object mode thinking or even to let the former replace the latter, I suspect that a feminist rethinking of these categories would result in new understandings of how, for instance, being receptive is a highly active process rather than a passive condition (feminists acknowledge listening as a legitimate form of discursive participation), and of how self-assertion is a necessary part of genuine cooperation rather than a synonym for aggression. Litke would no doubt accept that this is the case, but one might argue that he overemphasizes the necessity of a "choice" between the object and receptive modes of consciousness.

Another conceptual area that requires careful investigation is Litke's account of science and technology. Within his schema, science is a powerful manifestation of the object mode of consciousness and is characterized as exaggeratedly assertive, its practitioners obsessed with the technical manipulation of nature, and a competitive race for discovery. On this view of science, the development of nuclear technology appears almost inevitable. In support of his construal of science, Litke appeals to Brian Easlea's book, *Fathering the Unthinkable,* in which Easlea, building on the earlier work of Carolyn Merchant,[5] traces links between the rise of modern science in Europe, the resulting destruction of the environment, a new conception of masculinity, and newly repressive attitudes towards women. Easlea claims that the nuclear arms race is causally connected with male dominance and in particular with the sexual division of labor into the "domestic" and "public" spheres.

One of many problems with dichotomous conceptualizations is that there is often a hint of necessity and eternality in the picture they present. They suggest that the universe is constantly swinging between two poles and that health and safety lie in the maintenance of an equilibrium between these poles. The nature of women and men is permanently and irreconcilably opposed. The same assumption of eternality underlies the vision of science presented by Litke. He views science, in a positivistic way, as a transhistorical project and makes a number of generalizations about it. These include the claim that competition and an "obsessive drive toward control" are "integral to the pursuit of science and technology." An obvious implication of Litke's view would seem to be that the only way we can be sure of avoiding nuclear annihilation is by abandoning modern science and technology altogether.

Litke's conception of science and technology, in my view, is not supported by the work of Easlea, even though Easlea certainly does chronicle the competitive, domineering and patriarchal features of modern science. Easlea's feminist scholarship, together with that of Merchant, is indeed highly illuminating about the genesis of modern science and nuclear technology.

However, it is important to realize that both of these authors' works are essentially historical; they describe how science has been conducted in the past, but they do not license any inferences about its necessary conduct in the future. Indeed, if their research carries any implication at all about the what is to come, it is that future science, like the science of the past, will bear the marks of its social origins. The science that emerges from a competitive, racist, authoritarian, and male-dominant society inevitably will be competitive, racist, authoritarian, and male-dominant both in its objectives and in its methods. In a free and egalitarian society, however, we may hope for a science that will not be predestined for nuclear destruction but instead will provide the means for human welfare and liberation.

Litke's dichotomous conceptual framework presents us with limited options: think like a man, think like a woman, or think like each in turn. These options are simply too narrow; they are the options provided by a society that stands in desperate need of radical transformation. We do indeed need to change our consciousness, but we need to do so in ways that go far beyond balancing the modes of thinking that characterize the dominant and subordinate groups in existing society. The thinking of both groups is necessarily shaped and limited by their experience of hierarchy and domination.[6] What we need instead is to develop entirely new ways of conceptualizing social reality and far more imaginative visions of social alternatives.

Such radical changes in consciousness cannot be achieved simply by exhortation. Ways of thinking reflect and indeed *are* ways of life. Only as we engage in the process of political struggle (in both public and domestic spheres) shall we be able to generate new insights into the distortions of the dominant consciousness and new visions of social transformation. Marx once said, in a much quoted epigram, that "The philosophers have only *interpreted* the world, in various ways; the point, however, is to *change* it."[7] In fact, this dichotomy too is specious: the processes of interpreting and changing the world are ultimately inseparable.

Douglass College, Rutgers University and University of Cincinnati

NOTES

1 Jaggar, esp. Chap. 9. Cf. Echols, pp. 439-59.
2 The combination in one person of traits generally associated with prevailing stereotypes of masculinity and femininity.
3 See, for example, Rorty.
4 See, for example, Solomon.
5 Merchant.
6 Jaggar, Chap. 11.
7 Karl Marx, "Theses on Feuerbach," in Marx and Engels, p. 30.

Part IV   Issues to Think About and Discuss

1 Fox argues that "psychological fallout" from the arms race has distorted our thinking and prevented us from dealing with it in a rational way. Find an article in a
newspaper or magazine, or a letter to the editor of either, which manifests the kinds
of distortions Fox discusses, and analyze it in terms of Fox's point of view.

2 Hirschbein suggests that the members of a cult regress to a collective consciousness
marked by "an inability to resist malign authority." Suppose you were employed by
the military and were ordered to push a button which would begin a nuclear war. Would
the authority that issued the command necessarily be malign? Should you push the
button? Would doing so signify a lack of "autonomous thought, morality and
restraint"?

3 Zimmerman sees the sources of the arms race in "anthropocentric humanism," and
calls for us to "go forward in a way consistent with our deepest teachings, philosophical
and religious." On the other hand, us Secretary of the Navy John Lehman has said
that "What is needed today, more than ever, is a firm reaffirmation of the great religious
tradition that has always subtended our willingness to defend our Judeo-Christian
western values[,] ... those religious traditions that alone give our defense efforts meaning and value – and a sense of higher purpose." Can these viewpoints be reconciled?
If we have to choose, which (if either) should we choose and why?

4 "Anthropocentric humanism" yields acquisitiveness (consumption) which in turn
yields destruction of the world around us. Zimmerman derives this causal sequence
from Hannah Arendt, a follower of Heidegger. What do you think of this theory, and
does it have any relevance for the problem of nuclear war?

5 Santoni, like a number of other commentators on the arms race, concludes that standard thinking on the subject is "nuclear insanity." Referring to the features of such thinking discussed by Fox, Zimmerman, and others in this book, explain the considerations that lead Santoni to this conclusion. Is it justified?

6 Litke characterizes the arms race as the product of lopsided emphasis on certain
established modes of thinking. How, according to him, does deterrence demonstrate
this, and what alternatives do GRIT and *satyagraha* represent?

7 Jaggar raises the possibility that a more radical critique than Litke's is needed to explain the arms race – one which exposes our society's basic sexism and shows how the
cultural values it creates have led us to the nuclear brink. State and evaluate the reasoning by which she reaches this conclusion.

Part V   The Pursuit of Peace

Nuclear Arms Control:
Eluding the Prisoner's Dilemma

It hardly need be said that Western doubts about Soviet intentions create serious problems for nuclear arms control. However justified, the suspicion and hostility with which most Westerners view the Soviets does little to enhance constructive arms control agreements. On the contrary, it undermines confidence in the efficacy of such agreement and fosters a defensive attitude which disregards legitimate Soviet concerns. The outlook which reaches its extreme in Ronald Reagan's characterization of the Soviets as godless "monsters" who "reserve unto themselves the right to commit any crime, to lie [and] to cheat,"[1] does not provide fertile ground for arms control negotiations. It is in light of such sentiments that the West has rejected treaties like the Comprehensive Test Ban Treaty and the proposed Treaty of No First Use, and has adopted a policy of "peace through strength."

One way to deal with such an attitude is to argue for a more realistic view of Soviet interests and intentions. There is much that must be said in this regard, though I shall not address such matters here. Rather, I shall discuss the problem of mistrust in light of the "prisoner's dilemma," a classic problem in decision theory which arises in adversarial situations where one cannot be confident of an opponent's actions. It is in view of the antagonistic and competitive nature of the arms race that it apparently provides a paradigm instance of the dilemma and entails the conclusion that a concern for our own self-interest dictates a rejection of disarmament. As Anatol Rapoport suggests, such an analysis encapsulates "conventional wisdom" on the arms race, and illuminates one important aspect of the arguments against disarmament.[2] In order to show that such "wisdom" is misguided – at least in regard to nuclear weapons – I shall argue that any such analysis ignores important aspects of nuclear arms control. If I am not mistaken, the most extreme skepticism about the Soviets, coupled with a complete insensitivity to their international concerns, still entails the conclusion that NATO and its allies should pursue a variety of arms control agreements and a massive reduction in the present size of nuclear arsenals. There is a point at which the question of further reductions may confront us with a genuine prisoner's dilemma, but there is room for substantive disarmament before it becomes a problem.

In anticipation of our examination of disarmament, it is worth noting that the prisoner's dilemma plays an important role in contemporary moral thought. It appears to show that a pursuit of our own self-interest leads to non-cooperation in many situations, and it is the problematic nature of this conclusion that accounts for its importance. It is in light of the social, moral and political implications of non-cooperation, and the attempt by Gauthier and others to derive morality from rational self-interest, that the dilemma has drawn the attention of many recent commentators. We cannot consider their remarks in detail here, though we shall see that a discussion of disarmament can show that what appears to be the most serious practical instance of the dilemma can be straightforwardly resolved. It is equally important to see that disarmament need not be founded on altruistic sentiments, and is a natural consequence of the rational pursuit of our own self-interest.

The easiest way to construct the prisoner's dilemma is through a somewhat shady but straightforward instance of it. Suppose then that you wish to obtain some stolen diamonds from me for a specified amount, say $1000. Given the need for a secret transaction, you agree to deposit a check in my account tomorrow and I agree to place the diamonds in the mail. We both expect that we will never meet again and do not plan any future transactions. Tomorrow comes and you must decide whether you will deposit the check according to our agreement. Considering your own self-interest (which is all that concerns you anyway), it seems best not to deposit the check. Thus I will or will not put the diamonds in the mail. If I do, you will receive free diamonds. If I don't you won't receive the diamonds (which you wouldn't receive anyway), but you won't have lost your money. Either way you seem to be ahead. The problem is that I too am a rational individual and suspicious of your character. I must decide whether or not I should send you the diamonds. If I decide not to and you send your check I will be very pleased indeed. If I decide not to and you don't send a check, I won't have your money (which I wouldn't have anyway), but I will have the diamonds. Either way, I seem ahead. Both of us are rational individuals and wary of each other's motives, so you do not deposit your check and I do not send the diamonds. Our mutual concern for our own self-interest entails mutual non-cooperation, yet this puts both of us in a worse situation than if we both cooperated, for you want the diamonds and I want your money. Here we have a paradigm case where a concern for our own self-interest and suspicion of another's motives seems to make cooperation impossible, even though it would be to both of our advantages. This is one case of the prisoner's dilemma.

To see why the prisoner's dilemma is called the *prisoner's* dilemma, we might consider the standard instance of it. It arises in a situation where two criminals collaborate on a crime, are captured, placed in separate cells, and asked to confess. If neither confesses, they can only be convicted of a lesser offence, and spend a month in jail. If both confess, both receive a reduced sentence of five years. In the case where only one confesses, he or she goes free while the collaborator serves ten years. In deciding for or against confession, each prisoner must consider the likely outcome of any decision. We can represent the possibilities as follows.

	Partner Confesses	Partner Doesn't Confess
1 Confess	*Five Years*	*Freedom*
2 Don't Confess	*Ten Years*	*One Month*

Ignoring any moral obligations that might hold between the prisoners, we can consider the various outcomes from the point of view of the prisoners' own interests (the point of view of "economic rationality"). Taking such an outlook, it appears that a rational prisoner will confess, for this response has the best chance of producing a reduced sentence, taking into account her partner's decision options. If her partner confesses, for example, both will receive five (rather than ten) years, while a decision not to confess will mean no sentence rather than a month in jail. If both prisoners are rational, however, both will confess and both will receive five-year sentences – much more than they would receive if both refused to confess. It follows that cooperation is the best alternative, but an inability to rely on each other's actions entails a less desirable result.

To see how the prisoner's dilemma applies to the question of nuclear disarmament, consider Western nations and their position vis-à-vis the Soviet Union (for the sake of simplicity, we can ignore other nuclear powers in the present context). In deciding for or against disarmament, the West must consider the outcome of its decision as it relates to the decisions of the Soviet Union. From the Western point of view, we can represent the possibilities as follows.

	Soviets Don't Disarm	Soviets Disarm
1 Don't Disarm	*The arms race continues*	*We win the arms race*
2 Disarm	*We lose the arms race*	*Peaceful stalemate*

This representation of the outcomes is in some ways oversimplified, though it suffices for present purposes.[3] Given such an analysis, the rational decision seems to be a rejection of disarmament, for such a choice offers the best chance of a favourable outcome relative to the Soviet decision. If they decide against disarmament, it entails a continuance (rather than the loss) of the arms race, while if they decide to disarm, it allows us to "win" the arms race and the advantages that entails. The Soviet decision for or against disarmament mirrors the Western one, however, and it follows that if both act in a rational way, the arms race will continue. An endless arms race is fraught with dangers and expenses, however, and rather than pursue it, it seems obviously preferable to settle for a peaceful stalemate. It seems to follow that an agreement to disarm would be preferable to the present situation, but that it is not a viable alternative because the West cannot trust the Soviet Union to cooperate (and vice-versa). Given this lack of trust, there seems no way to avoid an escalating arms race, and probable disaster.

To see what is wrong with this analysis, we need to consider its uncritical acceptance of widely held, but problematic, assumptions about the arms race. It assumes, in particular, that winning the arms race is a valuable achievement (because it entails more security, international influence, etc.) and that losing the arms race is against our interest. The intuitions that lead to this assumption are illustrated in a poignant way in one of Daumier's lithographs on war. It shows the leaders of two armies graciously inviting one another to be the first to enter the *Bureau de Désarmement* ("Après vous," "Mais non, après vous," one can hear them say). The implication is, of course, that the first side to disarm will be at the mercy of its opponent. There is no doubt something to this suggestion in the case depicted, but things are not so straightforward when one considers contemporary nuclear arsenals. "Winning" the arms race in this context means having more or technologically superior nuclear weapons, and it is a mistake to assume that the possession of such weapons is in all cases to our advantage. In the original prisoner's dilemma, the value of the prisoner's goal (freedom or as little time in jail as possible) is not open to doubt, but the same cannot be said of the goal of nuclear superiority (or the West's professed goal of nuclear parity).

In order to assess properly the value of nuclear weapons from the point of view of our own self-interest, we must ask ourselves what purpose they serve and how it is best achieved. I shall argue (*1*) that the only rational use of nuclear weapons is for so called "strict deterrence;" (*2*) that such deterrence can be achieved with far fewer weapons than we now possess; and (*3*) that the possession of any other nuclear weapons or the pursuit of their technological development is *against* our own self-interest. I shall, in particular, argue that it is a

BUREAU
DE
DESARMEMENT

Honoré Daumier

mistake to think that our security depends on having an arsenal which is superior or even equal to that of the Soviet Union. The suggestion that we should keep abreast or ahead of the Soviets is founded on a drastic misunderstanding of nuclear weapons, their use, and our own self-interest.

In establishing a rational purpose for our nuclear arsenal, it is important to see that nuclear weapons are in some ways less useful than conventional weapons. There is, in particular, no situation in which it would be in our own self-interest to use nuclear weapons, for a nuclear war is not in our own best interest. Nuclear weapons cannot, for example, be used to achieve a meaningful victory over the Soviet bloc, for the West would be destroyed in the process. As George F. Kennan puts it in his critique of American nuclear strategy:

My opponents seem to see the nuclear explosive as just a weapon like any other weapon, only more destructive; and they think that because it is more destructive it is a better and more powerful weapon. It conforms, in my view, to none of the criteria traditionally applied to conventional weapons. It can serve no useful purpose. It cannot be used without bringing disaster upon everyone concerned. [4]

George Ball has similarly argued that nuclear weapons eliminate war in the traditional sense, and make mutual suicide the only remaining option. It scarcely needs to be pointed out that suicide is not in our own self-interest and it follows that the actual use of nuclear weapons is not a viable way to achieve our ends. Nor can this conclusion be avoided by an appeal to the notion of limited nuclear war, for all the evidence suggests that a limited engagement will lead to all-out war. [5]

Despite such considerations, some would argue that nuclear weapons do serve a "useful purpose," for they argue that they deter Soviet aggression. Such a use is distinct from the use of nuclear weapons in actual combat, and is the professed reason for having and expanding our present arsenal. According to the "official" Western view, nuclear weapons can in this way be used to prevent an actual war. In dealing with such claims, it is important to distinguish "strict" and "general" deterrence. [6] Strict deterrence is the use of the nuclear threat to deter the Soviets from the use of the nuclear weapons they possess. Without some such deterrence, it is arguable that they could use the threat of a nuclear attack or an actual attack to achieve their aims in international affairs. General deterrence is the use of the nuclear threat to deter conventional aggression, and is implicit in the NATO endorsement of the first use of nuclear weapons in Europe. It is this endorsement which is intended to deter the Soviets from conventional aggression on the European front.

The problems with general deterrence are numerous. The likelihood that the first use of nuclear weapons will lead to a full-scale nuclear confrontation makes such a strategy extremely problematic. The risk of destroying Western states (whether or not it is accompanied by the destruction of the Soviet Union) is too high a price to pay for averting a conventional attack. Indeed, NATO strategists have themselves expressed concern as to whether such deterrence is credible, arguing that the Soviets need not take seriously the possibility that the West would risk such damage to avert a conventional attack. [7] Others have argued that such deterrence is not needed. Hence conventional military wisdom holds that an attacking force needs at least a 3:1 margin of superiority to secure victory and independent analyses suggest rough parity between NATO and Warsaw Pact forces in Europe.[8] It is therefore arguable that a sufficient conventional deterrent already exists. Even if this were not the case, there is no intrinsic need to rely on nuclear weapons to deter a conventional attack and it would seem preferable to depend on conventional defense. Finally, the kind of reasoning we shall discuss shows that even the decision to pursue general deterrence does not imply a need for present arsenals and a never-ending arms race.

In contrast to general deterrence, strict deterrence is a plausible defensive strategy. Hence it is not clear that conventional weapons can be used to deter nuclear aggression and the cost of such aggression makes it imperative that it be deterred. Given strict deterrence as the most rational use of our nuclear arsenal, we must ask how we can most efficiently achieve it. It is here that the conventional analysis of disarmament (implied by the prisoner's dilemma) breaks down, for strict deterrence does not require improvements in weapons technology or the winning of the arms race. The ability to destroy the Soviet Union more quickly, more efficiently, or sixty rather than fifty times is irrelevant to such deterrence. As Kennan writes:

My opponents believe that differences of superiority and inferiority, in the statistical sense, have meaning: that if you have more of these weapons than your adversary has, you are in a stronger position to stand up against intimidation or against actual attack. I challenge that view, I submit that if you are talking, as all of us are talking today, about what are in reality grotesque quantities of overkill – arsenals so excessive that they would suffice to destroy the adversary's homeland many times over – statistical disparities ... are quite meaningless.[9]

Admiral Rickover has made essentially the same point.

Take the number of nuclear [powered] submarines. I'll hit right close to home. I see no reason why we have to have just as many as the Russians do. At a certain point you get where it's sufficient. What's the difference whether we have 100 nuclear submarines or 200? I don't see what difference it makes. You can sink everything on the oceans several times over with the number we have and so can they.[10]

Strict deterrence requires enough nuclear forces to make credible the threat of retaliation against Soviet nuclear aggression. It requires technology which is capable of such retaliation. Yet both these requirements were met many years ago and subsequent developments have been at best superfluous, at worst a threat to our own security.

What then is needed for strict deterrence? One way to answer this question is to turn to the present Western arsenal and ask how it can supply such deterrence. Nuclear submarines and the missiles they contain are the best candidates for such a role, for they are not vulnerable to a Soviet "disarming" first strike (a strike which would eliminate our arsenal[11]). Thus the launching of missiles can take place before they are detected, can occur outside the range of Soviet detection systems, and can be followed by an immediate change of location. The necessary visits to port can be staggered to insure that there is no time when a significant portion of the fleet is vulnerable to strikes against submarine bases. The traditional objection to submarine missiles is their alleged lack of accuracy and it is in part this which has led to the development of the Trident and the Navstar satellites which will guide its missiles. The kind of accuracy they will achieve is of interest only in the context of limited nuclear war, however (in the context of counterforce strikes against Soviet missile silos), and unnecessary for strict deterrence. It requires only that we be able to inflict unacceptable damage on the Soviets if they decide to use their arsenal. To see how easily this is achieved without the Trident, we can note that two American Poseidon submarines carry 320 nuclear warheads with the destructive power of 1000 Hiroshima bombs and enough missiles to destroy every Soviet city with a population over 100,000. Given such capacity, the thirty-one Poseidon subs in the American Navy more than suffice for strict deterrence. It immediately follows that the West could retain such deterrence, all the while eliminating the United States' 2000 land based ICBMs, the almost 3000 warheads on B-52 bombers, the American stockpile of 19,000 tactical and intermediate range weapons, as well as the French and British nuclear arsenals. In addition, such deterrence is compatible with the cancellation of the continuing deployment of cruise and Pershing II missiles, the production of Trident I and II, and the planned development of the MX and a variety of other weapons. Even if one chooses to pursue general deterrence, this can be accomplished by the addition of that fraction of NATO's tactical arsenal which this requires. In either case, deterrence is compatible with more than significant disarmament.

In proposing such disarmament, I do not suggest that it be undertaken without any consultation with the Soviets. Indeed, it would be a mistake not to use the opportunity to reduce the size of both arsenals, and thereby make the chance of war still more unlikely. This should not prove a problem, as the Soviets have (at least in recent times) been willing to accept equitable proposals. The problem with recent American initiatives (the "Zero Option" and the START proposals) has been their failure to take into account all Western missiles.[12] Be this as it may, I want to stress that it is a mistake to overemphasize the importance of multilateral agreements. Hence even if the Soviets rejected equitable arms control, it would still be in our interest to reduce our arsenal. To see why, we need consider a number of ways in which the possession of a nuclear arsenal beyond the minimum required is *against* our own self-interest.

The most obvious disadvantage of a more than minimal arsenal is its cost.

It is, in particular, extremely expensive to develop new weapons systems (the MX may cost $75 billion) and one should not underestimate the cost of maintaining present systems. The money used to finance the operation of American B-52s loaded with nuclear warheads (their maintenance, fuel, the cost of training and employing their pilots, etc.) could, for example, be diverted to conventional military uses, social programs, or a reduction of the American national debt. It is worth noting in this regard that military expenditures are not an effective way to provide employment[13] or achieve an increase in a country's standard of living.

A second reason for retaining only "minimal" deterrence is the consequent reduction in the chance of nuclear accidents. The likelihood of such accidents should not be overestimated, but the seriousness of their consequences means that they cannot be overlooked. The US airforce has, for example, admitted at least fifteen accidents involving planes carrying nuclear bombs. On the most serious occasion, a B-52 bomber carrying a ten megaton bomb (approximately 750 times more powerful than the Hiroshima bomb) crashed in South Carolina. The impact of the crash triggered four of the five interlocking safety devices guarding the warhead's trigger.[14] Accidents with B-52s would obviously be eliminated if the proposed plan were adopted, simply because there would be *no* B-52s loaded with nuclear warheads. The same can be said of accidents with the other missiles which would be eliminated, while other kinds of accidents (computer malfunctions, problems with early warning systems, misbehavior on the part of military officers, theft by terrorist groups, etc.) would still be possible, though much less likely.

A third advantage of minimal deterrence is its impact on international affairs. There can, in particular, be no doubt that a reduction in the size of our nuclear arsenal would do a great deal to reduce international tension and encourage other countries to disarm. It is not surprising that one of the most difficult problems with proliferation has been the apparently hypocritical stance of the major powers, who demand that other powers reject the nuclear option, all the while rejecting any meaningful limit on their own arsenals.

A fourth and final reason for rejecting nuclear development is the instability which results from technological development. The naiveté of the notion that technological advancement is to our own advantage can be seen if we consider the case of the Pershing II in Europe. Its prime feature is a speed of over 5000 MPH, which allows it to reach targets in the Soviet Union from points in Western Europe in less than eight minutes. Such a possibility gives the Soviets scant warning in the event that the Americans use the Pershing II (or the new Trident missiles) to attack their land-based ICBMs. Rather than allow the possibility that such weapons will be destroyed before they have time to retaliate, the USSR has threatened to develop launch on warning – a system which would delegate the responsibility for firing Soviet missiles to a computer programmed to detect an incoming attack. This is a worrisome possibility, as the United States has – despite its superior technology – experienced numerous problems with its early warning system. Similar accidents in the proposed Soviet system could accidentally launch Soviet missiles and entail an all-out war. Given that all Pershing II targets were previously targeted by other missiles, the only thing achieved by their deployment is an increase in the possibility of accidental nuclear war. It is hard to imagine anything more antithetical to our own interests.

Another example of the dangers of technological development is provided by the United States' apparent attempt to gain first strike capability. This would encompass the use of counterforce weapons and anti-submarine warfare to destroy Soviet missiles before they can be used. Given early warning systems and a variety of other factors (among them, the finding that such an attack would have irreparable ecological consequences for North America) such a strategy does not seem viable, though the United States continues to pursue it.[15] If present trends continue, American developments may succeed in creating the impression that the United States has first strike capability, but this will have disastrous consequences for international stability. As Frei writes:

> If ... by a preventive first strike, the opponent's capability to retaliate can be successfully knocked out and if both sides perceive the situation this way, they feel a strong urge to launch a disarming first strike. Under these circumstances ... the strategic system is highly unstable. In such a situation, a crisis confrontation is liable to trigger a nuclear war even if the Governments concerned do not intend to do so. It is the simple fear that the opponent might strike first which creates a powerful incentive for each side to keep at least one step ahead on the escalation ladder.[16]

Given the disastrous consequences which would accompany any escalation to all-out war, it is not in our own interest to create a situation in which an international crisis is likely to spark a nuclear confrontation.

Having noted why it is in our own interest to reduce our nuclear arsenal, we may return to the suggestion that a decision on disarmament presents us with a prisoner's dilemma. The crux of this suggestion is the claim that disarmament is a viable policy only if we can trust the Soviets to disarm to a similar extent. It should by now be clear that this is not the case. Hence previous considerations show that reductions in our arsenal are in our *own* interests regardless of Soviet decisions. If *they* wish to spend enormous sums of money adding to a superfluous arsenal (and creating all the disadvantages it implies), this is no reason for us to follow suit. The suggestion that we must match their arsenal is somewhat akin to the remarkably simplistic view (rejected by all businessmen) that a business' success is a function of its ability to match its competitors' technology and the number of their outlets. This is true in part, but there comes a point when such matching is against one's own interest. If a competitor is foolish enough to open a thousand outlets when ten will do, and insists on expensive new technology which is accident prone and superfluous, it would be foolish to follow suit. Yet it is just such mindless matching which characterizes the arms race.

We might finish our discussion by noting that the prisoner's dilemma may arise as a more serious problem for disarmament outside the present nuclear context. I will not deal with the dilemma as it arises in regard to the present build-up of conventional arms, though we should note that it arises when one asks whether the West or the Soviet Union should reduce its arsenal beyond that needed for strict deterrence. Looked at from the Western point of view, the possible outcome of a decision for or against such disarmament can be represented as follows.

	Soviets Don't Disarm	Soviets Disarm
1 Don't Disarm	*Stalemate*	*We win the arms race*
2 Disarm	*We lose the arms race*	*Preferred stalemate*

Such outcomes are superficially similar to those we discussed earlier, though there is a crucial difference. Hence winning the arms race in these new circumstances is not tantamount to the possession of superfluous weapons or technology. Rather, it allows one to have the ability to launch a nuclear attack while one's opponent does not have sufficient weapons for deterrence. From the Western point of view, it apparently follows that a decision not to disarm past the point of minimal deterrence is the best response to either Soviet decision (it leaves us with an advantage over the Soviets or a stalemate rather than a distinct disadvantage). The same reasoning holds from the Soviet point of view, however, and it appears that the rational move on both sides is the rejection of disarmament. Such moves leave us with a stalemate where both sides maintain enough of an arsenal for strict deterrence. This is much preferable to the present situation, yet less preferable to one where both sides continue to disarm (hence the best way to guard against nuclear war, accidents, the expense of armament, etc. is to eliminate both arsenals entirely). It seems to follow that the inability of both sides to trust one another entails a genuine prisoner's dilemma and a stalemate that is less desirable than complete disarmament.

Resolving this version of the prisoner's dilemma is not an easy matter. It may not become a practical problem for some time yet, but it deserves some comment. For present purposes, it suffices to note that the most plausible way to deal with it is to build mechanisms which can eliminate the need for trust, since it makes further disarmament irrational. Crucial to the original prisoner's dilemma was the inability of the prisoners to know their partner's decision. If, in contrast, both partners were telepathic and could anticipate each other's moves, there would be little chance that either would confess, for each partner could anticipate such a decision and act accordingly. Soviet research on parapsychology to the contrary, there seems no way to endow Western governments and the Soviets with telepathy, but there are ways to provide the information needed to judge an opposing country's actions on disarmament.

The verification of present arms control agreements provides at least some of the means necessary for monitoring disarmament.[17] Satellite observation is carried out by both superpowers and satellite photography can, with present technology, distinguish objects as small as one foot in length. Infrared photography allows observation at night, and is useful in detecting camouflage. Multi-spectral analysis is to some extent indicative of what goes on *inside* military buildings. Military activities (the building of missile silos, transportation of missiles to and from launch sites, the testing of new weapons, etc.) are readily observed. Submarines can be detected while in port. Further technological developments could make observation still more accurate, and observations could be enhanced by the formation of the proposed International Satellite Monitoring Agency, which would take observation out of the hands of the superpowers.[18] Ideally, such an agency would take an even broader scope, employing other kinds of observation. The power to undertake site inspections of military bases might be a further possibility.

Most aspects of nuclear monitoring need further development, but one aspect of verification which is already satisfactory is the detection of nuclear weapons tests. Discussions on a Comprehensive Test Ban Treaty were ended by the Reagan administration in 1982, but their claim that verification is impossible does not hold up to careful scrutiny (while the cessation of negotiations violates the Threshold Test Ban Treaty). Atmospheric testing is easily detected, and the alleged difficulties all involve underground tests. Such tests produce huge craters at the test site, however, and these are easily photographed from space. More significantly, seismic monitoring can be used to detect underground explosions as small as one kiloton.[19] Those who have questioned verification have argued that earthquakes would create difficulties, but the number of earthquakes which occur in the Soviet Union is very small and earthquakes produce seismic waves which are distinct from those created by nuclear explosions. Commentators have also suggested that verification might be eluded by holding tests in deep underground cavities mined for this purpose, but such cavities would have to be enormous and their mining would be an immense operation which could not escape detection by photo satellite. Any venting of radioactive debris would be detected by satellite air sampling and detection could be aided by on-site inspections and Western seismographic stations constructed in the Soviet Union – a method of detection to which the Soviets have agreed in principle. The problems with the monitoring of nuclear tests are not technological, but political.

Given our ability to detect nuclear explosions, there is no reason not to adopt a Comprehensive Test Ban Treaty. Trust is not a problem because we can rely on verification rather than trust when we (or the Soviets) question the actions of the "other" side. The exact consequences such a treaty would have for nuclear arsenals or the use of nuclear weapons is unclear, though military experts have suggested that military leaders would lack confidence in weapons that are not continually tested.[20] Much more importantly, an end to nuclear testing would put an end to the further development of a whole range of destabilizing weapons (weapons which represent the most serious threat to peace). The development of other means of verification are equally essential to any attempt to reduce nuclear arsenals beyond the point needed for strict deterrence and more work needs to be done in this regard (particularly when one considers such "undetectable" weapons as the cruise missile). It may nevertheless be said that a focus on verification can provide some of the means necessary to resolve the second version of the prisoner's dilemma.

We may finish our discussion by noting a final aspect of the prisoner's dilemma. I have argued that there is, at least in present circumstances, no reason to think of the question of disarmament as an instance of the prisoner's dilemma. It should nevertheless be noted that there is a sense in which the arms race is, from a *psychological* point of view, a genuine dilemma. Thus governments do believe that there is some advantage to nuclear superiority (and some disadvantage to nuclear "inferiority") and it is for this reason that the East and West seem locked in a never-ending arms race. If the arguments I have presented are correct, these beliefs are misperceptions, though it must still be asked how they can be defused. The psychological aspects of this problem are something I cannot consider here, though there is good reason to believe that suggestions by Michael Fox and others[21] could provide a remedy, and that Charles Osgoode's program of graduated unilateral initiatives could help fulfill this task.[22] Given earlier considerations, it may be said that some such program is essential to the pursuit of our own rational self-interest.[23]   *Wilfrid Laurier University*

NOTES

1 Scheer, pp. 42, 140, 149.
2 Rapoport, "Prisoner's Dilemma," pp. 17-18. See also Russett.
3 If we chose to disarm tomorrow, for example, and the Soviets did not reciprocate, it would be some time before we could be judged to "lose" the arms race, for the Soviets have a great deal of catching up to do. Note also that I use the word "disarm" in a broad sense, indicating any decision not to continue the present nuclear buildup.
4 George Kennan, "Two Views of the Soviet Problem," in Kennan, p. 158.
5 See my discussion in Part I on "Somerville, Gay, and Limited Nuclear War."
6 On this distinction, see Govier, "Philosophy, Nuclear Deterrence and the Real World."
7 On this point, see Govier, *ibid.* The latest incident in this debate was former Canadian Prime Minister Trudeau's suggestion that the risks it implies would prevent any American president from initiating a nuclear war in Europe.
8 See Cockburn, and the Center for Defense Information, "Soviet Military Power."
9 Kennan, p. 158.
10 Center for Defense Information, "Soviet Military Power," p. 9.
11 Though this is, it must be noted, a very remote possibility given the lack of accuracy in the Soviet missiles.
12 The Zero Option does not take into account American, British, and French submarine missiles. The START proposals do not take into account air and sea launched cruise missiles. On both proposals, see Webber et al.
13 A US Department of Labor Study ("The Structure of the US Economy, 1980-85") found that each $1 billion spent on needs like environmental control, alternative energy development, and mass transit yields, on average, 20,000 more jobs than $1 billion spent on military programs. For a short commentary on the economics of military spending, see Russett, pp. 52-54.
14 On nuclear accidents, see Cox, pp. 117-24.
15 See Simon Rosenblum, "The American Search for First-Strike Capability," in "Who's Ahead: The US or the USSR?", in Regehr and Rosenblum, eds.
16 Frei, p. xi.
17 On verification, see Cox, pp. 134-41, and Dahlitz.
18 See Dahlitz.
19 Sykes and Evernden, "The Verification of the Comprehensive Test Ban Treaty."
20 See the Center for Defense Information, "Stopping Nuclear Weapons Explosions."
21 See the selections in Part IV of the present book.
22 See C.E. Osgood; and Litke, in Part IV of this volume.
23 I am indebted to Gordon Graham for comments on an earlier version of this paper.

Commentary: The Deadly Logic of Deterrence

Leo Groarke has masterfully revealed a central myth of the arms race, namely, that it is not a *race* at all. One wins a race by outproducing one's opponent. Yet as Groarke indicates, the continued production of new and superior nuclear arms brings neither side closer to victory. Moreover, it is central to the very notion of a race that it can be won. But as he argues there is no sense in which either side can win the arms race. Without the possibility of victory, arms racing only perpetuates that which it is designed to halt – the very race itself.

We can easily be misled by language and, I submit, the notion of an arms race is a dangerously misleading metaphor. Each side squanders the wealth and labor of its people on new weapons of destruction while it uses these same weapons to hold hostage the civilian population of the other. The stated purpose of this hostage-taking is to deter each other from doing what is already unthinkable, putting an end to civilization as we know it. Meanwhile, the needs of the citizens of the superpowers, let alone the needs of the people of the Earth, go wanting. All of this is described in the playful language of a "race," as though the horrors of a nuclear holocaust are little more than the possible outcome of a harmless game or sport.

As I understand him, Groarke is offering a critique of the traditional notion that the prisoner's dilemma shows that winning the arms race (having more or technologically superior nuclear weapons) is rational, self-interested behavior. He does this by attempting to establish the following points.

(*1*) Strict deterrence (deterring the other from launching a nuclear strike by having a secure nuclear arsenal which would survive an attack and cripple the other in a retaliatory strike) can be achieved with far fewer weapons than we possess at present. Indeed, our nuclear submarine force is alone more than sufficient.

(2) Regardless of our trust of the Soviets or of Soviet intentions, the only rational use to which nuclear weapons can be put is strict deterrence. Extended deterrence (deterring the other from engaging in *any* activity of which we might disapprove by threatening to launch a first strike) raises significantly the likelihood of total nuclear war while strict deterrence does not.

(3) Therefore, contrary to the logic of the traditional prisoner's dilemma, the creation of any new nuclear weapons or even the technological development of such weapons is *contrary* to our own self-interest regardless of Soviet intentions or our trust of them.

(4) However, according to the logic of the prisoner's dilemma, total disarmament would be irrational while the other side still possessed nuclear weapons because of the inability of either side to trust the other.

I find Groarke's proposals to be a vast improvement over the actual practice of nuclear deterrence, yet several questions arise with respect to his central points. While his analysis seems plausible at present, the projected vulnerability of nuclear submarines may alter the situation considerably in the future. Although neither the US nor the USSR has yet attained the ability to detect and destroy nuclear submarines at sea, both are working diligently toward that end. Many experts believe that by the end of the century, if not sooner, both sides will have developed the needed technology,[1] although it must be said that American capabilities are far more advanced than the Soviets' to date. Moreover, the superior nature of US nuclear submarine forces (e.g. the Trident's ability to launch its missiles from virtually anywhere in the world, the fact that any two US submarines are capable of destroying the USSR, and the quieter and technologically superior nature of US submarines) makes it unlikely that the Soviets will be capable of mounting a disarming first strike against our submarines for some time.

There may, however, come a time when technological advances mean that a decision to rely on submarines would leave us vulnerable to a Soviet counterforce strike. Such vulnerability would leave us open to Soviet nuclear blackmail of the sort Groarke fears would befall us if we were to disarm beyond the point of strict deterrence. It is for this reason that the Pentagon has insisted on a tripartite nuclear arsenal which includes warheads on land, sea, and air, and which would make a disarming strike by the Soviets virtually impossible to coordinate. Although Groarke is correct in his claim that strict deterrence can be achieved with nuclear submarines alone, it is unreasonable to believe that that situation will maintain. Of course, this does not mean that the present Pentagon strategy is the best way to deal with changes in the strategic situation, and Groarke might argue that it is in our own self-interest to deal with it in other ways (e.g. by developing sophisticated warning systems to insure that we could not be caught unaware, or by making it clear to the Soviets that we would reintroduce the tripartite system should they continue to develop their antisubmarine war-fighting capabilities.

The second point raises similar questions. Even if Groarke is in fact correct in his claim that a first strike is too dangerous because of the high odds of escalation into total war, the possibility of threatening a first strike still remains. Nuclear strategy is as much a game of appearance as reality. Likewise, the decision to launch a nuclear war will be based as much on opinion as on fact.[2]

Let us suppose that the US is capable of mounting a credible first strike force. That is, suppose the US builds the MX and Trident II missiles, which have obvious first strike capabilities, and deploys the Pershing II and cruise missiles, both of which can be used in a first strike attack.[3] Suppose further that the US government takes a hard line with the Soviets, making provocative statements about its willingness to launch a nuclear first strike, its belief that it can survive a Soviet response, and the inevitability of conflict with communism. We might even imagine dialogue between the superpowers breaking down because of the heightened tension. Notice that the situation I am asking you to imagine bears a strong resemblance to present East-West relations.

Given these circumstances, at times of heightened international crisis the US could threaten the Soviets with a first strike unless they submitted to our will. The Soviets may well submit, as they did in Cuba, whether or not they believe that we can successfully launch a first strike. They might do so because they think we believe we can successfully launch such a strike, regardless of what they know. Either we launch and are successful, in which case they lose, or we launch and are unsuccessful, in which case they lose. In either case, the rational move for the Soviets would be to submit. Groarke might respond that there are alternatives that the Soviets could pursue. The Soviets might not take the threat seriously because of possible bad ecological and economic consequences for the West, including many of our allies. Or they might do what they are already threatening to do, adopt a launch on warning system which would make a disarming first strike virtually impossible. These points I leave for further discussion.

If one begins with the assumption that the deadly logic of nuclear deterrence is rational, it is not obvious that the production of new first strike nuclear weapons by the US is as irrational as Groarke contends. Only if both sides were to agree to a Treaty of No First Use and accept Mutual Assured Destruction (which the US has replaced with Countervailing as official policy) would extended deterrence be clearly irrational.[4] But such a treaty surely requires that we place some trust in Soviet intentions. Hence, Groarke's second and third points can be questioned.

Questions also come to mind about Groarke's last point. Although it may seem irrational to disarm if we consider only the immediate future, it is not clear that such a move is irrational if we project further into the future. While it may not be likely that we will engage in a nuclear war in the next five years, consider the next five decades, or the next five centuries. Consider the possibilities of accident or provocation due to nuclear proliferation; the possibilities of a demented leader or nuclear terrorist launching us into a nuclear holocaust; the possibilities of a lost gamble by one of the superpowers.[5] Ponder the horrors that such a nuclear holocaust would bring.[6] Remember that each new round of arms escalation by the superpowers creates new destabilizing situations and makes verification of arms control treaties more difficult. I believe that it is fair to conclude that the probability of nuclear war between the superpowers has increased since the 1950's and will continue to do so in the future. Polls indicate that few Americans feel that they are more secure now than they were in the 1950's even though we have spent hundreds of billions of dollars on new arms.

Now reflect on the fact that unilateral disarmament will almost insure that a total nuclear war will never occur. Might not the rational move for the US be to disarm slowly while inviting the Soviets to do the same, creating stronger economic alliances with its allies and the Soviets, and making it clear that we will not submit to nuclear blackmail? Why would the Soviets want to attack a disarmed America? There is little point in occupying an economically destroyed, highly radiated nation covered with teams of rotting corpses, and where diseased rodents and insects run wild. This is even more obvious when one considers that the long-term effects of the use of nuclear weapons is likely to have significantly bad consequences for the user of such weapons.[7] Insofar as the USSR is dependent on the US for wheat and economic trade, it is even less likely to attempt to destroy us. Whereas the inital risks of unilateral disarmament may be greater than the initial risks of deterrence, the risks associated with disarmament, once it is accomplished, decline rapidly while the risks associated with deterrence continue to mount in time. The longer we wait to disarm, the more difficult it will be to accomplish, while the more dangerous deterrence becomes.[8]

I find debates about what is rational, self-interested behavior with respect to nuclear strategy to be nonadjudicable and interminable. They prove nothing except how clever we can be in devising imaginary futures. Unfortunately, we can concoct far too many of these imaginary futures to delimit them with available facts even to a manageable few. Yet it is just such nonverifiable speculation which fuels the deadly logic of the arms race and makes us into prisoners of the dilemmas of deterrence. On the other hand, I find it rather obvious that it is morally wrong to use deterrence to hold hostage the innocent noncombatants of the other side – particularly so if it increases the odds that we will be involved in a nuclear war and kill hundreds of millions of noncombatants while ending civilization as we know it. Given that disarmament is a viable option and morally correct, I prefer disarmament to tinkering with deterrence. Like Socrates, I prefer to risk suffering evil rather than to risk doing it, especially if in risking the suffering of evil we diminish the possible bad consequences for humanity as a whole.   *Hamilton College*

NOTES

1 Aldridge, *The Counterforce Syndrome,* particularly pp. 45-55.
2 Scheer and Edward Zuckerman suggest strongly that the Reagan administration and the Pentagon actually believe their own rhetoric about successfully winning a nuclear war with the Soviets.
3 Aldridge, *The Counterforce Syndrome.*
4 See Bundy et al. for the classic statement of the need for such a treaty and what it would entail.
5 Calder explains why these scenarios are not as unlikely as one might suspect – in the present.
6 See Turco et al.,"The Climatic Effects of Nuclear War," for a discussion of the horrifying effects of nuclear war. Also see Turco et al., "Nuclear Winter."
7 *Ibid.*
8 See Lackey, "Missiles and Morals: a Utilitarian Look at Nuclear Deterrence," for a provocative treatment of this line of thought. For further discussion of the risks of deterrence see Bayles' contribution to this volume.
9 I am grateful to the Center for Dewey Studies for the John Dewey Senior Fellowship which supported me during the time this commentary was written.

Getting on the Road to Peace: A Modest Proposal

JAN NARVESON

1 Security, Mistrust and Insecurity

The world's superpowers and their allies currently maintain military establishments of unprecedented power and costliness. If we ask either of them what is the purpose of all this activity, we would be sure to get the same reply: "Defense" or "Security." If we were further to ask, "Security from what?," each would cite as the overwhelmingly major object of concern the other party. Neither has much to fear from anyone else, especially if the possible threateners are considered individually. Even the Russian concern about China is not one to call for the assembling of thousands of megatons of nuclear weapons to combat it. And certainly both the Soviet Union with its allies and the United States with its allies would strongly disclaim any aggressive intentions. The whole thing, they would insist, is for defense, and that's it. Thus what was once known as the War Department in the US government has for decades been called the Department of Defense.

There would seem to be something anomalous about this, if not downright absurd. How could each of two parties go to enormous trouble and expense to arm itself to the teeth against the other if each really believed that the sole reason the other was arming itself was for defense against the first party and no one else? Obviously, there must be some serious misunderstanding or mistrust on the part of at least one. On the part of both, actually; it can hardly be asymmetric. Imagine that Jones seriously mistrusts Smith's intentions, to the point that he equips himself with a revolver, but that Smith doesn't mistrust Jones

Reprinted, with slight changes, by permission of the author and The University of Chicago Press, from *Ethics,* 95 (April 1985). © 1985 by The University of Chicago Press. All rights reserved.

at all – he feels perfectly confident that Jones will never actually use the weapon in question. In that case, Smith will not arm himself in response, one would suppose; and one would further suppose that his refraining from doing so would eventually lead Jones to dismantle his revolver, or at least to leave it at home when a likely encounter with Smith is in the offing. It would be surprising, in the absence of mistrust or misunderstanding, if they did not soon resume normal, civil relations.

Mistrust can be a potent source of misunderstanding, as we know (and vice-versa of course, but the main effect is in this direction). Othello's readiness to believe that Desdemona is unfaithful betrays a strong streak of fear or mistrust. If he loved her in the right way, we take it, his standards of evidence for assessing charges of infidelity would be much more rigorous than the ones he actually employed – if indeed we can ascribe any "standards" at all. In the nuclear age, such attitudes bring with them perils of the worst kind. For a superb illustration, consider the notorious incident which occurred about the time this article was first written. Pilots of the Soviet Air Force, acting on explicit orders from higher up, shot down an airliner with some hundreds of civilians on board. That airplane had been deep in Soviet airspace, having departed from its normal flight path some hours previously, and had flown over some major Soviet military installations as a result. Upon being loudly accused of murder by the Western press, the Russians replied that the pilots had duly attempted to warn the intruder by means of shooting tracer bullets and other maneuvers, attempts that elicited no response from the airliner. Why didn't the pilot respond? Two hypotheses suggest themselves: (*a*) he was asleep, or the attempts were insufficient to get his attention; and (*b*) although he did see the warnings, he was in fact engaged on a spying mission which was of such importance, or would cause such a stink if uncovered, that he was constrained to fake response (*a*) in hopes that the Russian pilots would let him blunder onward and in any case in the realization that he could not permit capture even at the risk of death for all aboard. What interests us here is that the Russians adopted hypothesis (*b*). And this is interesting because that hypothesis is, on any reasonable assessment, incredible. The Americans, as the Russians well knew, fly on spy missions all the time in the area, not to mention having spy satellites all over the place. Moreover, the Soviet authorities are well aware that the American military people knew perfectly well that the Russians were quite capable of shooting down stray planes. And they knew perfectly well that no airplane on a spying mission could conceivably be unaware of the presence of Soviet fighter planes on its tail, and that any pilot attempting, in the circumstances, to fake it would have to be literally insane. In short, hypothesis (*b*) was completely incredible, whereas hypothesis (*a*) was certainly likely – to err, after all, is human, and straying was by no means unprecedented even if this was a more extreme case than usual. Nevertheless, the Russians stuck to the incredible story in preference to the credible one, and so persistently that one began to suspect that they actually believed it. In their minds, it seems, intruders on Russian airspace are assumed to be guilty until proven innocent beyond the shadow not only of a reasonable doubt but even of a quite outrageously unreasonable one.

Behavior of the kind illustrated by the Russians in this incident sends a chill down Western spines, and for good reason. Contemporary weapons systems are enormously complicated, but are operated, ultimately, by fallible humans. The possibility of error is inevitably appreciable. But the consequences of misinterpreted error, in the most important cases, are unfathomable. Thus the need to make allowances for the possibility of errors, to anticipate them and build in safeguards against rash response, is paramount. If the Soviet response in the airliner case is indicative of their standard frame of mind, then how is any sort of "security" to be possible in present technological circumstances?

What are we to think of those who exemplify, and still worse those who instill, such sets of mind? Our first impulse might be to write them off with a modishly clinical adjective: "paranoid." And no doubt the history of Russia provides some support for that description. But doing so seriously has two disadvantages. In the first place, the label is widely taken to be pejorative, and for good reason; but it can hardly be useful in the promotion of peace with another party to write him off with a pejorative label, especially in public. In the second, paranoia is a pathological condition, and the implication of such a diagnosis would be that there isn't much you can do with such people. And that attitude is dangerous. Moreover, I suggest, it is unjust.

It is unjust to assume that anyone is evil who cannot prove innocence beyond the shadow of an unreasonable doubt. It is also unjust to assume, without extremely good evidence, that he is irrational. Reason requires that we presume that those we deal with are not malevolent and not irrational. It does not require that we love them or share their ends; it does require that we not hate them, or at least that we refrain from acting as though we did. And it requires that we respect their right to pursue their ends so long as such pursuit is compatible with our pursuit of our own; and where it is not, that we be willing to negotiate on terms of moral equality regarding the division of concessions from our maximally preferred courses of action. It requires this because we will all be worse off if we act as the contrary assumptions would impel us to act. If I assume that you are out to get me by whatever methods you can as soon as you can, my obvious move is preemptive attack. If you assume that I have made this assumption, your obvious move will be pre-preemptive attack. And so on.

Of course the presumption is rebuttable, so the question is rebuttable. How?

A fair amount of military thinking proceeds on the "worst-case" maxim: assume the worst, and prepare for that. Military thinking concerns our dealings with known enemies, and within limits there is a certain rationality to making such assumptions when we know that. But when we deal not with known enemies, people who are known to be intent on killing us because they have already tried very hard to do so, but instead only with those who have differences of ideology or perceived interest, the worst-case assumption is quite another matter. In the worst case, my dear and good friend Bill would suddenly turn into a homicidal maniac, or it would suddenly become clear that he has for all these years been intent on my ultimate ruin, pursuing this with surpassing ingenuity that has deceived us all. Should I, then, shoot him now, just to make sure? Should I even be on my guard every moment, lest the dire issue of this worst case come about? After all, I cannot claim to know, for certain, that he won't do this. The epistemic situation here is merely that I have absolutely no reason to think that he will. This, however, is not the only reason for me to shun any behavior based on the hypothesis that he might, nevertheless. For there is also the fact that if I were to take up this strange stance – a slight stiffening, say, when Bill comes into view ("Uh-oh – does he know about the cleaver in the lower right-hand drawer of the kitchen cabinet next to the dishwasher?") – then I would be behaving in a way that invites Bill's fear, doubt, and suspicion. But he's my *friend,* for god's sake! Behavior of the type reasonably motivated by the belief that he is about to kill me, in addition to being idiotic under the circumstances, is also poisonous, insidious, intolerable. Who would want to live the sort of life called for by continuous application of "worst-case" reasoning at this level? How long could any friendship endure on such terms?

Now reason does not require that we be "friends" with, say, the Soviet Union. But there is an idea of "friendly relations" among States that doesn't really involve anything quite so personally commitive, and it is not unreasonable to suggest that friendly relations in that sense ought to be the norm in international dealings. We should not get hung up on verbal niceties. Whatever the minimal norms of international relations should be thought to be, it should surely be obvious that pointing large numbers of thermonuclear-tipped missiles at Nation x is not compatible with having such relations with x. That behavior invites fear, suspicion and response in kind; and the invitation has, unsurprisingly, been accepted. There is ample reason to think that American (or more generally, NATO) military policy in the years since the Second World War has been dominated by worst-case reasoning. We ought to ask whether such reasoning is justified in the circumstances that have prevailed since then.

It could be suggested that we are engaged in a zero-sum game with the Soviets, and that in such games, worst-case reasoning is, as is well-known, the *sine qua non* of rationality. It could be suggested, and one sometimes sees things in print that reflect such beliefs: but the suggestion is outrageous. Perhaps "we" are in some sense in "competition" with the Soviet Union – people talk about competition for the hearts and minds of the people, and that sort of thing – but the talk is loose, and when zero-sum is in question, it isn't just loose, but utterly wrong-headed. If I think that you are horribly in error about issue P, and I lose in my argument with you, your "gain" is, if I am in turn unconvinced, not my "loss," it's *yours,* or at least yours as well as mine. You are worse off for continuing in your wrong opinion, not I. The people of the Soviet Union are no doubt cursed with a miserable political and economic system, but that fact isn't an advantage to us, and failures to persuade them to change it are continued losses for them *and* us: if we were to win this ideological "battle," they wouldn't lose, they'd win! And if the Russians were to vaporize all of us with thermonuclear explosions, how would that be a gain for the program of ultimate world communism?

Of course the stakes in the nuclear era are very high, and with exceedingly high stakes, aversion to risk is indicated; and when it is, then worst-case reasoning begins to look better. What is at stake is the lives of hundreds of millions of people, or perhaps everybody; and they are "at stake" only because there is a threat by our supposed enemies to obliterate them all with H-bombs. But "because" implies "if"; *if* there is a real threat of that kind, then possibly a deterrent strategy designed to put them off from carrying it out is required. But what if there isn't a real threat, or rather, what if there wasn't such a threat, but the assumption that there was motivated us to engage in a form of behavior (acquiring an enormous nuclear weapons capability) that gave them very good reason for thinking that *we* were a threat, and their reasonable response to that now very real threat brought it about that they now are also such a threat to us?

And then another factor enters the situation. For once the nuclear arsenal reaches the level it reached a decade or so ago, there is now a risk of accidental employment. This risk is, one supposes, roughly linear with the size of the arsenal: so the more we try to reduce the risk of intentional use of these weapons by the other side, the more we increase the risk of accident. And that risk is going to stay around so long as the arsenal itself does, even if the real risk of intentional use is nonexistent or even always was nonexistent. Worst-case reasoning makes things worse, in short, and could make them so much worse that one wished one had never started thinking that way in the first place.

2 Two Views of Soviet Actions

Clearly, a rational defense depends on a rational appraisal of the sort of threat that exists. And that threat, in turn, must be presumed to be rationally motivated on the part of the presumed threatener, or else one must have very good evidence that the threatener is not rational, in specific ways. Now one hypothesis on the borderline between these two is that the opponent in question likes war. For there are individuals, and there have existed whole tribes and cultures, who positively preferred war to peace, or so it seems. If so, it is a preference that most of us, I imagine, do not very well understand. The sort of life afforded by the peaceful conditions such individuals visualize as the only alternatives to war must have been very dull indeed, or very miserable, to sustain such a preference. But be that as it may, the stakes in the present situation of the world are such as to eliminate any conceivable rational preference for war. Indeed, as has often been pointed out, nuclear war isn't really "war" as mankind has hitherto known it. Where is the sense of war in pressing a few buttons which will result in the impersonal extermination of millions of people with literally no possibility of defense other than a threat to do likewise? How could this engender the sense of camaraderie or courage, the elation of physical movement under danger, and such other goods as wars have no doubt afforded to at least a good many of those who participated in them on the battlefield? The prospect of nuclear war is of such unmitigated evil that one can only assume profound ignorance or lack of imagination on the part of any who might be animated to foment it by these obsolete martial motives.

Obviously the publicly professed motivations of the superpowers are entirely contrary to any such bellicose attribution of intentions. Both loudly proclaim the virtues of peace, and not just peace on their own ideal terms, but peace in the sense of coexistence with the other party. And while we cannot of course simply take their word for it, there is surely good reason to think that neither of them has any interest that would be promoted by full-scale war, nuclear or otherwise. In the case of nuclear war, there is, for one thing, the question how you go about "building socialism" (in the case of the Russians), or "building democracy" (in the case of the Americans) in an area rendered uninhabitable, as well as uninhabited, by a surfeit of H-bombs, even supposing that on one's own side one had anything left to do the building with. But conventional war also makes no sense for either. The stupefying costs involved, even if one were on the "winning" side, would render it a bad bargain for either one even if one didn't count the cost in lives, which would surely be staggering. And there are special reasons as well for doubting that the Soviet Union in particular could rationally contemplate a major war even if it could be confined to conventional weapons. It has been pointed out, for example, that it would be impossible for it to avoid reunifying Germany if it won such a war, and that the last thing the Russians want is a reunited Germany, socialist or no. These are of course questions of political fact, and I do not pretend to be an expert on such matters. But we surely owe the matter serious consideration: few students of the situation would dispute the general point, that even a conventional let alone a nuclear large-scale war is not in the interest of either of today's great powers.

Well, if there are only two "sides," and if both of them have nothing to gain from war, then why isn't there peace? Or rather, why isn't there a far less dangerous condition of non-out-and-out-war than the current situation? It must be that neither side really believes the other's professed interest in such a peace, since otherwise their current behavior would be completely irrational. So the question is, why don't they? And is it naive to believe that if the causes of the current uneasy situation can be found, then a less dangerous and expensive peace would be possible? Well, perhaps it is. But it is difficult to see what else there is to do but hope that it is not and press on.

We must, then, seriously address ourselves to those causes, with a view to asking ourselves what we can do that offers a reasonable prospect of improvement. We want to know the answers to two general questions: (*1*) Which Soviet actions constitute a reasonable cause of distrust, and what is the appropriate way to deal with them so as not to increase reasonable Soviet suspicion of the Western alliance? (*2*) Which Western actions constitute a reasonable cause of distrust on the part of the Soviet Union, and what alternatives might prevent such distrust from developing? (By "actions" here I of course mean to include policies and long-term trends as well as isolated or small-scale incidents.)

In general, the answer to question (*1*) is, apart from a few details, fairly easy. First, since the Second World War, the Soviet Union has acted to establish a ring of "buffer" states around its borders, insofar as possible, seeing to it, by force of arms or threat of such force where necessary, that only regimes under the thumb of the Soviet Union ruled in those states. (We may take it that Afghanistan is a further case in point.) And second, though obviously closely related to the first, the Soviet Union has consistently maintained a very large military establishment, in conventional and later in nuclear terms. Its conventional complement has consistently been maintained at an extremely high level; in particular, following the close of hostilities in 1945, the American army rapidly demobilized, whereas the Russian army repaired its war losses and maintained its size. The first of these facets of Soviet behavior led Americans to conclude that the Russians were embarked on a program of world conquest, presumably to spread socialism to all corners of the globe; the second backed up this conclusion, which was also reinforced by traditional Russian secretiveness and what was perceived, at least, as diplomatic intransigence. In short, the Soviet Union was perceived as a dangerous, militaristic imperialist power whose evil designs had to be met with re-establishment of American and European military power.[1]

Was this American construction of the postwar situation borne out by the facts? Possibly not. For there was, and is, a rival hypothesis: these Soviet actions can be construed as genuinely defensive in nature rather than essentially offensive, as the West, led by the Americans, supposed. The US enjoys excellent relations with its immediate neighbors, by world standards anyway, and has (a few overenthusiastic critics to the contrary notwithstanding) shown no tendency, of late anyway, to try to tamper with the internal politics of either Canada or Mexico, nor has it deployed significant military forces near its continental borders with a view to shoring up its security against them. The same has, happily, been true of Western European countries since the war. These facts undoubtedly contribute to American inability to contemplate this tamer hypothesis about Soviet intentions. We interpret moves to subvert neighbors as threats to *world* peace; but perhaps the Soviets see them as entirely reasonable means of securing its own borders against potential aggression of which, goodness knows, Russia has seen plenty in its history. It has also engaged in plenty of its own, of course, and this is a factor not to be ignored. But it is consistent with the facts, without stretching things unduly, to take it that Soviet movements in relation to border states have been essentially defensive. And the "American" hypothesis, as we might call it, does have one or two important counterexamples, notably the case of Finland, which has maintained its independence when the Russians could surely have subdued and occupied it militarily if that is what they really wanted to do; nor is Finland by any means a socialist state.

I am not saying that we should routinely accept the idea that one may secure one's borders by militarily subverting the governments of neighboring states when the latter themselves show no evident sign of hostile designs (and are in any case in no way capable of carrying them out!). Obviously this is unacceptable. But, quite apart from *tu quoque* arguments[2] we can surely take the view that the time for appropriate counter-action to the coups in Czechoslovakia, Hungary, and so on is long past, and that the situation has escalated to a vastly different level now. The point is that Russian actions may well be viewed in a way that makes sense *and* presents us with a much different, and distinctly less uncomfortable picture of the world situation. If Soviet intentions really are basically defensive, even if their view of what constitutes "defense" is rather strong stuff by our standards, that fact would have enormous implications for world security at the nuclear level. But first let us turn to the other of my two questions.

What Western behavior is occasion for reasonable distrust on the part of the Soviets? In part, they point to the past, citing such things as the sending of armies to aid the White Russians during the Bolshevik Revolution. As against such incidents, the West can reasonably respond, first, by pointing out that America contributed quite substantially to the Russian war effort against the Nazis, and second with a *tu quoque*: Russian military assistance, including the use of Soviet military personnel, has been frequently invoked in the recent past to shore up governments believed friendly to the Soviet Union or to assist revolutionary activity of types approved by them. More seriously, the Soviets can point out that the Americans have frequently been in the lead in the acquisition of nuclear arms. They were the first to build an atomic bomb, the first and still the only party to have used one in wartime, first with the H-bomb, first to develop the MIRV, and in the early stages of the nuclear arms race their stockpile of weapons was (as is now publicly known) very much greater than that of the Soviet Union.[3]

Of these, the second is much the more serious. On the hypothesis that Russian intentions are fundamentally non-defensive, Western (especially American) military activities in the nuclear sphere make a certain amount of sense. But on the lesser hypothesis, they decidedly do not. Let us try to frame a reasonably accurate global picture. For more than two decades after World War II, Russian conventional military forces were of a size that conceivably might, with some plausibility, be thought capable of supporting an invasion of Western Europe. It was this prospect that was always called upon to justify the development of battlefield nuclear weapons by the West, and for some time perhaps to have motivated the main strategic contingent of nuclear weapons as well. But in the recent past, it has been shown that the supposed immense superiority of Russian conventional forces simply does not exist.[4] It has also been argued that it never has existed, for that matter, but this does not concern us so much here.[5] What does matter is that Russian conventional strength has been enormously exaggerated, and Western weakness similarly overdrawn, so as to justify Western arms increments. Yet at the same time, it is commonly accepted that in order to mount a conventional invasion with good prospects of success, a great superiority in numbers and equipment is required, and not merely something approximating parity, which is at most what currently obtains. But if Russian conventional strength is in fact only sufficient for defending the Soviet Union against invasion from without, rather than sufficient to mount an invasion against Western Europe, then the hypothesis that Soviet actions are motivated by considerations of defense rather than more aggressive ends squares with the facts better than the hypothesis that seems to have attained cliché status in America. Under the circumstances, the American refusal to embrace a policy of no first use of nuclear weapons is evidently unjustifiable. That policy, indeed, constitutes prima facie evidence of aggressive intent in the eyes of the Russians. I suggest that the reason it strikes them that way is because it *is*.

How do we choose between these alternative hypotheses? I have already inveighed against worst-case reasoning both as a general rational strategy and in the present situation. In the light of the above considerations, "worst-case" would seem to be indefinable – what's the upper limit if irrational actions are envisaged? But trying to fix the worst rational case, the worst sort of thing our presumed enemies could do to us insofar as they are rational agents, depends upon our assessment of their goals. It cannot sensibly be attempted independently of such appraisals, since doing the worst with what they have is too insane to be worth contemplating as a possible course of action for a rational agent.

What we need is to select the appropriate response to actions lying within a spectrum that can reasonably be thought to include Soviet intentions, given purely defensive intentions on the part of the West. This is a fairly complex problem when one does not know precisely where those intentions lie, and especially when one's own actions are likely to influence those intentions. However, one would think that two guiding principles ought to be followed. (*1*) One should have a defensive capability that would be sufficient for mounting a defense against any probable aggression – if there is any such. (*2*) One's actions should be such as (*a*) to make it clear to the putative enemy that they are purely defensive, and (*b*) to make it possible for it to respond to one's actions in such a way as to confirm a hypothesis that its actions are likewise purely defensive, if they are – and on the other hand, to be clearly identifiable as aggressive if that is what they are.

In adumbrating these principles, I am of course assuming that a clear distinction between "defense" and "aggression" is possible. And it may be agreed that the distinction is not always easy to make out. That this is so is, actually, part of the motivation behind my formulation of (*2b*): for it may be that some possible actions would be ambiguous and others clear, and that some among the clear ones would be clearly defensive. In those cases, (*2b*) is intended to call upon the actor to choose the latter rather than the former. But I do not propose to try to analyze the notions of defense and aggression here. For my major purposes in this essay, a refined notion is unnecessary; so this can be left for another occasion.[6]

3 Options

It has become customary to distinguish four general nuclear strategies, as follows:

(*1*)   Superiority, or first strike capability: enough nuclear weapons to destroy the other side's nuclear capability at a single blow;

(*2*)   Parity: roughly match the other side's nuclear force;

(*3*)   Minimum Deterrence: enough strategic nuclear capability to make the launching of a first strike by the other side too unprofitable to contemplate;

(*4*)   Unilateral Nuclear Disarmament: dismantle all nuclear weapons, retaining only conventional forces.

The proposal to be advanced in this essay differs from all of these, lying somewhere between (*2*) and (*3*). By way of arguing for it, let us begin with a brief review of each of the four as characterized above.

(*1*) Little needs to be said about Superiority. It is generally thought to be impossible, and certainly thought not to obtain at present on either side. Given that it does not, then the attempt to attain it is exceedingly dangerous. If A is known to be working on a system capable of achieving that level by time t, then there is a motivation on the part of B to launch a preemptive strike at t_x, where the degree of nervousness generated among all parties approaches infinity as x approaches zero. And even if attainable, the condition of superiority would surely be at best temporary. If anything is agreed upon by serious students of these matters, it is that the policy of Superiority is tantamount to suicidal insanity. (One reflects grimly that American policy in recent years smacks rather too strongly of this folly.)

(*2*)   The official stance of each side today, no doubt, is Parity. Just what the rationale of parity is, is hard to say. It must be that the leaders of the superpowers today, and probably their publics, attach intrinsic significance to this. If A has more nuclear weapons than B, then A is a Greater Power than B, and being a Great Power is a Good Thing. But neither of these propositions will survive a moment's reflection, once we delete the upper case letters. Taken in and of itself, being a great power is not a good thing: it is, instead, expensive, dangerous, and downright silly. And having more nuclear weapons than the other fellow is only a sign of being able to kill more people than he can; if that qualifies one as a "great" power, then one's criteria of greatness are in need of serious re-thinking. In any case, there is a problem about making Parity a strategic goal. To begin with, nobody knows what it is. There are many measures of nuclear strength, and by different measures, different superpowers are today stronger.[7] One could in principle negotiate an agreement about what constitutes parity, but it would be arbitrary. Much worse, however, is that it would be unstable. The history of armaments negotiations in the recent past makes it eminently clear that an agreement specifying all sorts of levels of this and that type of hardware is treated by each side as an invitation to redouble one's energies at increasing the items *not* specified, and to fudge on every imprecise variable in the agreement. To aim at Parity is, for all practical purposes, to aim at continuing the arms race.

(*3*) Minimum Deterrence as a goal has its attractions. The main problem is that it is scarcely possible to identify it. One thought is that when you can wreck the other party's country totally, then that is enough if anything is. But perhaps twenty-five percent of his country is enough? How do you find out – *ask*?

(*4*) Unilateral Disarmament also has its attractions. It certainly rates an essay in itself, and so the present very quick dismissal of it should not be taken as a sign of contempt for it. What we can certainly say immediately is that it is politically impracticable: the public in Western Europe and the US is simply not about to do it, and any politicians advocating it seriously will soon find themselves out of office, we may be sure. (The British Labour Party did find itself out of office in the last British elections to a fair degree because of this very policy.) Apart from that, there are the usual questions about nuclear blackmail, although it is by no means clear how plausible they are. And there is a severe moral issue about whether it is not the only legitimate policy from the moral point of view. Without argument, I am going to assume that that is not so or at least not so obvious as to make other options not worth exploring.

It should be noted that all of the options discussed here are *unilateral*. Obviously one option always open is to attempt to negotiate mutual disarmament, and everyone hopes that this will eventually happen. But that's just the point: that it will happen is, strictly, a "hope," and advocating a policy of negotiated disarmament is equivalent to advocating no policy at all. The question is how we can make it likely that attempts at negotiation would have a useful result, and that is a question about unilateral policy. The option I propose is a unilateral one, and among its main virtues, I believe, is precisely that it would set the stage for stable mutual disarmament.

4 A Modest Proposal

What would the military establishment of a state concerned solely with defense look like? The answer, in principle, is in fact quite simple: *it would look distinctly less formidable than that of its opponents,* those against whom the agent in question sees a need for defense. If B, the "enemy," has various amounts of various kinds of military hardware and personnel, then A, our agent, will make sure to have less than that in each category, or in each relevantly corresponding category. There is one exception. Some weapons might be purely defensive. Anti-tank wire-guided missiles, for example, are apparently of no use for any purpose except to destroy tanks, and tanks are offensive weapons par excellence. A's tank force should be decidedly less numerous than B's, but we can allow A enough of these purely anti-tank weapons to provide against any invasion B might wish to mount with the aid of tanks.

Against nuclear missiles there is no "defense" as yet, although the Americans have recently had some luck with a true anti-missile missile. We will neglect, for present purposes, the possibility that such a weapon can be perfected and deployed in sufficient numbers to constitute a genuinely adequate defense against ICBM attack. Setting that aside, then, my proposal would have A opposing B with a *clearly inferior* force (quantitatively)[8] by *any reasonable measure* of nuclear force. By what margin of inferiority? It does not very much matter, in principle, so long as it be clear.

What is the rationale? Two different considerations converge here. First, aggression requires superiority. Inferiority, when clear and marked, is thus a guarantee that one is not planning aggression. At the same time, since inferiority is sufficient to defend against aggression when that agression is conventional, and to deter (if anything will) when it would be nuclear, this means that our hypothetical agent would not be unduly exposing himself to risk. Second, and equally important, this stance offers a clear inducement on the part of an opponent who claims to be acting defensively to reduce his military establishment in turn. Obviously, the extreme limit of this is mutual total disarmament, since if both parties make a point of arming themselves less than the other one, they must soon run out of arms to scale down. At some point short of this, however, the parties would achieve a level that is obviously insufficient for aggression, and at that point we have solved the problem this essay is concerned with. If every country in the world had an armed force no larger than Canada's, for example, then no country much larger than, say, San Marino would have anything to fear from any other.

My proposal has been crudely stated, to be sure. For example, a state might have more than one enemy, poised at very widely separated places along a very long border – the Soviet Union is an excellent example of this. Presumably this would justify making its total forces larger than those of any one of its enemies, even if the forces positioned against any one of them were appreciably smaller. We should have to make allowances for that. But, then, the context concerning us now is the situation in Western Europe in particular. NATO forces have been claimed to be much inferior to the Warsaw Pact forces opposing them, and this has been invoked to justify nuclear weapons and the refusal to adopt a no-first-use policy. It is decidedly not clear that Western forces are inferior in conventional terms to the Soviet forces relevantly opposing them, and obviously unclear that American nuclear forces are inferior to the Soviet nuclear armada. My principle would require a substantial unilateral reduction in the latter, and a careful appraisal of the former to see whether reductions might be in order. They probably are. But what do we do about the deployment of military forces in distant places where various alleged threats to American "security" may materialize? These too are problematic, and since the claim is that those who pose the threats are definitely not committed solely to defense, my proposed principle has no ready application there – except that it would call for a close and sympathetic analysis of the attributions of hostile intent we perhaps too readily make in those cases as well. For that range of cases, we need a sensitive principle about interventions, the limits of military support to friendly regimes under threat, and so on. I do not claim to have produced any such principles here.[9]

But the general principle proposed does seem to me to have application to the major context of the arms race, especially the nuclear arms race, between the major powers of today. This principle presupposes, of course, that our motives really are defensive only. Is it possible to defend the implied value-judgment: viz., that the only legitimate cause of war effort is to defend against threatened aggression? When the "war effort" we are considering consists in nuclear deterrence against nuclear threats, the case is surely easy to make. It is necessary only to appeal to the long-term self-interest of all concerned: mutual nuclear devastation must be worse than the mutual non-attainment of domination, revolution or whatever might otherwise be aimed at in any possible war between today's great powers.[10] Since that is scarcely deniable, it behooves us to do whatever necessary to avoid any such eventuality. Doing this requires renunciation of any ambitions beyond those of defense, and it requires them of all parties. But the implementation of peace in circumstances of international mistrust requires a careful gauging of others' intentions, rather than a cavalier attribution to them of aggressive aims; and it requires that we give others no good reason for attributing such aims to us. The principle suggested here is the only one I can think of that does not involve extravagant idealism or at least the appearance of it, and yet offers a clear way to the relaxation of tensions. Any other non-idealistic alternatives will leave us where we are: with an arms race whose dangers will increase with each successive wave of "improvements," ending who knows where?[11] Operation on the proposed principle will match our military deeds to our oft-reiterated words: viz., by being demonstrably confined to legitimate, defensive ends. This would seem to be both the most and the least that can reasonably be asked in a difficult world.[12]   *University of Waterloo*

NOTES

1 See Herkin for a full account of American attitudes following the war. For the development of such attitudes during the war, see Sherwin. For a synopsis of the Russian situation, see Ground Zero, *What About the Russians – and Nuclear War?*

2 See Powers, Chap. 15, "The Moral Fallacy," in which there is a superb series of "What About?" questions of the kind "What about Afghanistan?", "What about Vietnam?" – and so on. See pp. 118-19.

3 I presume I am speaking from common knowledge here, but a useful storehouse of

relevant information for all these claims may be found in Prins, ed., Chaps. 2-4 in particular.

4 See Prins, ed., pp. 178-79. More impressive is Cockburn. Chap. 6 in particular analyzes strengths numerically; the book as a whole gives a most interesting picture of the Soviet military machine, one which overwhelmingly disconfirms any idea that the Soviet army could overrun Western Europe in a matter of days. It would apparently have grave difficulties overrunning it in months, against no opposition whatsoever!

5 See Cockburn, p. 101.

6 One can hardly do better than consult Walzer, especially Part Two, pp. 56-126.

7 See the Harvard Nuclear Study Group, Chap. 6, pp. 115-32, for a thorough explanation.

8 Qualitative comparisons are another matter. It is evident that one cannot require a state to make inferior equipment when it could make superior equipment. Evident, too, is that the factor of personnel quality is of decisive importance. Would any contemporary military power contemplate attacking the Israeli army with a quantitative superiority of less than about ten to one? But obviously this factor cannot enter into the formulation of a principle of the kind I am proposing.

9 Again, Walzer has extremely interesting discussions of these subtle matters.

10 The basic argument for this is Hobbesian, in my view. For one go at it, see Narveson, "In Defense of Peace," in my anthology *Moral Issues*, pp. 59-71.

11 This may be over-hasty. I now think, for example, that cruise missiles are a major improvement over ballistic missiles. They are too slow to use as first strike weapons, and at the same time invulnerable because portable, so that the enemy could never target them stably even if it could find them in the first place. To start a nuclear war with cruise missiles, therefore, would be the sheerest folly; to retaliate with them, on the other hand, will always be possible. One might almost classify the cruise missile – its current form – as a "purely defensive weapon." Yet its development will undoubtedly stimulate further developments on the offensive side, in which case my dictum will again apply. Meanwhile, the principle proposed in this article would at least call for the drastic reduction, or perhaps even elimination, of ballistic missiles as the stock of cruise missiles increases.

12 I wish to thank the University of Chicago's Nuclear Study Group, which invited me to give what turned out to be the informal first version of this essay, for stimulation and a good deal of useful criticism. I am likewise grateful to comments from Leo Groarke and Bob Goodin on the first written version. I hope that the present version has benefitted from, as it has certainly been influenced by, their criticisms.

Commentary: Does Nuclear Deterrence Theory Rest on a Mistake?

STEVEN C. PATTEN

In "Getting on the Road to Peace: A Modest Proposal," Jan Narveson offers a number of acute observations and suggestions about lowering the risk of nuclear war. My comments are directed to the last two sections of his paper. Although I am sometimes critical of Narveson, my response should not be confused with that sort of philosophical chippiness that has been so much in vogue over the last twenty years or so. The patient reader will see that we begin fighting, but come out of it shaking hands if not sharing the same standard and banner.

(1) In arguing against nuclear parity Narveson touches on points with which we must all agree: how, given the variety of methods of assessing weaponry and means of delivery, are the two sides ever to agree that they have parity? And if they do reach agreement in some areas, won't this encourage dangerous acceleration in others? Despite such points, I do not expect the defender of nuclear deterrence strategy in its present form to be at all happy with Narveson's account of the rationale for parity (and of the nuclear arms race in general). Such a person will vehemently deny that NATO nuclear deterrence strategy is guided by the hypothesis suggested by Narveson that "if A has more nuclear weapons than B, then A is a greater Power than B, and being a Great Power is a Good Thing." Rather, our objector will insist, the motive force in creating more weapons is really a desire for greater security, the sort of security that comes from incrementally increasing the amount of fear. There is, I think, something deep and important (though mistaken) in this objection and I shall return to its guiding assumption in a moment.

Even if we grant, with Narveson, that "taken of itself being a great power is not a good thing," we cannot ignore that the alliance countries, in particular the US, would insist that they are not simply defending their great power status, but a set of "great" values – all those flagged under the label of "democracy." To be sure, we become as we age more and more suspicious of the ideological slickness of this response, but it cannot be ignored without rebuttal.

(2) Narveson's most important suggestions come by way of his "modest proposal." As he outlines it, his proposal is that if the military aim of the West *really is* one of defense then, by the nature of a position of defense, one requires far less in the way of nuclear weapons than those held at present. If we suppose that country A takes a position of defense against B, then his "proposal would have A opposing B with a clearly inferior force (quantitatively) *by any reasonable measure* of nuclear force." Here, then, we have an argument from the notion of defense to a position of unilateral partial disarmament. I have two points to make with regard to Narveson's plan. The first is the suggestion of another strategy for establishing a defense posture. The second is a counter-argument to protect Narveson's proposal from a tempting rebuttal.

(a) My first point is based on the idea that if there is an ethical justification for nuclear deterrence at all it must be to prevent *nuclear* war. In this I am referring to what is known as *strict deterrence.*[1] Thus, country A has nuclear weapons in order to deter country R from launching a *nuclear* attack. For most people it is precisely here that any ethical or defensive justification for the threat of the use of nuclear weapons must be found, if it is to be found anywhere. It is hard to disagree with the idea that any technique that prevents a nuclear exchange has the most compelling ethical or defensive justification possible.

When most of us think of the idea of contemporary deterrence and try to shoulder some comfort from that cold idea, it is strict deterrence we have in mind. However, it is often another kind of deterrence that gets confused in our minds with strict deterrence (and in some writings of NATO policy they seem to get confused on purpose): I have in mind what Trudy Govier speaks of as *extended deterrence.* Here one threatens to use nuclear weapons as a way of deterring a conventional war. Most famously it is often said that the Russians have been and are deterred from expansion into Western Europe by nuclear arms. I shall have more to say on the supposed ethical and defensive justification for such deterrence shortly.

We should mark off yet another deterrence class, what we might call *nightstick deterrence.* Here one justifies (or attempts to justify) the threat of nuclear response to protect one's perceived national or alliance interests (e.g. to protect Middle East oil supplies). Nightstick deterrence is at work when actions that go against certain interests are supposedly prevented or deterred by the threat of nuclear response.

Finally, reflect on what I call *mock deterrence.* With mock deterrence one postures toward nuclear deterrence, makes deft, feinting lefts armed with the threat of nuclear weapons, all the while really doing something else. Thus, some analysts have suggested that the supposed deployment of the neutron bomb in

1979 was just such a case of mock deterrence: the US pretended to be doing something that would add to Western deterrence credibility, all the while in actuality aiming to strengthen the Alliance. A similar account has been given of the US rationale for the deployment of Pershing II and cruise missiles.

Given these different kinds of deterrence, the important question is before us: Can one or more of these forms of deterrence be justified as a defensive or an ethical strategy? What I'm inclined to think is that whatever *may* have been the justification for extended deterrence in the past it is *not* believable in our times. It is not believable in two senses: First, it gives every indication of being incoherent (and this is one good ground for not thinking it a possible choice among our justifiable courses of action). Second, it is thoroughly incompatible with what is and should be our first interest in nuclear deterrence, viz., strict deterrence, the deterrence of nuclear war.

Consider first the *incoherence* of extended deterrence in Europe. Here is a quotation from *Nuclear Nightmares* by Nigel Calder:

[In Europe] Nuclear weapons became a cheap substitute for armored divisions. [Yet an] asymmetry exists: NATO is not, so it claims, deterred from starting a nuclear war by the latent firepower of the Soviet Union, but the Soviet Union is expected to be deterred from continuing the war by the latent firepower of the West. So ... , while the West promises to go crazy, the onus is on the Russians to be sensible. They [must be] presumed to be winning a conventional battle; why otherwise has NATO used nuclear weapons against them? Now they have been badly hurt and they cannot tell whether NATO will strike again. They still have their own schedule of nuclear strikes for destroying most of the West's "tactical" nuclear forces in Europe within the hour. But they are expected to pull back to the border, licking their wounds and regretting the adventure. Really?[2]

The incoherence of this application of extended deterrence should be transparent: the West *must* fail to be deterred by the very thing – use of nuclear weapons – which the Russians *must* be deterred by. But there is more. Suppose the Russians respond in kind. Suppose they initiate a responding attack in Europe. Again Calder:

The United States would regard a nuclear attack by the Soviet Union on any of its Allies as an attack on itself; if an H-bomb falls, say, on Amsterdam, the Americans are supposed to attack Soviet cities in retaliation. Presumed rationality goes out the window and is replaced by presumed American lunacy. The Russians are still supposed to be deterred, as reasonable chaps, by the threat of US destruction of Soviet cities, but the Americans pretend to be quite undeterred by the symmetrical threat of Soviet destruction of American cities. They promise to be so enraged by any nuclear bombing of their allies that, without thought for their own survival, they will let loose the final nuclear war. Really?[3]

Again the same transparent incoherence: that which does not deter the West *must* deter the Soviet Union. If there is an axiom that is at work in the strategy of extended deterrence in the contemporary world it must be something like "No rational persons (save us) would do the utterly irrational" – a principle of selective rationality at best.

The second way in which extended deterrence in its contemporary form fails to be believable is that at some point it undermines the defensive and ethical primacy of strict deterrence.[4] We should look at the list of kinds of deterrence that I marked off earlier as denoting a rank ordering of evils to be avoided. And above all, anyone who seriously propounds nuclear deterrence in this day must want to prevent a nuclear war, to defend us from that. They must want strict deterrence to work. And yet extended deterrence, actually played out, has (in this time) the consequence of full-scale nuclear war as a possible, if not likely, result. We cannot threaten a nuclear confrontation without risking one. So any one who proposes strict deterrence cannot consistently will and desire that we continue with a policy of extended deterrence. Extended deterrence simply is not believable given the primacy of the desire to deter nuclear war.

It should be apparent now what I think follows about the justifiability of nightstick deterrence and mock deterrence as well. Neither is believable in the same way that extended deterrence lacks credence, at least for contemporary times. It is incoherent to imagine a strategic deterrence plan that has one side asserting its interest by doing precisely what the other side is supposed to be rationally deterred from doing – making a nuclear strike. And it is surely unbelievable on ethical and defensive grounds to imagine that diplomatic or alliance interests should be so grand that they would encourage us to forget the primacy of strict deterrence – of avoiding nuclear war.

How do these reflections fit with Narveson's modest proposal? In just this way. I am suggesting that we can, to a large extent, adopt the desirable defense posture recommended by Narveson without dismantling even one of the present-day weapons. Rather, we need only insist that nuclear deterrence strategy must not ever be extended beyond its function *to prevent nuclear war.*

(*b*) With my second point I shall be briefer. Narveson has argued that if one's position is properly defensive this means that one will require substantially fewer weapons than one's aggressive foe. In general this may be true, but Narveson's proposal, in the way it is stated, seems to beg the question of deterrence strategy. The counter-account which concerns me claims first that deterrence with nuclear weapons *is* defensive, second that this defense comes by way of fear, and third that the amount of fear is roughly proportional to the quantity of nuclear weapons, so that one can incrementally increase the fear (and so increase the defense) by increasing the nuclear weapons. Nuclear deterrence strategy, I am suggesting, rests on the equation of "most feared" with "most deterrent,"[5] and if this equation is correct then I think Narveson's modest proposal must fail. posal must fail.

Yet I do not think it is correct. I think this equation is a part of the contemporary Western doctrine of strict deterrence and it is thoroughly dubious, dangerously so. It is a fallacious ideology that serves to drive us to behave in ways that are irrational and wrong. To be sure, military organization can have an inertia that aims toward greater growth of certain sorts; and complex technology has a way of breeding even more complex technology. But there is a psychology in all this too. It is tempting, but mistaken, to think that if one warhead creates fear and thereby deters, two warheads will create even greater fear and more deterrence. (And then think what 4000 or 10,000 or 20 million warheads might do.) My argument is that the equation is false, even if we grant that fear is increased by nuclear multiplication. I am arguing that what is sufficient to deter can be, will be, far below the most fearsome possibility imaginable.[6] Furthermore, it strikes me as a truth of human behavior that most of us have a breaking point in the face of terror. If someone is visited daily with ever-increasing fearful events of a personally threatening sort we should not be surprised by erratic and dysfunctional (if not destructive) responses. Is there any reason to think things might be different with the laws of psychology as they apply to nation states?   *University of Lethbridge*

NOTES

1 The first three kinds of deterrence specified below follow distinctions made by Govier, "Nuclear Illusion and Individual Obligations," 475.
2 Calder, p. 42.
3 *Ibid.*
4 Again, I am not saying strict deterrence is ethically justifiable: only that if any form of deterrence is justifiable on ethical grounds it must rest here.
5 The nature of the fallacy is eloquently displayed by Conway, 432f.
6 As an analogy, suppose that I am thirsty. You can rationally deter me from drinking the glass of water before me if you tell me that it will give me two weeks indigestion. I don't also need to know that ingestion will cause hepatitis, or kill me, before I am rationally deterred.

Realism, Deterrence, and the Nuclear Arms Race

CONRAD G. BRUNK

I

A fundamental assumption in philosophical discussions of nuclear weapons concerns the concept of deterrence. Most commentators assume that the whole point of nuclear armament (on "our" side at least) is to deter the other side from using nuclear weapons and hence to prevent nuclear war or reduce the probability of a nuclear confrontation. To a certain degree this assumption is valid. A primary aim of nuclear strategy on both sides since the ending of the American nuclear monopoly has been the prevention of nuclear war. But as anyone knows who has followed the developments in strategic doctrine since the late 1950s, the nuclear arsenals of the superpowers greatly expanded the role of deterrence to include the deterrence of aggression by conventional means – so-called "general deterrence" – and even more broadly, the deterrence of unfavorable policies likely to be adopted by the adversary. In this last function, the *threat* of nuclear weapons (which is indeed part of deterrence as such) becomes an integral aspect of the violent struggle for political advantage that is a normal feature of modern superpower diplomacy. It is commonly referred to as "extended deterrence."[1]

Of course it could be argued that it is only the simple deterrence of nuclear war that can stand up under ethical scrutiny, and so much the worse for the extended versions actually practiced by the superpowers today. This would certainly be an advance in the debate. Yet there is a further and in my view more fundamental difficulty with the concept of deterrence as it functions in modern nuclear strategy. It is this difficulty that I wish to elucidate in this article. My concern will be not so much with the *justifiability* of deterrence itself as with the dynamics of a deterrent strategy practiced under other assumptions about international diplomacy. The assumptions in question here are those of the modern school of so-called "political realism." This school is of special interest to philosophers because of its firm grounding in a philosophy of society and political order that is widely accepted.

My thesis is that some of the most significant aspects of the arms race, commonly ignored in the typical ethical analyses of deterrence, cannot be understood apart from the operation of these philosophical assumptions. There is within the logic of deterrence itself, at least deterrence practiced according to the tenets of modern *Realpolitik,* a kind of practical *reductio ad absurdum* in which deterrence refutes itself. In the very attempt to deter nuclear war "rational" strategies are adopted that make nuclear war *more likely.* Debates about the ethics of nuclear deterrence that fail to take into account this deadly logic are simply out of touch with the "real world" of nuclear strategy. In this "real world," the product of deterrence strategies is not the creation of the relatively stable system of what Churchill called "mutual terror" at some assumed level of force parity. Rather it is an accelerating escalation in the numbers and technical sophistication of nuclear weapons, which pushes each side into the adoption of hair-trigger launch strategies, and first strike or nuclear war-fighting strategies, and which pushes the whole world onto the increasingly precarious edge of the nuclear precipice.

Nearly everyone agrees that sooner or later (and probably *sooner*) the world must move into substantial nuclear disarmament. Even the idealized "simple" deterrence defended by the ethicists is justified only as a stop-gap measure on the way to ultimate disarmament. The question to which no one seems to have an answer is how to reach that goal from where we are now.

The difficulty is that the combined logics of deterrence and political realism prevent even this minimal step from being taken. For together they demand that the deterrent threat be made as effective and as credible as possible, so as to minimize the vulnerability to any possible attack by the other side and to maximize strategic advantage. Political realism, strictly adhered to, can never be content with simple minimum deterrence because it is maintained only by an acquiescence in mutual vulnerability by both sides. *Realpolitik* allows neither the acceptance of vulnerability to one's adversary nor the failure to exploit the adversary's vulnerability. It requires *maximum* deterrence through *maximum* threat. Consequently, it militates against both arms control and disarmament measures. I shall devote the remainder of my discussion to an elaboration of this point.

II

It may strike many readers as a kind of philosophical hubris to suggest that an important dynamic in the nuclear arms race could be a philosophical conception of the world and the social order. We are well-accustomed to explaining events of this social magnitude in terms of hard-nosed political and economic power struggles, and to minimize the role of ideas and ideologies. But as important as economic, political and technological factors may be in the race to oblivion, they are reinforced and legitimated by an ideology which also serves to discredit any voice of dissent or social pressures that might blunt or redirect these other forces.

All human activities, especially institutional activities, take place within a "symbolic environment" of abstract symbols and systems of symbols. This "symbolic environment" creates a reality all its own which can be far more significant in determining human behavior than the "real" biological and physical determinants in the non-symbolic environment.[2] No human activity is more conditioned by purely symbolic determinants than nuclear strategy, which has been formulated and reformulated over the past forty years in the virtual absence (thankfully) of any empirical experience of nuclear utilization. Strategies are formulated not on the basis of experience, then, but on the basis of highly theoretical prognostications, game theoretical models and speculations about the probable actions of national leaders, the probable accuracy, survivability, and destructiveness of the weapons systems. Deterrent strategy depends upon how each side *thinks* its own and its adversary's weapons are likely to perform or be utilized under varying conditions, knowing all the while that no one has a clue as to how they would *actually* perform or be utilized. Nor is it clear what possible political objectives might be served, or thought to be served, by the use of nuclear weapons. Nuclear strategy tends to develop in a highly insular, abstract world, determined by the internal dynamics of that world itself rather than by real disputes over substantive political issues in the real world. Hence, the arms race tends to be about the weapons themselves, each side at each step merely "fulfilling a theorem in deterrence theory" as British historian E.P. Thompson observes in a discussion about the likely cause of nuclear war.[3]

It is for this reason that the philosophical and political dogmas behind the strategic theorems directing the arms race are extremely significant and require careful scrutiny in any full accounting of it. The philosophical dogma involved here is primarily that of the American "political realist" school, associated with such well-known figures as Herman Kahn, Thomas Schelling, Hans Morgenthal, Raymond Aron, and Henry Kissinger.[4] The "political realism" of these writers has become a virtual orthodoxy in American foreign policy since the end of World War II. It establishes the ideological context in which the American and NATO buildup of nuclear arms has taken place, and its axioms have not remained unlearned or unappreciated by the Warsaw Pact countries, whose behavior has become a virtual "mirror image" of their Western realist adversaries.

In order to understand the realist school of thought and its strategic implications, it is necessary to go back to its philosophical beginnings, which, at least in the modern period, find their most comprehensive expression in the thought of Thomas Hobbes. Political realism holds basically that the international system is fundamentally a "state of nature" in which mutual reliance upon the respect and forbearance of others is impossible, adherence to moral or legal norms self-defeating and pointless, and in which, therefore, each party can act only out of sheer self-interest. The conditions essential to the establishment of a social, and therefore moral, order do not exist in the international system, hence international diplomacy must be conducted in an amoral atmosphere of absolute mistrust of one's adversaries.

Hobbes argued that adherence to moral principles of any sort requiring the subordination of self-interest to a larger good is impossible in the "state of nature." The latter he defined as that state in which there are no guarantees that other persons will act in other than completely egoistic ways, and hence no reason for anyone to expect the reciprocity of others. The "state of nature" is a state of "war of every one against every one,"[5] in which no person, no matter how strong, can guarantee his own security. Moral relations can be established among persons only where there exists a centralized coercive force which can guarantee the security and the reciprocity of all. Nations, being defined by Hobbes as social entities in which there exists just such a coercive power – a government with a monopoly on the use of force, have the power to create the conditions for moral action, hence persons within states can be subject to moral obligations. But nations find themselves as actors in relation to other nations in a situation in which no central coercive guarantee of state action exists. They remain, in other words, in the "state of nature," and, says Hobbes, "Where there is no commonwealth, there is nothing unjust."[6]

Several conclusions follow from the situation in which nations find themselves, according to this theory. First, while the internal morality of states is binding upon the citizens in their dealings with each other, it is not binding upon the state itself nor upon those who conduct the affairs of state in relation to other states. Here the only imperative is to maximize the national self-interest.

Second, international trust and cooperation are made impossible in situations of potential conflict of interest, for one nation can never be certain that its cooperation will not be taken advantage of by others. In Rousseau's well-known example, the five men who might cooperate to trap a stag and divide it among themselves find it to their own individual advantage to sabotage the cooperative project if doing so permits them to grab the hapless hare which happens across their path. Since no one's cooperation can be counted on, it is to no one's advantage to cooperate.

Third, in the absence of any monopolized coercive power at the international level there is no arbiter of disputes between nations other than the recourse to coercion on their own behalf and ultimately to war. As Rousseau puts it, war becomes a *necessary* occurrence within a situation of international anarchy. It is up to each state, then, to maximize its advantage in every way, including the threat and use of its military power. This systemic account of the place of war in international relations was merely elaborated by the nineteenth-century military theorist Carl von Clausewitz, with his oft-cited dictum that war is merely "the continuation of policy by other means"[7] – a normal aspect of the relations among states. Clausewitz viewed the international system as Hobbes' state of nature writ large, with no "Super-Leviathan" available to prevent the "war of every one against every one."

Of course just as the Leviathan – the sovereign ruler holding a monopoly on the use of force – is the Hobbesian solution to civil anarchy, so also is a "Super-Leviathan" – a World Government with a similar monopoly – the obvious Hobbesian solution to international anarchy. The problem is that such a solution has never actualized itself in the international arena, nor does it appear likely to do so in the near future. Further, no one has yet come up with a persuasive formula for bringing such a creature into being, and for many the prospect of such a monster suggests a cure that might be worse than the ailment. Nations are so tightly wedded to their own sovereign rights of self-defense and self-determination that there is little willingness to accede to even the barest minimum of international law and order.

The best "solution" thus far to the problem of constant war in the system of international anarchy is the modern "balance of power" theory of international diplomacy. It holds that while war between states can never be eliminated, its frequency and perhaps even its intensity can be reduced and controlled by each nation's pursuing a policy of deterrence through maintenance of military alliances in rough parity of military strength. "Balance of power" reduces the advantage gained by any one party initiating military hostilities and hence reduces its attractiveness to all parties. Within this school of diplomatic thought the worst mistake a nation can make is to permit another nation or alliance to gain clear military superiority. To do so is to invite war.

Contemporary diplomatic-military strategy, and its application to nuclear strategy in particular, can be understood only against the background of these Hobbesian assumptions about the "state of nature." Anatol Rapoport aptly calls contemporary political realists "Neo-Clausewitzians" because they embrace Clausewitz's understanding of the political nature of war.[8] They might also be called "Neo-Hobbesians" in view of their commitment to the Hobbesian principles just outlined. The axioms of political realism that most significantly influence the dynamics of strategic nuclear deterrence can be summarized as follows: First, in the international arena, nation-states cannot afford to govern their behavior by moral means, for where there are no guarantees that other nations will so govern their own behavior, to act morally is merely to place one's own nation at serious disadvantage.

Second, as a consequence of the amorality of international diplomacy, national policy must be guided by the principle of self-interest alone, though of course of the "enlightened" variety. Failure to maximize one's own advantage over others in the system only creates a weakness that will surely be exploited by others. Subordinating national interest to a larger international good will likely produce the same result. Or worse, national policy in the pursuit of some moral ideal (e.g., "liberty," "equality," "a world safe for democracy") will only upset the relatively stable balances of power and make *everyone* worse off.[9]

Third, in the international "state of nature" the war of all against all is a natural and normal state of affairs. War and the threat of war are normal instruments of national diplomatic strategy, not the consequence of breakdowns in diplomacy. War is best controlled by the stability of a system of alliances in rough balance of power where the *threat* of war rather than war itself becomes the major diplomatic tool. As the "power to hurt," as Schelling calls it,[10] becomes greater, so does the deterrent power of the threat of war.

Fourth, and most important for our discussion, is the realist adoption of the Hobbesian axiom that in the international state of nature it is irrational to trust other actors not to exploit one's vulnerability. There can be no covenants of mutual trust in the state of nature,[11] except where the parties can mutually extort compliance with the covenant. No nation, therefore, can afford to base its strategy and military preparedness upon an assessment of what adversary nations are *likely* to do, given what is known of their national aims and preferences, and certainly not upon what they might promise to do. Rather, one's own defense must be based upon what the adversary *could* do if he in fact had the very worst, and even irrational intentions. In contemporary strategic parlance, this principle is known as the "worst case hypothesis," under which one prepares to defend oneself not from any *likely* attack, but any *possible* one. This constitutes the banishment of even minimal trust from international affairs. It demands that one assume the worst of one's potential adversaries. This "worst case" thinking, implicit in the Hobbesian model, constitutes one of the most serious obstacles to meaningful arms control and disarmament measures, especially with respect to the contemporary race in nuclear arms. I will expand on this in the next section.

III

When nuclear weapons first appeared on the scene and it became clear that their possessors were not about to place them under the control of any international agency, early nuclear strategists began to hope that the very threat to human survival posed by them might be turned to an advantage. Nuclear weapons held out the promise of an unprecedented solution to the Hobbesian dilemma of security in the system of international anarchy. In the Hobbesian view the state of nature can be transcended only through the interposition of a monopolized coercive force. On the international level this translates into a World Government. This was the solution that some of the early atomic scientists, notably Albert Einstein, saw as the only feasible one to the threat of nuclear weapons. But the idea of world government continued to be viewed by most political theorists and policy-makers as either politically unfeasible in the short term (and a solution was required in the short term) or highly undesirable. Some form of balance of power seemed to be the only feasible solution, even if it had proven in the recent wars to be a notoriously fallible one.

Early nuclear theorists like Bernard Brodie hit upon the idea that nuclear weapons could in fact enhance the balance of power concept, because their awesome power could virtually guarantee the devastation of any state that chose to break the international order, regardless of its military strength. Here was the next best thing to the Super-Leviathan. It was a single deterrent force that could coerce peaceful behavior, even though it remained under the unilateral control of the sovereign nation-states which could thereby police each other. Out of this concept of deterrence – the concept that the primary function of weapons was not to fight wars, but to prevent them – arose an optimism about nuclear weapons that spanned the first two decades of the nuclear era. The early nuclear strategists assured us of a peaceful future through the deterrence provided by the ability of the nuclear powers to assure each other's destruction. Henry Kissinger even argued that the superpowers would be able, under the protection of this "nuclear umbrella," to carry on their diplomacy of violence, even to the point of medium-scale conventional war, without fear of escalation to total war.[12]

The promising aspect of nuclear weapons as deterrents to war lay in their unambiguous threat of retaliation. Unlike the old balance-of-power through conventional military strength, under which the misperception by one side or the other that the balance had swung in its favor constantly drew them into war, the new nuclear balance was far less likely to be mistakenly perceived. Even if one side perceived itself in a position of advantage, the risks of acting on the perception were far too high.

This vision of international stability under the new Nuclear Leviathan, which guarantees assured destruction of those who break the nuclear peace as well as those who retaliate for the breach, underlies most philosophical discussions of the ethics of nuclear deterrence. It holds out the promise of minimizing the potential violence and destruction of the system of international anarchy – the best that can be hoped for in a mean and unforgiving world. Though born of a tough-minded realism about the world, it has, in the strategic context of the 1980s, the appearance of an idealistic hope. To suppose today that the probabilities of nuclear cataclysm are so acceptably low as to stay the present course of nuclear competition itself requires a leap of faith in the face of evidence to the contrary. The actual evolution of nuclear strategy and technology under the doctrine of deterrence has, ironically, turned Hobbesian realism into its opposite. It has placed the human community upon a path of almost inevitable destruction, from which it seems powerless to extricate itself. The nuclear world in which we live today is far from the simple state of stable deterrence envisioned by the early nuclear optimists. It is a world where there are a hundred times more warheads in the nuclear arsenals than are needed for the mutual assured destruction of simple deterrence; where delivery systems have the accuracy to destroy the yet-unlaunched weapons of the adversary, thus tempting their possessors to mount a first strike and gain the strategic advantage; where the reaction time for the decision to launch an irreversible counter-strike has been reduced from the hours it took in the 50s to fly bombers across the pole, to the five or six minutes it takes the European-based Pershing IIs or SS-20s to reach their targets after initial detection. It is a strategic world where the threshold of nuclear war is lowered to increasingly tenuous levels by the deployment of "tactical" nuclear weapons among conventional forces, who would be forced early in a difficult battle to take recourse to their "nuclear option"; where the first nuclear explosion could so seriously disrupt the system of Command, Control, Communications, and Intelligence ("c^3i") that the entire weapons network would be cut loose from all central control and unleash its furor indiscriminately on the world. All these factors work to weaken seriously the stability of the ideal deterrence system by creating an increasingly sensitive "hair trigger" to a nuclear war that would be ever more destructive.

But there is a dynamic within the logic of the deterrence system itself that generates the destabilizing and perilous aspects of the nuclear arms race and illustrates the self-defeating or contradictory nature of deterrence, at least as it is practiced under Hobbesian assumptions. This dynamic is also of most interest philosophically, for it has to do with the concept of deterrence itself and the concept of rational choice within a system of deterrence. Simple deterrence through mutual assured destruction has always been plagued with the internal contradiction that if you limit your nuclear options to massive retaliation for a first strike, your adversary knows that you have little to gain by launching it, because you only bring greater destruction upon everyone, including yourself. Indeed, given the likely suicidal consequences of carrying out the retaliatory strike, it has all the deterrent credibility of a double-barrelled gun with one barrel pointed back at the gun holder. As Jonathan Schell observes, it might make sense to threaten a burglar wanting to enter your house with this gun, but it could never make sense to fire it.[13] Of course the burglar knows as well as you that it doesn't make sense. More importantly, the burglar knows that a single-barrelled gun pointed only at him would be a far more credible deterrent.

Herein lies the dilemma of nuclear deterrence. The threat of mutual suicide at least allows for the theoretical possibility of an agreed-upon level of nuclear weapons sufficient to guarantee a retaliatory strike without massive overkill, first strike or "prevailing" capacities. It therefore has the theoretical possibility of relative stability in the system: low incentive for first strike and high incentive for arms limitation and disarmament to the minimum levels necessary for deterrence. This is part of its attraction for the ethicists who defend nuclear deterrence.[14] But because its retaliatory threat is suicidal, it has low credibility, at least lower credibility than the threat to launch a "successful" preemptive, or damage-limiting strike. Any strategic theorist who takes seriously the Hobbesian-realist dogma that rational action in the state of nature requires minimizing one's own vulnerability and maximizing one's own strategic advantage is thus driven to strive for the stronger deterrent threat. The stronger, more credible, deterrent threat is not that of massive retaliation, but rather some threat of a preemptive, counterforce strike (i.e. one that destroys the enemy's weapons before they can be fired, not its population centers) that would limit the damage inflicted by the other side. In short, if I can convince the burglar that I can make him worse off than he can make me should he try to enter my house, I am more credible than if I threaten to kill us both.

This is precisely the reasoning that has informed the strategies on both sides of the present nuclear arms race. It is clearly articulated in the strategic literature on the Western side. Colin Gray, an advisor to the Reagan administration and apologist for its nuclear policies, clearly exemplifies this reasoning in a recent book on nuclear strategy.[15] Gray shows how American nuclear deterrence doctrine has moved through various stages. The first is the "Societal Punishment" doctrine of massive (and suicidal) retaliation, which Gray thinks was rightly abandoned because of its low deterrent credibility. The second stage was that of "Countervailing Strategy" or "Flexible Response" developed in the Kennedy administration, which involved developing the added capability to strike at Soviet war-waging structures, denying them victory and limiting the collateral damage. The third stage, adopted by the Reagan administration is a "Prevailing Strategy." It is a natural extension of the second stage to the development of the capability of imposing a military – and hence political – defeat on the Soviet Union, "to secure the achievement of Western political purposes at a military, economic, and social cost commensurate with the stakes of the conflict."[16] A credible American deterrence, says Gray, "would flow from Soviet belief, or strong suspicion, that the United States could fight and win the military conflict and hold down its societal damage to a tolerable level."[17]

It is clear that the recent developments in nuclear strategy toward nuclear war-fighting rather than retaliation capability, and toward first strike, counterforce technology, are in no way departures from the concept of deterrence, as they are commonly believed to be by the peace movement generally and deterrence ethicists in particular. They are "enhanced" or "extended" versions of deterrence. Again to quote Gray, "There is widespread agreement that a perceived ability to wage a nuclear counterforce ... war is probably critically important for the credibility of nuclear threats and hence for the stability of prewar [sic!] deterrence."[18] Deterrence through the ability to "prevail" in an actual nuclear war answers the old difficulty of simple deterrence – what do you do if deterrence fails? Its answer is that you carry out those threats not just because it is part of your threat policy but because it will actually serve your interests to fight the nuclear war – you will limit your own damage while maximizing your adversary's. The obvious question of what "damage limitation" actually means under these cataclysmic conditions is rarely addressed in any detail in these doctrines.

Enhanced deterrence by capability to "prevail" in an actual nuclear war also lends credibility to the extended deterrence doctrines mentioned earlier. Once deterrence is maintained by what the strategists want us to believe is a non-suicidal war-fighting strategy, it becomes more credible as an instrument of coercive diplomacy. Thus Gray argues in favor of a nuclear strategy he calls "Damage Limitation for Deterrence and Coercion." Under this strategy, "the fundamental purpose of the strategic forces is to deter, or help deter, hostile acts against vital US interests."[19] Gray also holds that this is the present policy of the Reagan administration he advises. Anyone who still believes that the sole purpose of nuclear weapons is to deter only nuclear war, as most deterrence ethicists do, then, is simply out of touch with strategic reality.

David Gauthier's recent argument about the rationality of deterrence is an all-too-common example of philosophical discussion out of touch with strategic reality.[20] Gauthier argues that if deterrence by threat of massive nuclear retaliation is a rational policy, then it could be rational to carry out a suicidal retaliatory strike if the deterrent failed. Gauthier argues, incredibly, that the carrying out of such a strike is rational (and therefore moral) no matter how monstrous the consequences of doing so. Even were Gauthier able to make this claim credible, it quite misses a more important point, which is implicit in his own game-theoretical approach to the question, just as it is in the Hobbesian-realist dogma. This point is that from the game-theoretical point of view, with its definition of rationality as the maximization of expected utility (for the actor), as for Hobbesian realism, the policy of deterrence by retaliation is itself judged irrational. This is because a threat to "prevail" over an enemy, should he behave aggressively, is itself more rational than a threat to commit suicide, which of course on its own terms is completely pointless and irrational. Rationality conceived in terms of "expected utility maximization" should therefore lead one to reject a policy of deterrence through mutual destruction in favor of extended deterrence through the threat of fighting and prevailing in a nuclear war. Gauthier, however, fails to follow the logic of his own theory of rationality, unlike the strategic theorists who design "real-world" strategies.

The problem of course is that both sides, having read the same strategic textbooks and used the same game theory, reason and act according to the same logic. This produces the irrational result that both sides develop nuclear arsenals designed to prevent nuclear war by being able to fight and win it. It is the classic "prisoner's dilemma" situation in which the apparent rational strategy, when adopted by both players in a two-person game leads to an irrational outcome for both. More accurately, in the nuclear case, it is a game of "chicken," because the payoff from adhering to the rational strategy is mutually disastrous. The irrational outcome here is the fact that the "rational" strategy locks both sides into a continuous race for nuclear superiority in which they each design more and more weapons, designed more and more to be *used*. In this deadly "game" there is no even theoretical equilibrium point where both parties can agree to freeze their deployment of new weapons. The only equilibrium point is the actual fighting of the war itself. The logic of deterrence under Hobbesian assumptions of rationality thus sets both sides on a course of preparation for warfighting that is bound to lead them into that war by the sheer inertia of the preparations themselves.

The strategy is "rational," however, only within the logic of the Hobbesian-realist dogma and the game-theoretical models that give it an air of mathematical precision and scientific objectivity. If it is assumed that the other actors in the system will exploit every vulnerability on your side to their maximum advantage; that only your own reciprocal exploitation of advantage can counter it; and hence, that every *possible* strategic advantage of the other must be forestalled regardless of the probabilities of its actually being exploited (the "worst-case" assumption), then the suicidal result becomes virtually inevitable. The Hobbesian logic requires that every "window of vulnerability" – no matter how small, or in how remote a part of the strategic attic – must be securely boarded up. It is instructive to note that the so-called "window of vulnerability" feared by the Reagan strategists was precisely the possibility that the Soviets might develop the ability to neutralize the US ability to "prevail" in a nuclear war, forcing the US to resort to mutual suicide.

Our present precarious situation of nuclear roulette with its growing risks of nuclear holocaust is a logical and predictable consequence of the Hobbesian-realist model. If policy-makers and strategists continue to be dominated by its orthodoxy, it will in all probability fulfill its own suicidal fears. The "balance of power" strategy may well have worked a utilitarian result in the pre-nuclear world where the consequences of the inevitable periods of breakdown in the balance and the resulting wars were less destructive than the consequences likely to accrue from a more idealistic or moralistic foreign policy. But in a nuclearized world where there are virtually no limits on the power to destroy, where the power of one actor no longer serves effectively to limit an adversary's power to destroy, and where the technological developments are increasingly destabilizing, this conception of the international system generates its own refutation.

There is no reason, consequently, to place any confidence whatever in the fact that nuclear weapons seem to have deterred nuclear war for forty years. Such confidence rests upon the fallacious assumption, among others, that the system of deterrence is not subject to the inherent dynamics of escalation toward war imposed upon it by Hobbesian realism. It assumes that the situation today is the same as in 1955 and will be the same tomorrow. It is for this reason that the assumption that nuclear weapons actually deter war could be, as one writer has aptly put it, "the most costly *post hoc* in human history."[21]

IV

If the preceding analysis is correct, it seems reasonable to conclude either that the Hobbesian model provides the best account of the international situation and we simply must learn to live with increasingly dismal prospects of survival, or that it is not accurate and we should therefore search about for a more workable alternative. But one of the greatest problems faced by those who believe some better way than the present nuclear course is possible and necessary, is that there seems to be no alternative model of international order that holds out a promise of effective control and reduction of nuclear arms.

The model most often appealed to by the nuclear disarmament community, beginning with Einstein and his colleagues, is the model of a World Government to which would be given the monopoly on nuclear and ultimately all weapons. On this view it is national sovereignty itself that has become obsolete and impossible in the nuclear world. This of course is itself a paradigmatically Hobbesian solution to the problem of war. Order can be created out of international anarchy only if it is maintained by threats backed up by the monopolized force of a "Super-Leviathan." But this solution has had little appeal among political theorists, least of all among the Hobbesian realists themselves.

There are some good reasons for skepticism about the World Government solution – some of them having to do with the weaknesses of the Hobbesian view itself. One important reason is that there seems to be no way under Hobbesian assumptions to implement the solution. It is not "rational" for any nation to give up its sovereign right of self-defense when it cannot rely upon others to do so as well or not to take some advantage of its vulnerability. The Hobbesian solution is a Catch-22 from which Hobbes himself and all Hobbesians have difficulty extricating themselves. It is a fundamental flaw in Hobbes' entire view of the social contract. While he holds on the one hand in the "Second Law of Nature" that "all men seek to abandon the state of nature by laying down their right of self-defence," and as a law of reason "To endeavor peace, as far as he has hope of obtaining it,"[22] he recognizes that this cannot be done unilaterally. And in the absence of the Leviathan to guarantee the performance of all others in the laying down of their right, there is no possibility of multilateral action either. Hobbesianism can find no way, consistent with its own axioms, to transcend the state of nature.

This is precisely the dilemma of the nuclear arms race viewed in the light of Hobbesian principles. Nearly everyone recognizes that before this competition pushes both sides, perhaps unintentionally, into the nuclear holocaust there must be some kind of bilateral agreement to freeze the weapons development, to reduce the numbers of the weapons through disarmament procedures, to eradicate the hair trigger launch-on-warning policies that threaten accidental war, and to reach some at least provisional agreement to live with a parity of deterrent force. But even these minimal steps to preserve the security of the world require cooperative, non-guaranteeable initiatives. Even if, on the way to meaningful de-nuclearization of the world, we need to step back to the "good old days" of mutual assured vulnerability, we can do it only if we are willing to live with vulnerability and give up the Hobbesian urge to maximize our security and our advantage.

In the long run, of course, we must rid the world of nuclear weapons. But given that the extremity of the present situation requires a short-run solution, perhaps we shall have to live for a time with some form of deterrence at lower and more stable levels of nuclear weapons systems. This means that the immediate, urgent need[23] is not only for a freeze in the development of new weapons, but also for disarmament to the minimum levels required for simple deterrence. Ultimately deterrence, if it functions at all, will have to be essentially non-nuclear.

But there is no way to achieve even these limited goals if we do not break the grasp of the Hobbesian-realist dogma that demands continued escalation to inevitable war. The first tenet of Hobbesian orthodoxy to be thrown off must be the assumption that there can be no even minimal reliance upon the nuclear adversary not to break through every tiny "window of vulnerability." Arms control, disarmament, even a stable system of deterrence, requires a degree of cooperation based upon a certain reliance upon others not to exploit that cooperation to their own maximum advantage. This, it seems to me, merely reflects a simple fact about the necessary conditions for human social life and community that the strict Hobbesian model fails to recognize. There is no way to transcend the "state of nature" without the willingness to take unilateral initiatives that rely upon a certain faith in the reciprocal action of others. It is perhaps a symptom of the massive self-deception of our life in the nuclear shadow that the overwhelming evidence from the study of conflict management which demonstrates the necessity of unilateral gestures in reversing conflict escalation is universally rejected in strategic theory. It is rejected in favor of the thesis that one's adversary can be deterred from escalating a conflict only by a threat of superior force. One must always "negotiate from strength." No thesis has been more thoroughly discredited by empirical studies of conflict management than this one. It almost always guarantees escalation of a conflict. This should not surprise anyone of common sense. One need only reflect upon what he would do, following Hobbesian principles, if the other party to a conflict "negotiated from strength."

It should be pointed out that the strict Hobbesian dogma against the possibility of non-enforced cooperation and in favor of maximizing strategic advantage is rejected not only in the theory of interpersonal conflict but in the theory of non-military international diplomacy as well. Few nations today, and certainly not the superpowers, conduct themselves on the assumption that non-enforceable treaties or canons of international law carry no weight whatever in international affairs. The international system of commerce and non-military diplomacy simply is not a "state of nature," nor do most nations act as if it were. Trust in the reciprocal action of others is essential to the functioning of the system, and it is not maintained solely by threat of force. It is only in matters of strategic military doctrine that the Hobbesian dogma is involved as religious orthodoxy.

We are here at the heart of a fundamental philosophical question about the nature of human society. It puzzled not only Hobbes, but Rousseau, Hume, Kant, and others as well. It is the question of the rationality of acting in accord with ideals or principles that put one at serious disadvantage vis-à-vis others if they cannot be counted on to act reciprocally. Hobbes believed that it was not rational except where the performance of others could be guaranteed by coercive sanctions. Hence, as we have seen, he finds himself trapped in the state of nature where the "laws" of reason and nature show him the rationality of everyone's getting out but not the rationality of any *one* person doing what is necessary to get there. Gauthier has argued that those moral philosophers who disagree with Hobbes' view of the matter must necessarily invoke, as did Locke and Kant, a religious faith in a God whom one hopes will turn one's own unilateral performance of one's duty to ultimate good even if others do not perform likewise. [24] Gauthier complains that many contemporary moral philosophers have abandoned the faith in this deity yet cling to a morality of unilateral performance of duty. But once the faith is gone, one has to accept the Hobbesian conclusion, as Gauthier does himself.

It may be for this reason that the nuclear disarmament movement in North America and Europe has been most strongly supported by religious institutions and persons. But the strategists who are responsible for the interests and security of their nations have never felt it responsible to rely entirely upon Providence without at least providing God a sufficient military backup. To the strategist the peace movement's call for cooperative disarmament measures initiated by non-maximizing policies of restraint appear naively idealistic, resting upon the all-too-tenuous faith that God might bring them to fruition.

Annette Baier has argued persuasively in response to Gauthier that some faith in the reciprocation of others to one's own moral actions is absolutely essential to the building and maintaining of a moral community. [25] Where there is no belief in God to sustain this faith, then it must and can be a "secular faith." Moral community is not possible unless there is some faith, not necessarily that others are essentially good, but only that they are not absolutely and unconditionally evil and prone to taking full advantage of every vulnerability of their peers. Indeed, as Baier quite rightly points out, even Hobbes himself could not escape this reality. For while he accepted it as a "rule of reason" that "every man ought to endeavor peace," and hence end the state of nature, he found it necessary to place upon this law the qualification, "as far as he has hope of obtaining it." [26] Only *hope* for a reciprocation that cannot be absolutely guaranteed, Baier observes, can get even Hobbes out of the state of nature. [27]

There simply cannot be progress in the control and reduction of nuclear arms, and the development of some more stable structure of international security unless nations are willing to renounce the desire to maintain maximum advantage through unilateral escalation. They must be willing to take unilateral steps that forego advantage or the need to maximize every vulnerability. [28] What is required today is not naive faith that the Soviets (or Americans) will be good if the other side completely renounces its right of defense, but the recognition that we can step back from the nuclear abyss only if we find ways of relying on each other's interest in that goal while showing the willingness to forego absolute guarantees. Moral community, and in this case survival, requires mutual reliance and cooperation even where reciprocation cannot be certain. We must learn to accept this fact or else resign ourselves to the fate which Hobbes himself saw as intrinsic to the "state of nature." Under the conditions of a nuclear state of nature our life as a species on this planet will indeed be "poor, nasty, brutish, and short."   *Conrad Grebel College, University of Waterloo*

NOTES

1 This position founders always on the question of whether it is possible to make a credible nuclear threat without actually *intending* to carry out that threat, and if not, whether it is morally justifiable to intend to do what it would be immoral to do. This is especially problematic given the fact, usually ignored in this discussion, that the corporate intentions of a government or nation entail a kind of institutional commitment to carry out the threat that is virtually irreversible when the threat fails to deter the unwanted action of the adversary. In institutional behavior there is such a strong link between the issuing of a threat and the carrying out of the threat, that any moral distinction in theory between the two is immaterial in practice. For a contrary view of this matter, see Shaw.

2 For an excellent analysis of this idea, see Rapoport, *Conflict in a Man-Made Environment.*

3 Thompson, p. 22.

4 See, for example, Kissinger, *Nuclear Weapons and Foreign Policy;* Schelling; Aron; and Robert Osgood.

5 Hobbes, *Leviathan,* Chap. 14.

6 *Ibid.,* Chaps. 13, 15.

7 Clausewitz (Penguin edn.), p. 119.

8 Rapoport, "Introduction," in Clausewitz.

9 See Kissinger's discussion of the immorality of being moral in international diplomacy in *A World Restored,* pp. 108 ff.; and Noble's discussion of Kissinger's view.

10 Schelling, pp. 1-34.

11 Hobbes, Chap. 14.

12 Kissinger, *Nuclear Weapons and Foreign Policy.*

13 Schell, *The Abolition,* p. 54.

14 Assuming that one dispenses with the morally unpleasant fact that it involves holding populations of innocent people hostage by threatening them with nuclear annihilation. See the contributions by Wasserstrom, McDonald, and Nielsen in this volume.

15 See Colin S. Gray.

16 *Ibid.,* p. 2.

17 *Ibid.,* p. 3.

18 *Ibid.,* p. 7. The President's Commission on Strategic Forces (the Scowcroft Commission) embraced the same concept, that the best deterrent is a war-fighting capability. *Report of the President's Commission on Strategic Forces,* p. 7.

19 Gray, p. 79.

20 Gauthier, "Deterrence, Maximization and Rationality."

21 Govier, "Nuclear Illusions and Individual Obligations," 480.

22 Hobbes, Chap. 14.

23 In *The Abolition* Schell puts forward a novel scenario for nuclear disarmament which does not rely on a Hobbesian World Government to guarantee compliance. Schell argues for a form of deterrence through a combined system of *conventional* defenses against nuclear weapons and complete nuclear disarmament to the level of maintaining the industrial/technical capacity to build nuclear weapons. Deterrence would then consist in the threat to build up nuclear arsenals in "retaliation" for the adversary's buildup. This would be a much safer deterrence system, in Schell's view, because it would increase the time for diplomatic initiatives to head off the hostile actions before nuclear war could be fought. This is a form of deterrence that could be maintained only on non-Hobbesian principles.

24 Gauthier, "Why One Ought to Obey God."

25 Baier, "Secular Faith."

26 Hobbes, Chap. 14.

27 Baier, 134.

28 For more on the unilateral initiatives that might be taken, see Narveson's contribution to this volume.

Commentary: Trust, Risk, and Possible Benefits

Conrad Brunk's central argument can perhaps be summarized as follows. Political realist nuclear deterrence strategy rests on three fundamental assumptions: (*1*) In the international arena, one cannot trust others to act even in their own rational self-interest. (*2*) Analysis of nuclear strategy must thus be based solely on considerations of one's self-interest. (*3*) One's strategy should be to minimize the worst possible outcome. These assumptions originally led to a balance of power retaliation strategy; one could deter others from attacking if one had sufficient power to insure that equally massive destruction would be inflicted on an aggressor. However, this strategy evolved through a countervailing strategy to a prevailing strategy, that is, to one of having sufficient power to inflict damage on an enemy disproportionate to that suffered by oneself. A prevailing strategy is in one's rational self-interest, because it is better to be able to inflict more rather than equal damage on one's adversary. Mutual adoption of a prevailing strategy produces an arms race to gain superiority and an increased rather than decreased chance of nuclear war. A world government is a way out of this problem, but it is not rational for countries to surrender their sovereignty. (Arms control treaties with guarantees of no violation are also a way out; unfortunately, no system of mutual inspection seems capable of providing such guarantees.) Brunk concludes that the first fundamental assumption should be dropped and some minimal mutual trust should be conceded and acted upon.

Brunk assumes that the alternative is so bad (a nuclear cataclysm or holocaust) that minimal trust or hope must be chosen. However, some might argue that there are reasons for thinking that a policy based on minimal trust is immoral or irrational. First, it is morally permissible to take greater risks with one's own life than it is with the lives of others. Government officials are responsible for protecting their citizens' lives from aggressors. Thus, it might not be morally appropriate for them to risk citizens' lives by policies of minimal trust even if they are willing to risk their own lives. There are two responses to this point. If one believes, as Brunk seems to, that without minimal trust massive nuclear destruction is nearly inevitable, then such trust is the lesser evil and therefore is justifiable. Whether this is true is a factual question that cannot be discussed here. Alternatively, a government which has its citizens' consent (however that should appropriately be determined) to a policy of minimal trust, can legitimately exercise that trust.

Second, the grounds for minimal trust being rational do not appear strong. Brunk holds that the study of conflict management shows the necessity of unilateral gestures in reversing or preventing conflict escalation. But the vast majority of that literature concerns disputes between neighbors, labor and management, spouses, and so on within a common society; its conclusions might not be applicable between societies. (Brunk assumes that unilateral gestures require minimal trust; such trust may justify the gestures, but I would argue that unilateral gestures do not really require even minimal trust.) Grounds for minimal trust among nuclear powers do not seem very strong. At the time I am writing, the Soviet Union seems willing to negotiate to limit weapons in space, but not missiles in Europe; and vice-versa for the United States. The Soviet Union is thought to be behind the United States in developing space weapons, but ahead in nuclear weapons in Europe. If an adversary is willing to discuss limiting weapons in your area of superiority but not in its own area of superiority, not even minimal trust seems warranted.

More importantly, unilateral gestures may be necessary, but they do not always work. A rational basis for minimal trust to justify unilateral gestures seems even weaker when one looks into the not too distant future. At present, at least six countries have nuclear weapons – Britain, China, France, India, the USSR, and the US. Israel and Pakistan may also have them, and a large number of other countries, including Egypt, Argentina, and South Korea, could develop them. Unilateral gestures often do not work with fanatics and psychotics. Unfortunately, such people do sometimes have control of governments. If they do, a strategy of minimal trust is probably doomed to failure. The only saving grace is that many of these countries likely to have or be capable of developing nuclear weapons in the future will lack the capacity to deliver them all over the world in large quantities. At least for a while (fifty years?), they will be individually limited to blowing up one continent with a few other scattered areas. Yet collectively, they will be capable of destroying vast areas – Africa, the Middle East, South America, and much of Asia.

Brunk thinks that the alternative to minimal trust is unacceptable. Most people automatically assume that nuclear war is the worst possible outcome – and it is. Nonetheless, one should ask both why it is and how bad it would be. Would a nuclear war be bad because it would mean the end of the human species? I have elsewhere argued that the continuation of the human species is not intrinsically desirable. [1] Would it be bad because of the way people would die? One-third or so of the North American population will probably die of cancer, and death by vaporization seems preferable to death by at least some cancers. Would it be bad because some people would survive in primitive conditions? Many people today live in primitive conditions without adequate shelter, food, or clean water. Would there be more or fewer such people? Would it be bad because millions, probably billions, of people would die sooner than otherwise, would lose a valuable part of their lives just as victims of homicides and automobile accidents do? This certainly is so. Many persons would suffer a "premature" death.

But let us for a moment weigh these effects against the possible benefits stemming from unilateral peace initiatives that might reasonably be undertaken. [2] Every day millions of people risk their lives for things that to many others do not seem to be of great value – climbing mountains, riding motorcycles, smoking, jay-walking, driving while impaired, and so on. If the billions of dollars and hours of labor committed to the arms race were devoted instead to other activities – growing and transporting food, providing decent housing and clean water, etc. – every human being on Earth could be significantly better off. The harm of a nuclear war is great, but the possible benefits of nuclear arms limitation or reduction are also great. It may be that these benefits will be realized only when one superpower undertakes some unilateral disarmament initiative, accepting a somewhat greater risk. The benefits seem worth an increased risk of death as much as many other things for which people risk their lives.

Brunk rejects the assumption of no trust and advocates minimal trust. There is little basis for such trust, but unilateral gestures need not rest on trust and can be recognized as risks. The assumption of no trust is correct, the worst case strategy is not. If one tries only to minimize the worst possible outcome (all-out nuclear war), one may forgo great possible benefits. It is reasonable for each citizen to accept an increased risk of the worst possible outcome for an increased chance of the best possible outcome, so it is also reasonable for leaders to do so on their behalf. How much of an increased risk is acceptable depends on how bad one thinks the worst possible outcome is. I suggest that it is premature death for many or most of us, so we should be willing to take as much risk as we do normally. Even the most cautious of us take some risks with our lives, often for less valuable benefits than could result from a halt to the nuclear arms race.

University of Florida

1 Bayles, pp. 15-18.
2 See, for example, Narveson's contribution to this volume.

The Abolition of War

BEVERLY WOODWARD

Peace is preferable to war, or so most reasonable people believe. But there agreement stops. For what is the way to peace? Indeed, what is peace? And is it attainable?

The same "reasonable people" who believe that peace is preferable to war tend to believe that the elimination of armed conflict is not possible. In this view the risks of an armed world will always be preferred to the risks of a disarming or even disarmed world. (Even in a disarmed world, there will remain the knowledge of how to wage war and the risk that this knowledge will be applied.)

The advent of nuclear weapons has, of course, changed drastically the risks inherent in the war system. Some, therefore, have raised their voices to warn that drastic changes in human behavior are necessary if humankind is to survive. Einstein's warning is the most famous: "The unleashed power of the atom has changed everything save our modes of thinking, and thus we drift towards unparalleled catastrophe." Einstein believed that the abolition of war was an urgent necessity and that it could be achieved only through the creation of a world government, a point he argued in a piece which appeared in the November 1945 issue of the *Atlantic Monthly*. Einstein's advice, as we know, was not taken. The proclaimed policy instead has been that of "deterrence." Under this policy the assurance of nuclear retaliation in the case of a nuclear first strike is counted upon to deter an opponent or potential opponent from launching a nuclear war.

Since 1945 there has been no nuclear war. It is not clear, however, how large a role deterrence has played in this outcome. At least part of the time the non-use of nuclear weapons may have been due to factors other than the fear of retaliation. We know also that in some instances the use of nuclear weapons has

Reprinted, with slight changes, by permission of the author and the editor, from *Cross Currents*, 33 (3), Fall 1983.

been contemplated in spite of the possibility or even likelihood of retaliation if they were used.[1] The explicit refusal of the government of the United States to adopt a policy of "no first use" is in fact a refusal to admit that the US will necessarily be deterred by an opponent's nuclear weapons and a clear indication that the fear of defeat (a conventional military fear) might be permitted to override the fear of a more encompassing and extraordinary disaster. That the world may have to be destroyed in order to "save" freedom is indeed a notion that has dominated a great deal of Western political and military thinking since the dawn of the nuclear age.

Recent developments in nuclear strategizing and in the speed, accuracy, and destructiveness of nuclear weaponry appear to have increased the chances that a nuclear war will take place.[2] The alarm generated by these developments has led to the resurgence of anti-nuclear movements and to campaigns to prevent the deployment of the new weapons. Nevertheless, discussions about issues of national security remain fundamentally unchanged. The vast majority continue to believe that an armed defense is indispensable in order to counter armed threats. (The discussion is practically never about the merits of a non-military as opposed to a military defense, of which more will be said later.) The basic structure of the world political order, a world of armed states, is generally not put in question. In short, arguments about national security tend to concern only the details of a military defense: Exactly what sorts of weapons do we need at a given time? How many of a particular variety are needed? Are we adequately armed to meet military challenges on several fronts at once? Discussion about the foreign policy assumptions linked to a particular defense strategy is often simplistic: all the usual ideas about enemies, who they are, what they want, etc., are accepted *or* rejected with little attempt to make an independent assessment of what should be considered a "threat" and what threats actually exist.

Because most of us have been socialized to think in terms of national interest and national security rather than in terms of global interest and global security, we generally fail to look at the war system *as a whole* and to ask what that system or particular policies within it are likely to bring about for humanity as a whole. Those who adopt this broader perspective, however, are concerned about the cumulative effect of the arms race and particular arms policies for humankind in general.

Nuclear proliferation is a case in point. In the current world situation every nation may consider it in its own "self-interest" to possess at least some nuclear weapons. (Some or all nations may in fact err in coming to this conclusion, but given conventional wisdom about what promotes national self-interest one can see how this conclusion may appear reasonable.) It is not difficult to see, however, how the multiplication of nuclear actors increases the risk of a nuclear conflagration.

In some respects, then, we are faced in the sphere of military competition with something resembling the "tragedy of the commons" of which Garrett Hardin has written. In the tragedy of the commons a multiplicity of individual actors, in this case English sheep grazers of the 1700s and 1800s, by pursuing their own private advantage destroyed the basis both for the common good and for their own individual well-being. Although it appeared to the advantage of each individual farmer using the common pastures to increase his herd and thus reap more profits, the combined effect of many farmers following the same course was to destroy the common grazing lands. If the combined result of many nations pursuing their own "national security" is to increase the risks of a disastrous world war and if such a war in fact takes place, humanity will be the victim of a far vaster "tragedy of the commons."

For those who are opposed to war primarily on "instrinsic" moral grounds the possibility of doomsday is not the central issue. In their view what must be emphasized are not the contingent results of the practice of war, but the fact that the conduct of war *necessarily* contravenes fundamental moral principles. In 1946, at the same time that he was warning of nuclear catastrophe, Einstein invoked this argument when he wrote: "Up to now, controversies among nations have been settled by military force, either by war or the threat of war. This is and always was morally wrong. The question of right and wrong can never be decided by force. ..."[3] While the more just cause *may* prevail in a war, there is nothing in the method that guarantees this result. Moreover, the central means of coercion in war, i.e., killing, is an act that our moral codes hold "on its face" to be wrong. It is an act that needs a moral "justification" to be acceptable.

The moral point here is fundamental and indicates why there have always been some individuals who have refused to participate in armed combat. But in our time this *a priori* argument cannot be separated from the seemingly more contingent point that war may now lead to what John Somerville has termed "omnicide," i.e., the annihilation of all life on Earth. Some partisans of "limited war" have argued against this outcome on theoretical grounds. In his famous treatise *On War* (1832) Clausewitz described war as the continuation of politics by other means. Building on this dictum, those who have held that war *can* and *should* be limited have maintained that there is a kind of "political illogic" in carrying extermination beyond a certain point or in using grossly cruel or unfair methods for the sake of victory.

Unfortunately, the conceptions of theorists do not always correspond to the realities of the world. Clausewitz also wrote that: "All beyond this [i.e., beyond the political objectives of war] which is strictly peculiar to War relates merely to the peculiar nature of the means which it uses. ...[T]he means must always include the object of our conception."[4] In modern times the "peculiar nature of the means" of war has become more apparent. Throughout this century (the era of "total war") there have been clear-cut demonstrations that the means of war and of preparations for war have the capacity to overwhelm war's objectives rather than to be informed and controlled by them. Just as preparations for war can bring about in the life of a nation some of the changes that armed defense is meant to prevent – e.g., loss of freedom and damage to the economy – the weapons of war can shape the course of battle and in the process alter the objectives of battle.

The elimination of individuals, of groups (genocide), of humanity, and of all life (omnicide) indicates a quantitative progression in the application of the method of war. The moral objection to the killing of individuals is correct. The unrestrained application of the method, however, intensifies the moral evils with which we are confronted (as actual or possible events). Little in the behavior of contemporary nation-states indicates that there is an inherently self-limiting factor in the application of the method. When it became possible to create the weapons that can eliminate all life, they were created. Thermonuclear weapons have not yet been employed by two sides in a conflict. But our governments can provide no reliable assurance they will not be employed or that present policies are the ones that most effectively minimize the risk that they will be employed.

War, of course, continues to be waged. Since World War II the battlegrounds have most often been in Third World countries. Not many in the Third World are ready to renounce violence. To those engaged in bitter struggles for power and justice violence appears an indispensable means. The superpowers aid and abet this violence. Local conflicts provide the occasion for superpower confrontation with surrogate armies on surrogate battlefields. In these complex situations, forces for human advancement and liberation may prevail, although generally at a high cost. These costs include not only the immediate and obvious ones, but that reinforcement of the war system that occurs whenever there is a resort to armed struggle. In many current situations it appears that the use of violence may be "justifiable" by important moral criteria and yet ultimately ineffective or even counterproductive. Every gain achieved by violence risks being wiped out by the still greater violence that the war system can unleash.

The possibility of a man-made apocalypse undermines our usual modes of reasoning and provides nothing in their place. Understandably, many would like to return to "the way things were." Can we not eliminate nuclear weapons and carry on war the way we used to? The "disease" of the nuclear age, however, is not encapsulated in the nuclear weapons that have been produced (or may be produced). The mentality that supported the development of nuclear weapons is the same mentality that has supported recent developments in "conventional" weaponry, leading to the creation of weapons of unprecedented accuracy and destructive capacity. According to Michael Klare, the new high-tech weapons "will certainly produce a new more lethal battlefield, where anything that moves or gives off heat or sound will be targetable by precision-guided munitions with near-total effectiveness."[5] He quotes Julian Robinson, who has asked: "May it not be the case that, as more and more of the militarily valued effects available from nuclear weapons come to be provided by a variety of non-nuclear means, a non-nuclear battlefield may come closer and closer to resembling a nuclear one ... ?" History, it appears, has no reverse gear.

Arms control and the "law of war" (i.e. international agreements not to perform certain acts during a war) are the accepted "moderate" response to the problem of war. Efforts to control the arms race tend to fail, however, because they are carried on in the same spirit and by the same personnel as the arms race itself. Each side seeks to maintain some advantage under whatever agreements are reached. If there are agreements with regard to quantitative limits on arms, then the contending parties put their major efforts into achieving qualitative improvements that may strengthen their military standing. The perspective of the participants in the negotiations is persistently partisan rather than global. Consequently, the net effect of arms control efforts till now has been to channel and in some measure "legitimize" the arms race rather than arrest it.

Arms control fails – in practice and in theory – because arms control does not have to do with the principles of war and their negation, but with the details of war and their modification. Whether killing is carried out by chemical warfare or by atomic warfare is, in some crucial respects, a detail. Whether threats and acts of destruction, and in particular the destruction of human life, will continue to be the means by which some political disputes are settled is not a detail, but a central (perhaps the central) moral and political issue of our time. If threats to lives are an acceptable weapon, then potentially the threat to *all* human life is an acceptable weapon – and that is precisely the situation in which we find ourselves at present. All human life is now hostage to nation-state politics. The concern to protect civilians has been part of the "law of war" and a concern of some war planners, but a restraint that has repeatedly been swept aside when "military necessity" conflicted with its requirements.

It is not easy to devise a strategy for overcoming the present impasse. Some discount the risks of catastrophe. Others believe that if catastrophe is to occur, there is nothing we can do about it. Many believe that the choice is between the risk of worldwide destruction and the risk of worldwide slavery, and profess to prefer the former. That is, they prefer it as a risk; it is not clear they would prefer it as a reality.

Although the question of how to get from here to there has long defied human powers of reason and persuasion, the alternative to the war system is less of a conundrum. The alternative to a war system is a peace system. For quite some time there has been discussion – and debate – about the key elements of such a system. Six important elements (described in very general terms) might be the following: (*1*) universal and complete disarmament (including the disarmament of internal police to minimal elements); (*2*) international institutions (both regional and global) to mediate and adjudicate international disputes and those domestic disputes that threaten world peace; (*3*) the replacement of military forces by international unarmed peace-making forces and by a capacity for non-violent struggle and nonviolent defense on the part of the nations *and* other social entities with a perceived need to defend their rights; (*4*) massive educational efforts on behalf of the values and behaviors associated with a nonviolent orientation; (*5*) the creation of more effective institutions to protect the basic political, social, and economic rights of individuals and groups; (*6*) efforts by the more industrialized countries to adopt less resource-consumptive economies and by the less industrialized countries to find alternatives to present models of development.

These six elements are interdependent. That is, it is not difficult to see how the effectiveness of each element will be increased by the presence of the others. The second and third elements provide the substitutes for the use of violence to settle political disputes. The fourth element is meant to assist the profound cultural, psychological, and behavioral transformation that the shift to a peace system would require. (The experiences of the nonviolent movement in training for nonviolent action and for nonviolent conflict-resolution would be important in this regard.) The fifth and sixth elements are meant to deal with some of the causes of conflict.

The first element is the one to which peace movements and organizations tend to devote most of their attention and efforts; it is also given the most attention at the governmental level. This is probably because the arms race is at present the most obviously dangerous part of the war system. Even governments with little interest in genuine disarmament may wish to "control" this race or at least wish to appear to be trying to do so. Not to appear to be trying to do so is to risk losing legitimacy.

Disarmament, however, even if sincerely pursued, is insufficient as a goal and as a vision. Even if all weapons could be destroyed (which in fact is not possible; many of the common objects of the world can be turned into lethal weapons if that is desired), that would not in itself eliminate the tendency to take up armed struggle. Even after disarmament it would be extremely difficult to prevent a return to the manufacture of weapons, as long as a need for weapons was perceived on the part of any group with minimal technical capabilities.

It is the prevailing forms of political organization and of the organization of "defense" that provide the most crucial support for the war system. As the Norwegian peace researcher Johan Galtung has pointed out, it is not weapons alone, but the readiness to use these weapons that makes our world such a dangerous place – a readiness which depends largely on the existence of the military with its hierarchies of command and obedience. Military forces in their turn generally rely on the framework of political organization provided by the nation-state. Indeed Rumanian peace researcher Silviu Brucan argues that it is the very existence of political organization that makes war possible, that politics itself is at the heart of the problem. Tracing the development of the war system, he writes: "To the degree that a social group lost its autonomy and was assimilated into a larger unit – from band to tribe and [then] to tribal units or confederations – force became the inevitable companion of politics and required some sort of military organization."

The form of political organization which undergirds the violence system (or the war system) is the nation-state. In his *Politics as a Vocation,* Max Weber argued that the nation-state was to be defined by its relation to the means of violence. The nation-state, he wrote, is the entity that arrogates to itself the sole power to use violence *legitimately.* This monopolization of "legitimate violence," as we know, has been held to be justifiable on the ground that it best secured the *minimization* of the use of violence – the very claim that must now be questioned. If we conclude that the nation-state is a failure with respect to minimizing international violence, certain further conclusions seem to follow. (Even the achievements in the domestic arena must be questioned in a time when the typical war is both a civil and an international war.) These conclusions pertain to a necessary redefinition – and transformation – of the nation-state and with it a transformation of our understanding of politics.

The *elimination* of politics, as Brucan seems to concede, is unimaginable at the present state of our development. Barring nuclear catastrophe, it is unlikely that we can return to the life of nomadic tribes. We cannot now dispense with the effort to achieve new levels and kinds of human cooperation and human integration. War and politics have been inextricably interlinked in the past, because it was mainly by war that integration was achieved. But the situation has changed. As Brucan indicates: "The historical context today is totally different. ... Whatever the effectiveness of military force in various international conflicts, it simply does not work in the process of supranational integration. ... Indeed, the use of force in unification processes defeats its purpose by generating such deep and intense anger and alienation that integration is actually postponed for a long time thereafter." The point is clear. The achievement of a peace system requires a measure of political integration that we have not hitherto attained. But this form of integration cannot be achieved by force and any effort of this kind can only have destructive results.

We cannot consider here precisely what shape governmental institutions might take or should take in a world where governmental violence was no longer considered legitimate. Where the process of governing had been demilitarized, however, governance clearly would assume new forms. For this reason it would be appropriate to speak of a "transformation of politics." Most debates about "world government" in the past have assumed that world government would simply be some kind of a global version of national government, probably even more powerful and therefore more dangerous. The delegitimization of violence, however, would involve a cultural and behavioral transformation that would necessitate and make possible political and legal institutions that functioned quite differently at all levels – national, regional, and global.

Some legal theorists, to be sure, have argued that a legal system *must* rest on commands and that commands *must* ultimately be backed by violent sanctions in order to be effective. An opposing point of view was offered by William O. Douglas who argued that "the true gauge of law is not command but conduct. Those who move to the measured beat of custom, mores, or community or world mandates are obeying law in a real and vivid sense of the term." From this perspective, parts of our existing legal systems are already "nonviolent legal orders." What is at issue is how to expand their scope while diminishing and finally eliminating those parts of our national and international legal systems which rest on violence as the ultimate means of law enforcement.

When presented as an end goal, the institution of a peace system appears highly desirable, but also utopian (i.e. a very unlikely achievement). The institution of such a system appears to require widespread, coordinated, multilateral action on a scale that we have yet to see in human affairs. Not one nation has indicated that it was willing to undertake all the steps outlined above. (Perhaps Sweden, in spite of its position of "armed neutrality," has gone furthest in indicating a willingness to proceed in this direction.) Each nation can explain and excuse its own stance simply by pointing to the attitudes and behaviors of other nations.

The institution of peace, however, should be seen mainly as a *process* rather than an ultimate goal with static content. Peace is not some wonderful object that we can possess once certain prescribed steps have been accomplished, but a way of living and struggling that can begin now and that will have to continue (with its attendant difficulties) even after many desirable institutional changes have been achieved. The peace *process* involves risks and problems that are not so apparent when peace is considered simply as an end state. To undertake the peace process entails an acceptance of the attendant risks and difficulties as "worth it" – as a challenge, as a source of individual and/or collective "growth" and well-being, or from a negative point of view, as less terrible than the risks and difficulties of continued participation in the war system.

Participation in the peace process will involve attempts to build nonviolent relationships where violent relationships currently exist. In some cases it will involve unilateral nonviolent initiatives. The threat and the use of violence will be renounced in situations where their employment might well be considered "justified." This choice is likely to cause alarm among those who are convinced that nonviolence does not "work" or that it "works" only where the opponent is "reasonable" and shares one's own moral values. To these arguments we may respond: (*1*) The opponents of nonviolent initiatives generally employ a double standard which minimizes the costs and failures of violence while exaggerating the costs and failures of nonviolence. The alternative courses are not evaluated fairly. (*2*) Violent action may succeed in the short-run, but the deleterious long-term results of the practice of violence are obvious. We live in a world that bears the burden of those results. It cannot be proven that nonviolent initiatives will undo the violence system, but we believe that they are worth trying. (*3*) Nonviolent action is based only in part on our moral persuasion and shared values. Nonviolent methods can, if necessary, be forceful and coercive.[6]

Whatever peace initiatives are undertaken, it is desirable that they form part of a coordinated strategy and that one's ultimate objective be communicated in many ways to the global community, at both leadership and popular levels. To disarm unilaterally, for example, whether partially or completely, without taking other related measures, would not appear to be an effective approach. One can imagine, however, steps (i.e. a *set* of steps) that might be undertaken by one or several nations in pursuit of a "peace policy" aimed at the eventual establishment of the peace system described earlier. Such steps might include: (*1*) unilateral measures of disarmament, e.g., the elimination of tactical nuclear weapons, of first strike weapons, and of weapons designed for "nuclear warfighting"; (*2*) the creation of a capacity for nonviolent defense: (*3*) acceptance without reservation of the jurisdiction of the International Court of Justice and/or efforts to create regional institutions to mediate and adjudicate disputes between particular groups of nations; (*4*) rationing of gasoline so as to reduce consumption of a limited resource; (*5*) the revising of elementary history textbooks to emphasize nonmilitary, nonviolent values.

The peace process must eventually involve governments in actions such as those just described, but governmental action will not occur without massive popular pressure. It is not only that governmental elites benefit in certain respects from the war system; just as importantly, they have habits of thought which severely inhibit them from embarking on new paths. Governmental figures excuse their "conservatism" in these matters by pleading that they are doing what the "people" want and expect. It is therefore up to the people to indicate that they (we) want something else.

Fortunately, this state of affairs has considerable advantages for the people. It means that the road to peace, or rather the road of peace, is also the road of our own self-empowerment. This, then, is one of those positive factors that may encourage some to engage in the struggle for peace. In struggling for a peaceful world order and against those aspects of our own behavior which obstruct peaceful relations, we will diminish our sense of alienation and achieve a new sense of capability to affect the world and the course of our lives.

In some cases pragmatic concerns may cause governments to give attention to one or more of the elements of a peace strategy. Some governments, for instance, have already manifested an interest in nonviolent (or "civilian-based") defense, a key element in a peace strategy. A number of smaller European countries have shown an interest in this form of defense, based on the limited capacity of their armed forces to protect them against an invader.[7] Given their size and location, these countries have had to accept the fact that no military defense can for long protect them against the invading army of a greater military power and that a military defense carried on too long can have worse consequences than the cessation of military struggle.

The situation of the smaller countries is not altogether unique in a world of proliferating nuclear arms. Larger countries may find themselves compelled to choose between risking nuclear attack or preparing a nonviolent defense to meet the risk of foreign occupation. While a nonviolent defense may not be effective in protecting territorial integrity in the short-run, it has shown itself to be effective in certain circumstances in protecting human life and a country's social institutions (as in the Norwegians' successful resistance against the Nazification of their schools and churches during World War II).[8] If nuclear devastation is threatened, clearly a key advantage of armed defense is lost, since such an attack would be even more damaging to territorial integrity and a country's resources than an invasion. In such a situation, a nonviolent defense may seem the best option.

Nonviolent defense denies a usurping power (whether externally or internally based) control over a population by refusing cooperation and obeisance. The methods and tactics that may be employed in this regard are very numerous, as Gene Sharp, a leading researcher in this field, has shown. Nonmilitary forms of struggle include social, economic, political, and psychological measures. Some of these measures are aimed at subverting "the loyalty of the attacker's troops and functionaries and [promoting] their unreliability in carrying out orders and repression. ... "[9] The ultimate aim is "to deny the attacker his desired objectives."[10] Because this form of defense has not yet been made the official policy of any government, we have yet to witness a case of fully prepared civilian-based defense. The considerable power of the method has been illustrated recently, however, in two cases of internally imposed (and externally abetted) dictatorship – against the Shah's regime in Iran and against the official political leadership in Poland. The Shah's overthrow was a considerable political achievement, however much one may lament political developments in Iran since then, and in Poland the official leadership is by no means in control of the country's social and political life.

A capacity for nonviolent struggle is crucial to the establishment of a peace system, since groups must have a way to assert and defend their fundamental rights. When institutional mechanisms to mediate and adjudicate disputes fail, nonviolent means of carrying on conflict must remain. The fact that the war system has reached a point where there are practical as well as idealistic reasons for concerning ourselves with this form of struggle provides some basis for hope in the midst of an increasingly ominous global situation.

Moreover, in an era in which the vast majority of the civilian population may be passive victims in a war, it seems appropriate that the alternative form of defense is one that engages nearly the entire population of a country actively. While a nuclear war would involve a minute proportion of a country's population in an active role and represents an extreme application of technological prowess, nonviolent defense involves almost the total population in an active way and more nearly engages the total personality of those taking part in the struggle. Thus it can be said that the adoption of nonviolent means both humanizes and democratizes intergroup struggle. For those who are pursuing a more humane and democratic world order, these are further factors in favor of such a course.

Will war persist? Must war persist? Lacking prophetic powers, we cannot provide certain answers. However, one conclusion does appear justified. The problem of war does not confront us exactly with an intellectual puzzle, although the intellect may assist in its solution. The problem we confront is fundamentally a problem that regards human will and human action. And although it is not usually put in these terms, it is a problem that regards human dignity. Humankind will have little claim to dignity if we fail to undertake a concerted struggle against the war system and all that it entails and portends for our species.   *International Seminars on Training for Nonviolent Action*

NOTES

1 In his introduction to Thompson and Smith, eds., Ellsberg notes instances in which the use of nuclear weapons has been threatened by US presidents – in some cases against opponents without nuclear weapons. Even in such cases, of course, the possibility of Soviet retaliation cannot be excluded. (Ellsberg uses publicly available publications, for the most part memoirs of public officials, to document his claims.)

2 These developments include the production of first strike (or "counterforce") weapons which may severely limit an opponent's capacity to retaliate, the deployment of cruise, Pershing II and ss-20 missiles in Europe, and the promulgation of doctrines of "limited nuclear war."

3 Nathan and Norden, eds., p. 390.

4 Clausewitz (Kegan Paul edn.), Vol. 1, p. 23.

5 See Klare and note Calder's remark that "The precision of modern weapons can be used ... to place napalm and other incendiary weapons on a city in patterns that will produce a fire storm and so kill almost as many people as a nuclear weapon." It is true, of course, that the threat of ecological catastrophe posed by nuclear weapons is not posed at present by "conventional" weaponry.

6 This point has been well documented in the work of Sharp.

7 These include the Netherlands, Sweden, Norway, and Denmark.

8 For a summary account of the Norwegian resistance see Jameson. The resistance included the refusal of the vast majority of Norway's teachers to join a new Teachers Association set up on Nazi lines. Some 1300 teachers were arrested, but within the same year were released and the new association never came into being. The Norwegian resistance was supported morally and spiritually by the clergy; 93 percent "resigned their administrative functions as officers of the State Church, though retaining their spiritual functions towards the people." (Information on the Norwegian resistance can also be found in Sharp's *The Politics of Nonviolent Action.*) The possible uses of nonviolent defense in contemporary Europe are discussed by Sharp in *Making Europe Unconquerable.*

9 Sharp, *National Security Through Civilian-Based Defense.*

10 *Ibid.* Further discussion of nonviolent defense is found in the following publications: a special issue of the *Bulletin of Peace Proposals* on "Alternative Defense and Security," No. 4, 1978 (this includes articles by a number of European researchers); Mahadevan, Roberts, and Sharp, eds.; and *US Defense Policy: Mainstream Views and Nonviolent Alternatives,* International Seminars on Training for Nonviolent Action, 1982 (a study guide and packet of readings available from ISTNA, Box 515, Waltham, MA 02254).

Commentary: The Abolition of Fire, Disease, and Bad Weather

STEPHEN M. ANDERSON

In her article on the abolition of war Beverly Woodward suggests that human-kind's survival depends not so much on a new way of thinking, as Einstein put it, as a new way of acting. This suggestion deserves to be reinforced. Edging as we are toward a cliff, it will not do to be paralyzed by the persuasion that our survival hangs on a new way of thinking we have yet to discover (as suggested, for example, by Michael Zimmerman elsewhere in this volume).

The barriers to changing our ways of acting are already great enough. It does not say much for us as a species that it takes a confrontation with the specter of annihilation to set a few of us on the search for alternatives to violence when the futility of war has been so evident for ages. Looked at in one way, our resistance to change can only add to a profound pessimism already sowed and watered by the political bestiality of our times.

This attitude is one-sided, however. If humans have proven themselves capable of almost anything, we have also shown a remarkable ability to adapt to changing circumstances, and this is one of the most noteworthy characteristics of our species. A brief look at examples of how we have mastered some serious threats to our well-being may be instructive.

Confronted with extreme conditions, severe weather for instance, we either change the situation by building shelters or get used to the new environment. Most often we do both, until some acceptable state of livability is achieved. Faced with external threats to health and life, like infectious diseases, we either learn to live with or attempt to eradicate them. More likely we do both.

In the nuclear age it is nuclear war that threatens us, all of us together and all at once. The way things are now, it only takes a few individuals coincidentally doing the wrong things. Whether they are motivated by rage, fear, misinformation, miscalculation, or mistake will not much matter. How shall we adapt to this threat?

Our adaptability can be a two-edged sword, since one way to adapt to a threat is, as I've suggested, by getting used to it. Some social critics call this "psychic numbing," but I am not so sure it should rate as an emotional defect, as the term implies. One can of course ignore a serious threat at one's peril, and to do this hardly seems healthy. But it might be encouraging to discover that this is not what we do as a rule. Our record, again as a species, is generally one of doing whatever we can to remove what threatens us, when we can see a way to do it. [1]

The forest-dweller learns to live with the permanent threat of fire. Yet we have, in time, worked out ways of controlling forest fires. Will this two-edged adaptation serve as a model for how we shall adapt to the threat of nuclear war? If so, then we shall, as Woodward suggests, develop ways to reduce the risks of escalating violence. But while we create our controlling mechanisms – whether they are treaties or supranational peacekeeping forces or civilian-based defenses or massive consciousness-raising schemes or all of these things – the fire may still engulf us at any time, and this is something we have to learn to live with.

I have not yet distinguished the ways we adapt as individuals from the ways we adapt collectively. But each of the examples I've used illustrates the contrast in a different way. Protection from the weather by providing shelter and clothing for oneself is basically an individual or small-group effort, though the supply of goods necessary to this end, like houses and clothes, may depend upon a complicated economic system. One can reduce the risk of infectious disease to oneself by taking precautions. (It may be a purely unintended side-effect that this reduces the risk to others.) But the complete eradication of a disease, as with smallpox, takes cooperative efforts of the most intricate and durable sort. One person alone can do relatively little to stop a forest fire, but over the years we've figured out how a group of people working together can do it.

In each of these cases the *collective,* as opposed to the *individual* effort to overcome some threat to our well-being has been managed by a relative few who took a special interest in the matter, located the like-minded, achieved consensus on how to proceed, and convinced the rest to go along. Perhaps those interested in preventing nuclear war could benefit by studying such cases.

I have only one suggestion about where such a study might lead. Some peace advocates shun politics because they think, as Woodward describes one such position, that "politics itself is at the heart of the problem." Woodward does not claim this herself, though she does speak of the kind of change she requires as a "transformation of politics." I find these expressions obscure. It seems to me that whenever a group adopts a policy affecting some other group, there is politics. And whenever some within a group are selected to represent the rest in choosing policy, communicating it, or carrying it out, there is politics. Nor do I see how politics, thus defined, is avoidable, whether or not it has yet been "transformed."

More to the point, it is clear that some societies afford more opportunities than others for individuals to select for themselves a role in policy-making. Those are the societies in which individuals are relatively more free to research policy questions, advocate changes, attain positions of responsibility, and organize efforts to insure that the most qualified representatives are selected. It should also be clear that, in our time, we are one of those societies.

Any threat which can be met only by collective efforts is seen for what it is more clearly by some individuals than by others. It seems reasonable to me that those who understand also bear a greater responsibility than the rest to participate in the process of change in whatever way is open to them. If the corrective measures Woodward prescribes for a global order in which the capacity for violence is diminished and the inhibitions against its use are reinforced, or any equally appealing alternative recommendations[2] begin to be realized, it will be through some political process or other, and it will happen because those with opportunities to participate took the lead in organizing the necessary changes.

Concerned Philosophers for Peace

NOTES

1 Bettelheim tells of his concentration camp experiences: those who when confronted with extreme circumstances, in this case dehumanizing treatment by the ss, failed to make some accommodation in thought and behavior to the new order, failed to survive; those who accommodated too much, failing to protect at least some fragment of self-respect from the relentless assault on individual dignity, also perished, somewhat later. Peace advocates see nuclear arsenals as an extreme circumstance threatening the survival not just of individuals but of societies. Just how Bettelheim's lesson applies to our case I will leave to the reader to investigate.
2 See, for example, the well-defined, step-by-step proposal of Forsberg.

Commentary: Cultural Adaptation and Hope

MAJ.-GEN. LEONARD V. JOHNSON (RETD.)

Our species, *Homo sapiens sapiens,* is differentiated from all others by its cultural mode of adaptation, by its inventiveness and ingenuity in developing tools and techniques to survive in widely differing habitats without physical change. The primary attributes of this evolutionary advantage are a large brain and the capacity for speech. We think, we act, and therefore our species survives in an evolving biosystem in which the survival of any species is exceptional.

Before Hiroshima, doubt about the survival of our species probably never entered the conscious mind. The four decades since then have made the possibility of extinction a pressing concern, however. Nuclear weapons and delivery systems are tools of a culture become maladaptive and which now threatens to destroy its creators. Our culture is in urgent need of change. This can happen only through reason and persuasion, but first there must be demand for change, a moral sensibility that condemns nuclear deterrence on ethical grounds and rejects it as delusion. Generation of moral sensibility is the responsibility of secular and religious leadership.

Beverly Woodward rightly suggests that we also need a new way of acting. The beginning must be to stop the drift to war, to subordinate lesser interests to mutual necessity, to take acceptable risks for peace, and to prevent the holocaust for today and tomorrow. There is no shortage of good proposals to do this. All that is lacking is political courage and will. Generation of this is the democratic responsibility of every citizen.

With the time made available by this holding action, we need to develop and transmit an ideology of peace. The ideology of war so cogently described by Conrad Brunk must be replaced with a secular version of "love thy neighbor as thyself," an ideology that recognizes the need to pursue the common good in inter-state relations. Hobbes and Clausewitz must be relegated to philosophical curiosities that were irrelevant long before Hiroshima. This change is the responsibility of the intellectual, who must articulate the ideology of peace and teach it to others.

Cultural evolution is not a military campaign achievable by a deliberate strategy. It proceeds instead by what Eric Lindblom of Yale University called "disjointed incrementalism," the British technique of muddling through. Small steps lead to small gains via small risks. This process, if motivated and guided by an ideology of peace, could lead to world government and the six key elements of the peace system Woodward describes. We can strengthen the United Nations: as imperfect as it is, it remains our best hope. Until we reach Utopia, it is sufficient to steer toward it.

War is not the product of human nature, but of the state, a human institution. Only the state can deploy the resources to threaten other states; only states build empires and extend their influence through force. The behavior of states can be changed by those who lead them. We need better leaders, men and women who will choose peace, not war. Voters can choose better leaders, if they will.

Although general and complete disarmament is not achievable at present, inter-state war could be prevented if states renounced preparations for offensive war and kept their armed forces at home for manifestly defensive purposes. Only a few states, notably the US and the USSR, now have the capacity to threaten others. Moral suasion can be exerted on them.

Nature is indifferent to the survival of any species, including our own. Michael Bayles suggests that our survival is not inherently desirable, and members of other species might well agree. But it is not for us to choose extinction. As long as we have memory of what happened at Hiroshima, and even though we are mortal, our humanity calls us to avert the holocaust. We can avert nuclear war, but we must exert our minds and our wills to do so.

Generals for Peace and Disarmament

Part V   Issues to Think About and Discuss

1 According to Groarke, "deterrence is compatible with more than significant disarmament." How does he argue his case, and does it strike you as convincing? Explain your answer.

2 Why does Werner suggest that *total* unilateral disarmament may be preferable to deterrence? Do you agree or disagree? Why?

3 Do you share Narveson's conviction that "[Western] military policy in the years since the Second World War has been dominated by worst-case reasoning"? Explain in your own terms what this means. If you agree with him, evaluate his analysis of the flaws in this reasoning. If you disagree, what flaws do you find in Narveson's own account?

4 Patten argues that deterrence makes no sense because it assumes that our threats to use nuclear weapons will deter the Soviets, but that their threats will not deter us. Explain his argument. Is it convincing?

5 Some strategic theorists, like Colin Gray, assert that under certain conditions, in Brunk's words, "it will actually serve your interests to fight [a] nuclear war." Could this ever be the case? Justify your answer.

6 "Unilateral gestures need not rest on trust and can be recognized as risks." (Bayles) Discuss.

7 "Peace ... should be seen mainly as a *process* rather than as an ultimate goal with static content." Why does Woodward say this, and what role does she assign in this process to nonviolent actions and policies?

8 In Anderson's view, the lesson of human history and evolution is that threats to our survival as a species, like the threat of nuclear war, must be met by collective action. What forms of action can you think of that would offer hope for survival, and how might you participate in them? Is the nuclear freeze proposal to which Anderson refers in footnote 2 a promising option? Explain.

9 "It is not for us to choose extinction. As long as we have memory of what happened at Hiroshima, and even though we are mortal, our humanity calls us to avert the holocaust." Johnson suggests here that while it may not matter from an evolutionary point of view whether our species survives, it does matter from other standpoints. State whether you agree or disagree and why.

10 Johnson suggests that the "generation of moral sensibility" and "political courage and will" are the keys to solving the nuclear crisis. Explain what you think he means and how such sensibility might be fostered.

Bibliography

Adams, Ruth, and Susan Cullen, eds. *The Final Epidemic: Physicians and Scientists on Nuclear War.* Chicago: Educational Foundation for Nuclear Science, 1981.

Aldridge, R.C. *The Counterforce Syndrome: A Guide to US Nuclear Weapons and Strategic Doctrine.* Washington: Institute for Policy Studies, 1979.

_____. *First Strike: The Pentagon's Strategy for Nuclear War.* Boston: South End Press, 1983.

Alford, John. "A Skeptical View of 'No-First-Use'." *Conflict Quarterly,* Winter 1984.

American Friends Service Committee. *Questions and Answers on the Soviet Threat and National Security.* Philadelphia: AFSC, 1982.

Arendt, Hannah. *The Origins of Totalitarianism.* Cleveland: World Publishing, 1958.

Aron, Raymond. *Peace and War: A Theory of International Relations.* Garden City, NY: Doubleday, 1966.

Aronson, Ronald. *The Dialectics of Disaster.* London: Verso, 1983.

Attfield, Robin. *The Ethics of Environmental Concern.* Oxford: Blackwell, 1983.

Ayres, R.W. "Policing Plutonium: The Civil Liberties Fallout." *Harvard Civil Rights-Civil Liberties Law Review,* 10 (2), Spring 1975.

Baier, Annette. "Secular Faith." *Canadian Journal of Philosophy,* 10 (March 1980).

Barnet, Richard. *The Economy of Death.* New York: Atheneum, 1970.

Bayles, Michael D. *Morality and Population Policy.* University, AL: Univ. of Alabama Press, 1980.

Beardslee, William and John Mack. "The Impact on Children and Adolescents of Nuclear Developments." *Psychosocial Aspects of Nuclear Developments.* Task Force Report #20. Washington: American Psychiatric Association, 1982.

Bellenson, Laurence, W. "Accepting Our Nuclear Age." *Journal of Civil Defense,* February 1983.

_____, and Samuel T. Cohen. "A New Nuclear Strategy." *New York Times Magazine,* January 24, 1982.

Bender, David L., ed. *The Arms Race: Opposing Viewpoints.* St. Paul: Greenhaven Press, 1982.

Benson, H. *The Relaxation Response.* New York: Avon, 1975.

Beres, Louis René. *Apocalypse: Nuclear Catastrophe in World Politics.* Chicago: University of Chicago Press, 1980.

_____. *Mimicking Sisyphus: America's Countervailing Nuclear Strategy.* Lexington: Lexington Books, 1983.

_____. "Presidential Directive 59: A Critical Assessment." *Parameters: Journal of the US Army War College,* XI (1), 1982.

Berman, Morris. *The Reenchantment of the World.* Ithaca: Cornell Univ. Press, 1981.

Bernstein, Barton. *The Atomic Bomb: The Critical Issues.* Boston: Little, Brown, 1976.

Best, Geoffrey. *Humanity in Warfare: The Modern History of the International Law of Armed Conflicts.* New York: Methuen, 1983.

Bettelheim, Bruno. *The Informed Heart: Autonomy in a Mass Age.* New York: The Free Press, 1960.

Blake, Nigel and Kay Pole, eds. *Dangers of Deterrence: Philosophers on Nuclear Strategy.* London: Routledge & Kegan Paul, 1983.

Bookchin, Murray. *The Ecology of Freedom.* Palo Alto, CA: Chesire, 1982.

Bracken, Paul. *The Command and Control of Nuclear Forces.* New Haven: Yale Univ. Press, 1983.

Brennan, Andrew. "The Moral Standing of Natural Objects." *Environmental Ethics,* 6 (1), Spring 1984.

Broad, William J. "Nuclear Pulse (I): Awakening to the Chaos Factor." *Science,* May 29, 1981.

_____. "Nuclear Pulse (II): Ensuring the Delivery of the Doomsday Signal." *Science,* June 5,

1981.

_____. "Nuclear Pulse (III): Playing a Wild Card." *Science,* June 12, 1981.

Brodie, Bernard, ed. *The Absolute Weapon.* New York: Harcourt, Brace, 1946.

Bronfenbrenner, Urie. "Why Do the Russians Plant Trees Along the Road?" *Saturday Review,* January 5, 1963.

Brouwer, D.R., ed. *On the Fate of the Earth.* San Francisco: Earth Island Institute, 1983.

Brown, William M. *The Nuclear Crisis of 1979.* Washington: US Government Printing Office, 1976.

Buber, Martin. *I and Thou.* Trans. by Walter Kaufmann. New York: Scribner's, 1970.

Buchan, Glenn C. "The Anti-MAD Mythology." *Bulletin of the Atomic Scientists,* 37 (4), April 1981.

Bundy, McGeorge, George F. Kennan, Robert S. McNamara, and Gerald Smith. "Nuclear Weapons and the Atlantic Alliance." *Foreign Affairs,* 60 (Spring 1982).

Bunn, M. and K. Tsipis. "The Uncertainties of a Preemptive Nuclear Attack." *Scientific American,* 249 (5), November 1983.

Calder, Nigel. *Nuclear Nightmares.* Harmondsworth, Middlesex: Penguin, 1979.

Caldicott, Helen. *Missile Envy: The Arms Race and Nuclear War.* New York: William Morrow, 1984.

_____. *Nuclear Madness: What You Can Do!* New York: Bantam, 1980.

Callahan, Daniel. "What Obligations Do We Have to Future Generations?" *American Ecclesiastical Review,* 164 (4), April 1971.

Capra, Fritjof. *The Turning Point.* New York: Simon & Schuster, 1982.

Carey, Michael J. "Psychological Fallout." *Bulletin of the Atomic Scientists,* 38 (1), January 1982

Carver, Field Marshal Lord Michael. "Towards a No-First-Use Policy." *Conflict Quarterly,* Winter 1984.

Center for Defense Information. "Soviet Military Power: Questions and Answers." *Defense Monitor,* XI (1), 1982.

_____. "Stopping Nuclear Weapons Explosions: The Vital Next Step." *Defense Monitor,* XI (8), 1982.

Charney, Israel, ed. *Towards Understanding, Intervention and Prevention of Genocide.* Boulder: Westview Press, 1984.

Clark, Ian. *Limited Nuclear War.* Princeton: Princeton University Press, 1982.

Clausewitz, Carl von. *On War.* Baltimore: Penguin, 1968.

_____. *On War.* Trans. by J.J. Graham. London: Kegan Paul, Trench, Trubner, 1918.

Clayton, Bruce. *Life After Doomsday.* Boulder: Paladin, 1980.

Cockburn, Andrew. *The Threat: Inside the Soviet Military Machine.* New York: Random House, 1983.

Cohen, Avner and Steven Lee, eds. *Nuclear Weapons and the Future of Humanity.* Totowa, NJ: Littlefield, Adams, 1984.

Committee for the Compilation of Materials on Damage Caused by the Atomic Bombs. *Hiroshima and Nagasaki: The Physical, Medical, and Social Effects of the Atomic Bombs.* Trans. by Ishikawa and Swain. New York: Basic Books, 1981.

Common Cause. *Up in Arms: A Common Cause Guide to Understanding Nuclear Arms.* Washington: Common Cause, 1984.

Conway, David. "Capital Punishment and Deterrence: Some Considerations in Dialogue Form." *Philosophy and Public Affairs,* 3 (4), Summer 1974.

Cox, John. *Overkill: The Story of Modern Weapons.* Harmondsworth, Middlesex: Penguin, 1981.

Crownfield, David. "The Curse of Abel: An Essay in Biblical Ecology." *North American Review,* 258 (2), Summer 1973.

Dahlitz, Julie. *Nuclear Arms Control.* Boston: Allen & Unwin, 1983.

Deikman, Arthur J. *The Observing Self: Mysticism and Psychotherapy.* Boston: Beacon Press, 1982.

Deutsch, M. *The Resolution of Conflict: Constructive and Destructive Processes.* New Haven: Yale Univ. Press, 1973.

Dworkin, Ronald. *Taking Rights Seriously.* Cambridge, MA: Harvard Univ. Press, 1977.

Easlea, Brian. *Fathering the Unthinkable: Masculinity, Scientists and the Nuclear Arms Race.* London: Pluto Press, 1983.

Echols, Alice. "The New Feminism of Yin and Yang." In Snitow, Ann, Christine Stansell, and Sharon Thompson, eds. *Powers of Desire: The Politics of Sexuality.* New York: Monthly Review Press, 1983.

Ehrlich, Paul R. et. al. "Long-Term Biological Consequences of Nuclear War." *Science,* December 23, 1983. (Reprinted as *The Cold and the Dark: The World After Nuclear War.* The Conference on the Long-Term Worldwide Biological Consequences of Nuclear War. New York: W.W. Norton, 1984.)

Ellsberg, Daniel. "Nuclear Weapons: Will We Use Them?" *Current,* 233 (1981).

Etzioni, A. "The Kennedy Experiment." *Western Political Quarterly,* 20 (2, Part 1), June 1967.

Fairley, W. "Criteria for Evaluating the 'Small' Probability." In D. Okrent, ed. *Risk-Benefit Methodology and Application.* Los Angeles: UCLA School of Engineering and Applied Science, 1975.

Feld, Bernard T. "The Consequences of Nuclear War." *Bulletin of the Atomic Scientists,* 32 (6), June 1976.

Ferguson, Marilyn. *The Aquarian Conspiracy: Personal and Social Transformation in the 1980s.* Los Angeles: J.P. Tarcher, 1980.

Fischer, Dietrich. *Preventing War in the Nuclear Age.* Totowa, NJ: Rowman & Allanheld, 1984.

Fischhoff, B. et al. "How Safe is Safe Enough?" *Policy Sciences,* 9 (2), 1978.

Fisher, Ronald. *Social Psychology.* New York: St. Martin's Press, 1982.

Fiske, S.T., B. Fischhoff and M.A. Milburn, eds. *Images of Nuclear War. Journal of Social Issues,* 39 (1983). (9 papers)

Ford, Daniel F. *The Cult of the Atom: Secret Papers of the Atomic Energy Commission.* New York: Simon & Schuster, 1982.

Ford, John C. "The Morality of Obliteration Bombing." *Theological Studies,* 5 (1944).

Forsberg, Randall. "Confining the Military to Defense as a Route to Disarmament." *World Policy Journal,* 1 (Winter 1984).

Frank, Jerome D. "The Nuclear Arms Race: Sociopsychological Aspects." *American Journal of Public Health,* 70 (September 1980).

———. *Sanity and Survival: Psychological Aspects of War and Peace.* New York: Vantage Books, 1968.

Frankl, Viktor. *The Doctor and the Soul: From Psychotherapy to Logotherapy.* Trans. Richard and Clara Winston. 2nd edn. New York: Random House, 1973.

Freeman, Harold. *This is the way the world will end, this is the way you will end, unless....* Edmonton: Hurtig, 1983.

Frei, Daniel. *Risks of Unintentional Nuclear War.* Published in Cooperation with the United Nations Institute for Disarmament Research. Totowa, NJ: Allanheld, Osmun, 1983.

Freud, Sigmund. *Group Psychology.* New York: W.W. Norton, 1961.

Friedman, M. and R.H. Roseman. *Type A Behavior and Your Heart.* Greenwich: Fawcett Publications, 1974.

Gardiner, Robert W. *The Cool Arm of Destruction: Modern Weapons and Moral Insensitivity.* Philadelphia: Westminster Press, 1974.

Garrett, B.N. and B.S. Glaser. *War and Peace.* Berkeley: Institute of International Studies, 1984.

Gauthier, David. "Deterrence, Maximization, and Rationality." *Ethics,* 94 (April 1984).

_____. "Why One Ought to Obey God: Reflections on Hobbes and Locke." *Canadian Journal of Philosophy*, 7 (3), September 1977.

Gay, William. "Myths About Nuclear War." *Philosophy and Social Criticism,* 9 (Summer 1982).

Gewirth, Alan. *Human Rights.* Chicago: Univ. of Chicago Press, 1982.

Gilligan, Carol. *In a Different Voice.* Cambridge: Harvard Univ. Press, 1982.

Glasstone, Samuel and Philip Dolan, eds. *The Effects of Nuclear Weapons.* us Department of Defense. Washington: us Government Printing Office, 1962.

Glucksmann, A. *Discours de la Guerre.* Paris: L'Herne, 1968.

Goldman, D.S. and W.M. Greenberg, eds. *Preparing for Nuclear War: The Psychological Effects. American Journal of Orthopsychiatry,* 52 (4), October 1982. (7 papers)

Goodpaster, K.E. "On Being Morally Considerable." *Journal of Philosophy,* 75 (6), June 1978.

_____ and K.M. Sayre, eds. *Ethics and Problems of the 21st Century.* Notre Dame: Univ. of Notre Dame Press, 1979.

Goodwin, Gregory L., ed. *Ethics and Nuclear Deterrence.* London: St. Martin's Press, 1982.

Govier, Trudy. "Nuclear Illusion and Individual Obligations." *Canadian Journal of Philosophy,* 13 (4), December 1983.

_____. "Philosophy, Nuclear Deterrence and the Real World," *Ethics,* 95(3). April 1985.

Gray Colin S. *Nuclear Strategy and Strategic Planning.* Philadelphia: Foreign Policy Research Institute, 1984.

_____ and Keith Payne. "Victory Is Possible." *Foreign Policy,* 39 (Summer 1980).

Gray, J. Glenn. *The Warriors: Reflections on Men in Battle.* New York: Harcourt Brace Jovanovich, 1959.

Green, H. "Cost-Benefit Assessment and the Law." *George Washington Law Review,* 45 (5), 1977.

Green, Philip. *Deadly Logic: The Theory of Nuclear Deterrence.* Columbus: Ohio State Univ. Press, 1966.

Griffiths, Franklyn and John C. Polanyi, eds. *The Dangers of Nuclear War.* Toronto: Univ. of Toronto Press, 1979.

Ground Zero. *Hope: Facing the Music on Nuclear War and the 1984 Elections.* New York: Pocket Books/Longshadow Books, 1983.

_____. *Nuclear War: What's In It For You?* New York: Pocket Books, 1982.

_____. *What About the Russians – and Nuclear War?* New York: Pocket Books, 1983.

Halifax, Joan. *Shamanic Voices.* New York: E.P. Dutton, 1979.

Halloran, Richard. "Pentagon Draws Up First Strategy for Fighting a Long Nuclear War." *New York Times,* May 30, 1982.

Hardin, Russell. "Unilateral versus Mutual Disarmament." *Philosophy and Public Affairs,* 12 (3), Summer 1983.

Harvard Nuclear Study Group: *Living With Nuclear Weapons.* New York: Bantam, 1983.

Heidegger, Martin, *The End of Philosophy.* Trans. Joan Stambaugh. New York: Harper & Row, 1973.

_____. *Basic Writings.* Ed. David Farrell Krell. New York: Harper & Row, 1977.

_____. *What Is Called Thinking?* Trans. Fred D. Wieck and J. Glenn Gray. New York: Harper & Row, 1972.

_____. *An Introduction to Metaphysics.* Trans. Ralph Mannheim. Garden City, NY: Doubleday, 1961.

_____. *Nietzsche, II.* Pfullingen: Gunther Neske, 1961.

_____. *Poetry, Language, Thought.* Trans. Albert Hofstadter. New York: Harper & Row, 1971.

_____. *Heraklit: 1. Der Anfang des abendländischen Denkens.* Ed. Manfred S. Frings. Lectures at the Univ. of Freiburg, Summer 1943. In Martin Heidegger, *Gesamtausgabe,* Vol. 55. Frankfurt am Main: Vittorio Klostermann, 1979.

Heller, Steven, ed. *Warheads: Cartoonists Draw the Line.* Harmondsworth, Middlesex: Penguin, 1983.

Herkin, Greg. *The Winning Weapon.* New York: Knopf, 1980.

Hersey, John. *Hiroshima.* New York: Modern Library, 1946.

Hilgartner, Stephen, Richard C. Bell, and Rory O'Connor. *Nukespeak: The Selling of Nuclear Technology in America.* Harmondsworth, Middlesex: Penguin, 1982.

Hobbes, Thomas. *Leviathan.* London, 1651.

Holden, Constance. "Military Grapples with the Chaos Factor." *Science,* September 11, 1981.

Holloway, David. *The Soviet Union and the Arms Race.* New Haven: Yale Univ. Press, 1983.

Horsburgh, H.J.N. "The Distinctiveness of Satyagraha." In James Rachels and Frank A. Tillman, eds. *Philosophical Issues.* New York: Harper & Row, 1972.

Independent Commission on Disarmament and Security Issues. *Common Security: A Programme for Disarmament.* London: Pan Books, 1982.

Jaggar, Alison M. *Feminist Politics and Human Nature.* Totowa, NJ: Rowman & Allanheld, 1983.

Jameson, A.K. "Unarmed Against Fascism." *Peace News,* April 1963.

Jervis, Robert. *The Illogic of American Nuclear Strategy.* Ithaca: Cornell Univ. Press, 1984.

Johnson, James T. *Can Modern War Be Just?* New Haven: Yale Univ. Press, 1984.

Joseph, Paul. "From MAD to NUTS: The Growing Danger of Nuclear War." *Socialist Review,* 12 (61), January/February 1982.

Jungk, Robert. *Brighter Than a Thousand Suns.* New York: Penguin, 1982.

Kahn, Herman. *On Thermonuclear War.* Princeton: Princeton Univ. Press, 1960.

_____. *Thinking About the Unthinkable.* New York: Horizon Press, 1962.

Kaldor, Mary. *The Baroque Arsenal.* New York: Hill and Wang, 1981.

Kaplan, Fred. *The Dubious Specter: A Skeptical Look at the Soviet Military Threat.* Washington: Institute for Policy Studies, 1980.

_____. *The Wizards of Armageddon: Strategists of the Nuclear Age.* New York: Simon & Schuster, 1982.

Katz, Arthur. *Life After Nuclear War.* Cambridge, MA: Ballinger, 1982.

Kavka, Gregory. "Doubts About Unilateral Disarmament." *Philosophy and Public Affairs,* 12 (3), Summer 1983.

_____. "Some Paradoxes of Deterrence." *Journal of Philosophy,* 75 (6), June 1978.

Kennan, George F. *The Nuclear Delusion: Soviet-American Relations in the Atomic Age.* Expanded, updated edn. New York: Pantheon, 1983.

Kennedy, Robert F. *Thirteen Days.* New York: New American Library, 1969.

Kissinger, Henry A. *Nuclear Weapons and Foreign Policy.* Abridged edn. New York: W.W. Norton, 1969.

_____. *A World Restored.* Boston: Houghton Mifflin, 1957.

Klare, Michael. "Leaping the Firebreak." *The Progressive,* September 1983.

Kovel, Joel. *Against the State of Nuclear Terror.* Boston: South End Press, 1983.

Lackey, Douglas. "Missiles and Morals: A Utilitarian Look at Nuclear Deterrence." *Philosophy and Public Affairs,* 11 (3), 1982.

_____. *Moral Principles and Nuclear Weapons.* Totowa, NJ: Rowman & Allanheld, 1984.

Laszlo, E. and D. Keys, eds. *Disarmament: The Human Factor.* Oxford: Pergamon Press, 1981.

Lewis, Kevin N. "The Prompt and Delayed Effects of Nuclear War." *Scientific American,* 241 (1), July 1979.

Lifton, Robert Jay. *Death in Life: Survivors of Hiroshima.* New York: Random House, 1967.

_____. and Richard Falk. *Indefensible Weapons: The Political and Psychological Case Against Nuclearism.* New York: Basic Books; Toronto: CBC Enterprises, 1982.

Lovins, Amory and L.H. Lovins. *Energy/War: Breaking the Nuclear Link.* San Francisco: Friends of the Earth, 1980.

Lowrance, W. "The Nature of Risk." In R. Schwing and W. Albers, eds. *Societal Risk Assessment.* New York: Plenum, 1980.

Luttwak, Edward N. "How to Think About Nuclear War." *Commentary,* August 1982.

Macy, Joanna. *Despair and Empowerment in the Nuclear Age.* Philadelphia: New Society, 1983.

Mahadevan, T.K., A. Roberts, and G. Sharp, eds. *Civilian Defense: An Introduction.* New Delhi: Gandhi Peace Foundation; Weare: Greenleaf Books, 1967.

Malcolmson, Robert W. *Nuclear Fallacies: How We Have Been Misguided Since Hiroshima.* Montreal and Kingston: McGill-Queen's Univ. Press, 1985.

Mandelbaum, Michael. *The Nuclear Question.* Cambridge: Cambridge Univ. Press, 1979.

Marcuse, Herbert. *One-Dimensional Man.* Boston: Beacon Press, 1964.

Marx, Karl and Friedrich Engels. *Selected Works.* New York: International Publishers, 1968.

Mavrodes, George. "Conventions and the Morality of War." *Philosophy and Public Affairs,* 4 (2), Winter 1975.

McNamara, Robert S. "The Military Role of Nuclear Weapons: Perceptions and Misperceptions." *Foreign Affairs,* Fall 1983.

Medvedev, Roy and Zhores. "The U.S.S.R. and the Arms Race." *New Left Review,* December 1981.

Merchant, Carolyn. *The Death of Nature: Women, Ecology and the Scientific Revolution.* New York: Harper & Row, 1980.

Meyer, Stephen M. *The Dynamics of Nuclear Proliferation.* Chicago: Univ. of Chicago Press, 1984.

Milgram, Stanley. *Obedience to Authority: An Experimental View.* New York: Harper & Row, 1974.

Mills, Claudia. "Not With a Bang: The Moral Perplexities of Nuclear Deterrence." *Report from the Center for Philosophy and Public Policy,* 3 (3), Summer 1983.

Mitcham, Carol and Robert Mackey, eds. *Philosophy and Technology.* New York: The Free Press, 1972.

Modgliani, A. "The Public and the Cold War." *War/Peace Report,* September 1973.

Morris, Christopher. "A Contractarian Defense of Nuclear Deterrence." *Ethics,* 95 (3), April 1985.

Myerson, Michael and Mark Solomon. *Stopping World War III.* New York: US Peace Council, 1981.

Myrdal, Alva. *The Game of Disarmament.* Revised and updated edn. New York: Pantheon, 1982.

Nagel, Thomas. "War and Massacre." *Philosophy and Public Affairs,* 1 (2), Winter 1972.

Narveson, Jan, ed. *Moral Issues.* Don Mills, Ontario: Oxford Univ. Press, 1983.

Nathan, Otto and Heinz Norden, eds. *Einstein on Peace.* New York: Schocken, 1968.

Nield, R. *How to Make Up Your Mind About the Bomb.* London: Andre Deutsch, 1981.

Noble, Cheryl. "Political Realism, International Morality, and Just War." *The Monist,* 57 (4), October 1973.

Novick, S. *The Electric War.* San Francisco: Sierra Club, 1976.

Orwell, George. *Collected Essays.* London: Mercury Books, 1961.

Osgood, C.E. *An Alternative to War or Surrender.* Urbana: Univ. of Illinois Press, 1962.

Osgood, Robert. *Limited War: The Challenge to American Strategy.* Chicago: Univ. of Chicago Press, 1957.

Partridge, Ernest, ed. *Responsibilities to Future Generations.* Buffalo: Prometheus, 1981.

Paskins, Barrie and Michael Dockill. *The Ethics of War.* Minneapolis: Univ. of Minnesota Press, 1979.

Passmore, John. *Man's Responsibility for Nature.* New York: Scribner's, 1974.

Perry, Thomas, ed. *The Prevention of Nuclear War.* Vancouver: Physicians for Social Responsibility, 1983.

Peterson, Jeannie, ed. (for *AMBIO*). *The Aftermath: The Human and Ecological Consequences of*

Nuclear War. New York: Pantheon, 1983.

Powers, Thomas. *Thinking About the Next War.* New York: Knopf, 1982.

Pringle, Peter and William Arkin. *s.i.o.p.: The Secret u.s. Plan for Nuclear War.* New York: W.W. Norton, 1983.

———. and James Spigelman. *The Nuclear Barons.* New York: Avon, 1981.

Prins, Gwyn, ed. *Defended to Death.* A Study of the Nuclear Arms Race from the Cambridge University Disarmament Seminar. Harmondsworth, Middlesex: Penguin, 1983.

Ramberg, Bennett. *Destruction of Nuclear Energy Facilities in War.* Lexington: D.C. Heath, 1980.

Rapoport, Anatol. *Conflict in a Man-Made Environment.* Harmondsworth, Middlesex: Penguin, 1982.

———. "Prisoner's Dilemma." In Rapoport, ed. *Game Theory as a Theory of Conflict Resolution.* Boston: D. Reidel, 1974.

Rawls, John. *A Theory of Justice.* Cambridge, MA: Harvard Univ. Press, 1971.

Regan, Tom. *All That Dwell Therein: Animal Rights and Environmental Ethics.* Berkeley and Los Angeles: Univ. of California Press, 1982.

Regehr, Ernie and Simon Rosenblum, eds. *Canada and the Nuclear Arms Race.* Toronto: James Lorimer, 1983.

Rickover, Hyman. "Advice from Admiral Rickover." *New York Review of Books*, March 18, 1982.

Rifkin, Jeremy, with Ted Howard. *The Emerging Order: God in the Age of Scarcity.* New York: G.P. Putnam's Sons, 1979.

Riordan, M. *The Day After Midnight: The Effects of Nuclear War.* Based on a Report by the US Office of Technology Assessment. Palo Alto, CA: Cheshire Books, 1982.

Rorty, Richard. *Philosophy and the Mirror of Nature.* Princeton: Princeton Univ. Press, 1979.

Rothchild, Emma. "Delusions of Deterrence." *New York Review of Books,* 30 (6), April 14, 1983.

Roussopoulos, Dimitrios, ed. *Our Generation Against Nuclear War.* Montreal: Black Rose Books, 1983.

Russett, Bruce. *The Prisoners of Insecurity: Nuclear Deterrence, The Arms Race, and Arms Control.* San Francisco: W.H. Freeman, 1983.

Sagan, Carl. "Nuclear War and Climatic Catastrophe." *Foreign Affairs,* 62 (Winter 1983/84).

Santoni, Ronald E. "A Reply to Professor Garver on Philosophy and Pacifism." *Philosophy Today,* 11 (Summer 1967).

———. "The Arms Race, Genocidal Intent, and Individual Responsibility." *Philosophy and Social Criticism,* Fall 1984.

———. "Omnicide and the Problem of Belief." *The Churchman,* August/September 1980.

Scheer, Robert. *With Enough Shovels: Reagan, Bush and Nuclear War.* New York: Random House, 1982.

Schell, Jonathan. *The Abolition.* New York: Knopf, 1984.

———. *The Fate of the Earth.* New York: Knopf, 1982.

Schelling, Thomas C. *Arms and Influence.* New Haven: Yale Univ. Press, 1962.

Seager, William. "Is Nuclear Deterrence Paradoxical?" *Dialogue* XXIII (2), June 1984.

Sharp, Gene. *Making Europe Unconquerable: The Potential of Civilian-Based Deterrence and Defense.* New York: Taylor & Francis, 1984.

———. *National Security Through Civilian-Based Defense,* forthcoming.

———. *The Politics of Nonviolent Action.* Boston: Porter Sargent, 1973.

———. *Social Power and Political Freedom.* Boston: Porter Sargent, 1980.

Shaw, William H. "Nuclear Deterrence and Deontology." *Ethics,* 94 (January 1984).

Shawcross, William. *Sideshow: Kissinger, Nixon and the Destruction of Cambodia.* New York: Simon & Schuster, 1979.

Sherwin, Martin J. *A World Destroyed.* New York: Knopf, 1975.

Shrader-Frechette, K.S. "Economics, Risk-Cost-Benefit Analysis and the Linearity Assumption." In P.D. Asquith and T. Nickles, eds. *PSA 1982,* Vol. 1. East Lansing, MI: Philosophy of Science Association, 1982.

————. "Energy and Ethics." In Tom Regan, ed., *Earthbound: New Introductory Essays in Environmental Ethics.* New York: Random House, 1983.

————. *Nuclear Power and Public Policy.* 2nd edn. Boston: D. Reidel, 1983.

————. *Risk Analysis and Scientific Method.* Boston: D. Reidel, 1984.

————. "Risk-Assessment Methodology and the Challenge to Jeffersonian Democracy." *Energy Policy Studies,* 1 (1983).

————. "Technology Assessment, Future Generations and the Social Contract." *Humanities and Technology,* 1 (1), 1979.

Singer, S. Fred. "The Big Chill? Challenging a Nuclear Scenario." *Wall Street Journal.* February 3, 1984.

Sivard, Ruth Leger. *World Military and Social Expenditures 1983.* Leesburg, VA: World Priorities, 1983.

Solomon, Robert C. "Emotions and Choice." In Amelie Oksenberg Rorty, ed. *Explaining Emotions.* Berkeley and Los Angeles: Univ. of California Press, 1980.

Somerville, John. *The Crisis.* London: Menard Press, 1982.

————. *The Peace Revolution.* Westport, CT: Greenwood Press, 1975.

————, ed. *Soviet Marxism and Nuclear War: An International Debate.* Westport, CT: Greenwood Press, 1981.

Sommers, F.G. and T. Dineen. *Curing Nuclear Madness: A Prescription for Personal Action.* Toronto: Methuen, forthcoming.

Starr, C. and C. Whipple. "Risks of Risk Decisions." *Science,* June 6, 1980.

Sterba, James, ed. *Morality, War and Nuclear Deterrence.* Belmont, CA: Wadsworth, 1984.

————. "On Achieving Nuclear Deterrence." *Concerned Philosophers for Peace Newsletter,* 8 (March 1984).

Stobaugh, Robert and Daniel Yergin, eds. *Energy Future: Report of the Energy Project at Harvard Business School.* New York: Random House, 1979.

Stockholm International Peace Research Institute. *The Arms Race and Arms Control.* London: Taylor & Francis, 1982.

————. *The Law of War and Dubious Weapons.* Stockholm: SIPRI, 1976.

Subcommittee on Energy Research and Production of the Committee on Science and Technology of the US House of Representatives. *Nuclear Power Plant Safety After Three Mile Island.* Washington: US Government Printing Office, 1980.

Suddaby, Adam. *The Nuclear War Game: Facts and Information Everyone Should Know.* Aurora, IL: Caroline House, 1984.

Sykes, Lynn R. and Jack F. Evernder. "The Verification of a Comprehensive Test Ban Treaty." *Scientific American,* 247 (4), October 1982.

Teller, Edward. "Dangerous Myths about Nuclear Arms." *Reader's Digest* (US edition), November 1982.

The President's Commission on Strategic Forces (The Scowcroft Commission). *Report of the President's Commission on Strategic Forces.* Washington: US Government Printing Office, April 1983.

Thompson, E.P. *Beyond the Cold War.* New York: Pantheon, 1982.

———— and Dan Smith. *Protest & Survive.* New York: Monthly Review Press, 1981.

Tobias, Sheila et. al. *The People's Guide to National Defense (What Kinds of Guns Are They Buy-*

ing for Your Butter? A Beginner's Guide to Defense, Weaponry, and Military Spending).
New York: William Morrow, 1982.

Truitt, Willis H. and T.W. Graham Solomons, eds. *Science, Technology, and Freedom.* Boston: Houghton Mifflin, 1974.

Tsipis, Kosta. *Understanding Weapons in a Nuclear Age.* New York: Simon & Schuster, 1983.

Turco, Richard P. et al. "The Climatic Effects of Nuclear War." *Scientific American,* 251 (2), August 1984.

_____. "Nuclear Winter: Global Consequences of Multiple Nuclear Explosions." *Science,* December 23, 1983.

Turner, John. *The Arms Race.* Cambridge: Cambridge Univ. Press (Modern World Issues series), 1983.

UN. *Nuclear Weapons: Report of the Secretary General.* Brookline, MA: Autumn Press, 1980.

US Congressional Budget Office. *Planning US Strategic Nuclear Forces for the 1980's.* Washington: US Government Printing Office, 1978.

US General Accounting Office. *Countervailing Strategy Demands Revision of Strategic Force Acquisition Plans.* Washington: US Government Printing Office, August 1981.

_____. *The Economic and Social Consequences of Nuclear Attacks on the United States.* Prepared for the Joint Committee on Defense Production, Congress. Published by the Committee on Banking, Housing and Urban Affairs, US Senate. Washington: US Government Printing Office, 1979.

US Government. *DCPA Attack Environment Manual.* Washington: US Government Printing Office, 1973.

_____. "Questions and Answers on Crisis Relocation Planning." *Information Bulletin* No. 305, April 20, 1979.

US Office of Technology Assessment. *Application of Solar Technology to Today's Energy Needs.* 2 vols. Washington: US Government Printing Office, September 1978.

_____. *The Effects of Nuclear War.* Washington: US Government Printing Office, 1979.

US Senate. *Civil Defense.* Hearings Before the Committee on Banking, Housing and Urban Affairs. Washington: US Government Printing Office, 1979.

_____. *Nuclear War Strategy.* Hearings Before the Committee on Foreign Relations, Ninety-Sixth Congress, Second Session, on Presidential Directive 59. Washington: US Government Printing Office, 1981.

Walzer, Michael. *Just and Unjust Wars.* New York: Basic Books, 1977.

Wasserman, Harvey and Norman Solomon. *Killing Our Own: The Disaster of America's Experience with Atomic Radiation.* New York: Delacorte Press, 1982.

Wasserstrom, Richard. "Conduct and Responsibility in Time of War." In Wasserstrom, *Philosophy and Social Issues: Five Studies.* Notre Dame: Univ. of Notre Dame Press, 1980. 1980.

_____. "The Laws of War." *The Monist,* 56 (1) January, 1972.

_____. "On the Morality of War: A Preliminary Inquiry." *Stanford Law Review,* 21 (1969).

_____. "Review of Michael Walzer, *Just and Unjust Wars.*" *Harvard Law Review,* 92 (1978).

_____. "Review of Telford Taylor, *Nuremberg and Vietnam.*" *New York Review of Books,* June 3, 1971.

Webber, Philip, Graeme Wilkinson, and Barry Rubin. *Crisis Over Cruise: A Plain Guide to the New Weapons.* Harmondsworth, Middlesex: Penguin, 1983.

Wells, Donald A. *War Crimes and Laws of War.* Lanham, MD: Univ. Press of America, 1984.

Weston, Burns H., ed. *Toward Nuclear Disarmament and Global Security: A Search for Alternatives.* Boulder, Westview Press, 1984.

White, Lynn. "The Historical Roots of Our Ecologic Crisis." *Science*, March 10, 1967.

White, Ralph K. *Fearful Warriors: A Psychological Profile of US-Soviet Relations*. New York: The Free Press, 1984.

_____. "Images in the Context of International Conflict: Soviet Perceptions of the US and the USSR" In Herbert C. Kelman, ed. *International Behavior: A Social-Psychological Analysis*. New York: Holt, Rinehart and Winston, 1966.

Wieseltier, Leon. *Nuclear War, Nuclear Peace*. New York: Holt, Rinehart and Winston, 1983.

Wilber, Ken. *The Atman Project*. Wheaton, IL: Quest, 1980.

_____. *Up From Eden: A Transpersonal View of Human Evolution*. Boulder: Shambhala, 1981.

Wilkinson, Loren. *Earthkeeping: Christian Stewardship of Natural Resources*. Grand Rapids: Eerdman's, 1980.

Willrich, M. *Global Politics of Nuclear Energy*. New York: Praeger, 1976.

Wolfe, Alan. *The Rise and Fall of the "Soviet Threat": Domestic Sources of the Cold War Consensus*. Washington: Institute for Policy Studies, 1979.

Yellin, J. "Judicial Review and Nuclear Power." *George Washington Law Review*, 45 (5), 1977.

Yudkin, Marcia. "When Kids Think the Unthinkable." *Psychology Today*, 18 (4), April 1984.

Zimmerman, Michael. "Beyond Humanism: Heidegger's Understanding of Technology." *Listening*, 12 (Fall 1977).

_____. *Eclipse of the Self: The Development of Heidegger's Concept of Authenticity*. Athens, OH: Ohio Univ. Press, 1981.

_____. "Humanism, Ontology, and the Nuclear Arms Race." In Paul T. Durban and Carl Mitcham, eds. *Research in Philosophy and Technology, VI*. Greenwich, CT: Jai Press, 1983.

Zuckerman, Edward. *The Day After World War III*. New York: Viking Press, 1984.

Zuckerman, Solly. *Nuclear Illusion and Reality*. London: Collins, 1982.

Zwicker, Barrie. "Inside the Mushroom Cloud"; "Journalism and the Bomb"; "Our Portrayal of the Soviet Union Dooms Ourselves"; and "Study of Coverage of USSR in US Media." *Sources: The Directory of Contacts for Editors, Reporters and Researchers,* Summer 1983.

Index